About This Book

Why is this topic important?

The number of corporate universities around the globe continues to increase rapidly. But beyond sheer numbers, the significance of corporate universities lies in the ways that organizations are using their corporate universities strategically to help develop people and expand organizational capabilities. As corporations increasingly rely on their corporate universities as strategic tools, they have discovered innovative ways to use these universities to move the organization forward. This book provides a window into some of the most innovative corporate universities and their inventive approaches.

What can you achieve with this book?

The book is intended for corporate university professionals—those who run corporate universities, work in them, and, especially, are charged with creating them. A who's who of corporate university professionals contributed chapters designed to give practical, hands-on tips for how to strategically use corporate universities to add value. After reading this book, corporate university professionals will be armed with numerous proven techniques.

How is this book organized?

The book is organized around four major themes: (1) corporate universities as strategic business partners, (2) internal corporate university functions, (3) distinctive settings for corporate universities, and (4) next-generation corporate university functions. Within each of these parts are chapters expanding on these concepts and offering case studies of real-world success stories. You may read the book sequentially or select the chapters that have the most relevance for you. Either way, the book is designed as a resource to help you get the most value out of your corporate university.

About Pfeiffer

Pfeiffer serves the professional development and hands-on resource needs of training and human resource practitioners and gives them products to do their jobs better. We deliver proven ideas and solutions from experts in HR development and HR management, and we offer effective and customizable tools to improve workplace performance. From novice to seasoned professional, Pfeiffer is the source you can trust to make yourself and your organization more successful.

Essential Knowledge Pfeiffer produces insightful, practical, and comprehensive materials on topics that matter the most to training and HR professionals. Our Essential Knowledge resources translate the expertise of seasoned professionals into practical, how-to guidance on critical workplace issues and problems. These resources are supported by case studies, worksheets, and job aids and are frequently supplemented with CD-ROMs, Web sites, and other means of making the content easier to read, understand, and use.

Essential Tools Pfeiffer's Essential Tools resources save time and expense by offering proven, ready-to-use materials—including exercises, activities, games, instruments, and assessments—for use during a training or team-learning event. These resources are frequently offered in looseleaf or CD-ROM format to facilitate copying and customization of the material.

Pfeiffer also recognizes the remarkable power of new technologies in expanding the reach and effectiveness of training. While e-hype has often created whizbang solutions in search of a problem, we are dedicated to bringing convenience and enhancements to proven training solutions. All our e-tools comply with rigorous functionality standards. The most appropriate technology wrapped around essential content yields the perfect solution for today's on-the-go trainers and human resource professionals.

www.pfeiffer.com

Essential resources for training and HR professionals

The Next Generation of Corporate Universities

Pfeiffer™

The Next Generation of Corporate Universities

Innovative Approaches for Developing People and Expanding Organizational Capabilities

Mark Allen, Editor

John Wiley & Sons, Inc.

Published by Pfeiffer
An Imprint of Wiley
989 Market Street, San Francisco, CA 94103-1741
www.pfeiffer.com

For additional copies/bulk purchases of this book in the U.S. please contact 800-274-4434.

Pfeiffer books and products are available through most bookstores. To contact Pfeiffer directly call our Customer Care Department within the U.S. at 800-274-4434, outside the U.S. at 317-572-3985, fax 317-572-4002, or visit www.pfeiffer.com.

Pfeiffer also publishes its books in a variety of electronic formats. Some content that appears in print may not be available in electronic books.

Library of Congress Cataloging-in-Publication Data

The next generation of corporate universities: innovative approaches for developing people and expanding organizational capabilities / Mark Allen, editor.
     p. cm.
   Includes index.
   ISBN-13: 978-0-7879-8655-1 (cloth)
   1. Employer-supported education. 2. Employees—Training of. 3. Organizational learning. I. Allen, Mark.
   HF5549.5.T7N473 2007
   658.3'124-dc22

                                                                                    2006101890

Acquiring Editor: Lisa Shannon
Director of Development: Kathleen Dolan Davies
Senior Developmental Editor: Susan Rachmeler
Production Editor: Nina Kreiden

Editor: Beverly Miller
Manufacturing Supervisor: Becky Carreño
Editorial Assistants: Caitlin Clarke and Marisa Kelley
Illustrations: Lotus Art

Printed in the United States of America

Printing   10   9   8   7   6   5   4   3   2

CONTENTS

PART TWO: INTERNAL CORPORATE UNIVERSITY FUNCTIONS

PART THREE: DISTINCTIVE SETTINGS FOR CORPORATE UNIVERSITIES

PART FOUR: NEXT-GENERATION CORPORATE UNIVERSITY FUNCTIONS

ACKNOWLEDGMENTS

MOST BOOKS are the result of a collaboration of several people, but this book required the contributions of many talented professionals. Above all, I thank the chapter authors for generously contributing their time, talent, and expertise, all out of a genuine desire to help corporate university practitioners.

I am deeply grateful to two wonderful friends, Stephanie Wilcox and Lisa Zamastil, for their support, counsel, encouragement, inspiration, and, especially, friendship.

I also thank Lisa Shannon, Susan Rachmeler, and the team at Pfeiffer for their help in getting this book to you.

Finally, I thank my wife, Dayna, and my two amazing boys, Skyler and Dylan, who make it all worthwhile.

PART 1

Corporate Universities as Strategic Business Partners

Part One provides an overview of how corporate universities are used as strategic tools to advance organizations. Whereas subsequent parts in this book deal with the specific how-tos of the various activities and functions that corporate universities engage in, Part One is devoted to the overarching philosophy of a corporate university as a strategic tool.

Chapter One discusses what a corporate university is and how it is a strategic part of its parent organization. The chapter provides a description of the next generation of corporate universities—those that go beyond training into numerous innovative approaches for developing people and expanding organizational capabilities. Chapter Two describes how Booz Allen Hamilton's corporate university takes a holistic approach to learning by linking all people processes with the organization. Chapter Three looks at the topic of learning as a competitive business variable and provides insights into how learning, when done properly and used strategically, can be a source of competitive advantage for an organization.

1

What Is a Next-Generation Corporate University?

Mark Allen

CAN IT BE THAT corporate universities have actually been around long enough for there to be a second generation? The first corporate universities date back at least as far as the 1940s, but the real growth started in the 1990s, so many corporate universities are now entering their second decade. As these entities grow in size and sophistication, the answer to my opening question is yes, and it is time to start talking about a new generation of corporate universities—ones that go beyond training and development, go beyond merely calling themselves a corporate university, and offer a variety of innovative services that help develop people and expand organizational capabilities. It is those corporate universities and their innovative approaches that are the subject of this book.

The two questions I am most frequently asked about corporate universities are, "Isn't a corporate university just a fancy name for a training department?" and "What exactly is a corporate university?" A corporate university is not a fancy training department. The best way to distinguish a training department from a corporate university is to look at the span of activities that each offers. A training department does training. A corporate university does training and many, many other things.

Corporate universities are responsible for developing people and growing organizational capabilities. Lest you think I am discounting training, I believe training is an excellent way to develop people—possibly the best way. However, there are many other ways to do it as well. A bit later in this chapter I list those ways (training is near the top of the list), and it is quite a long list.

So that brings us to the other question: What exactly is a corporate university? In *The Corporate University Handbook* (2002), I offered this definition: "A corporate university is an educational entity that is a strategic tool designed to assist its parent organization in achieving its mission by conducting activities that cultivate individual and organizational learning, knowledge, and wisdom" (p. 9). The most important word in that definition is *strategic*. Although training departments are important, they are usually tactical and operational and are often not tied directly to an organization's strategy. In order to be considered a true corporate university, the entity must be mission driven and tied to strategy.

This leads us to another question that people often ask: Is it appropriate for my organization to have a corporate university? As much as I am an advocate for corporate universities as vehicles for adding tremendous value to organizations, the concept is not right for every organization. It is not right to create a corporate university when it is viewed merely as a marketing gimmick. If people aren't coming to your training programs, relabeling them a corporate university may initially treat the symptom—low attendance—but it won't cure the disease (which is usually a case of having programs that people perceive as lacking value).

The other reason for not creating a corporate university is not having a clear and compelling reason to do so. I have spoken to dozens of people who told me that they were starting a corporate university because their boss read something about corporate universities and said, "I gotta get me one of them." Someone in the organization was then picked to create a corporate university. Since the mandate can be as nebulous as, "Create a corporate university," it is easy to succeed at reaching that low bar. However, it is virtually impossible to have any real success in terms of adding value to the organization and making a difference when there is no real strategic intent behind the plan. Without any purposeful objectives tied to organizational strategy, it is generally not a good idea to create a corporate university for the sake of having one. In fact, this can be quite damaging to an organization if, sometime later, a genuine strategic corporate university is conceived. People will remember the ill-fated marketing gimmick and will not embrace the concept when there is a real need for it.

So when should you have a corporate university? When there is a genuine strategic need for one. If there is a clearly identified need that involves the development of people, a corporate university can be a valuable strategic tool. Remember: a true corporate university is a strategic tool tied directly to helping an organization achieve its mission.

Corporate University Functions

Although *strategic* is the key word in defining a corporate university, this book is devoted to the part of the definition that discusses activities. The definition uses some fairly specific words to define a corporate university, but the word *activities* is quite vague, and deliberately so. The reason for this ambiguity is that there are many different ways that a corporate university can fulfill its role of cultivating individual and organizational learning, knowledge, and wisdom. At the time the definition was written, I knew I could not possibly name all of those different ways and that many had not yet even been conceived.

As I've spoken to numerous corporate university professionals over the years, I have compiled a list of these various activities. The list is long, but it is not meant to be comprehensive. First, I am sure I have overlooked some viable developmental methods. More important, I am even more certain that by the time you read this, innovative corporate university professionals will have created new and exciting ways for corporate universities to develop people and add value.

Here is the list of activities and functions that corporate universities can engage in:

- Needs assessments
- Designing training programs
- Delivering training programs
- Designing managerial and executive development programs
- Delivering managerial and executive development programs
- Assessing technology options
- Delivering e-learning or blended learning programs
- Hiring vendors
- Managing vendor relationships
- Marketing programs internally
- Marketing programs externally
- Evaluating programs
- Evaluating the corporate university
- Managing university partnerships
- Executive coaching
- Mentoring
- Career planning
- Strategic hiring
- New employee orientation
- Succession planning
- Culture change
- Strategic change
- Knowledge management
- Wisdom management
- Library and electronic collections of information
- Research and development

Although this list is not intended to be exhaustive, it is nonetheless instructive. The first lesson it demonstrates is that there are many ways to develop people in addition to training. Beyond that, many of the functions listed—knowledge management, succession planning, coaching, mentoring—are not new ideas. What is a recent development, however, is the notion that these functions can be managed as part of a corporate university. Not only can they be part of a corporate university, I would argue that they should be managed by a corporate university, or at least have some degree of corporate university involvement.

When I work with people charged with creating new corporate universities, I give them this list and ask them to create four columns, labeled "responsible for," "involved with," "outsource," and "won't do." For each item on the list, I ask them to think about whether their corporate university will be responsible for this function, involved with it, outsource it (which still might involve oversight by the corporate university), or just won't do it at all.

The last column is perfectly acceptable because although every function on the list could be managed by a corporate university, I know of no corporate university that could do everything on the list, nor would it need to. Depending on the size of the organization, its goals, and a number of other variables, some of the functions on the list might not be necessary.

However, what every function on the list does have in common is that they all relate to people and their development. And while some items on the list are traditionally the responsibility of other departments (for example, human resources usually is involved with strategic hiring and new employee orientation), all of these are development opportunities, and therefore corporate university involvement makes sense.

Consider the example of new employee orientation. At one end of the spectrum are the companies that do half-day orientation sessions explaining the benefits plan and other basic information (for example, how many holidays employees get). At the other end are the strategic efforts to accelerate the acculturation and engagement of new employees, vital components of new employee success. When I speak to groups of corporate university professionals, I ask how many are involved with the various functions on the list. Five years ago, I saw only a few hands go up as I asked this question about new employee orientation. Now I routinely see more than half the hands in the room raised. What was formerly a standard human resource function has become a strategic corporate university function. And this is true of most of the activities on the list.

It is also interesting to note some things that are not on the list, for example, degree programs. Programs leading to associate, bachelor's, master's, or doctoral degrees remain the exclusive province of traditional universities. A study in 2000 went in search of degree-granting corporate universities and discovered fewer than ten in all of the United States and Canada (Thompson, 2000). The trend for corporate universities to stay out of the degree-granting business has not changed since that study. Due to the complexities of degree programs and the barriers to entry (primarily accreditation), corporate universities that wish to provide degree programs (sometimes customized) for their employees have found it much more efficient to form a partnership with a local traditional university. That's why "managing university partnerships" is on the list but not "offering degree programs."

Also missing is academic research, the kind that traditional research universities undertake. Publishing articles in academic journals would not help develop people or expand organizational capabilities, so it is generally avoided by corporate universities. However, research and development is on the list. Most large companies have a separate research and development department, but some have embraced the idea of having the corporate university administer the process of employees' conducting research that will benefit the company. One of these, Enclos Corp., is profiled in Chapter Nine. Enclos University administers innovation grants that offer money or time away from other tasks (or both) in order to create a new product, service, or process that the company will be able to use.

The absence of degree programs and academic research demonstrates that despite the similarity in names, corporate universities and traditional universities do not have overlapping functions. They certainly cannot be viewed as competitors, except possibly for the very narrow space of executive development programs. These programs are typically not a core part of a traditional university's mission, although many do perform this function. So in some cases, internal corporate universities can be viewed as competitors to university-based executive development programs. But in other cases, savvy university-based business schools collaborate with corporate universities to create customized degree and nondegree programs.

How This Book Is Organized

Some chapters in this book are dedicated to many of the functions already noted in this chapter. In fact, this book is devoted to telling stories about how corporate universities have successfully integrated these functions into their responsibilities for developing people and organizational capabilities. A next-generation corporate university is one that goes beyond training to integrate numerous methods for the strategic development of people.

The chapters in Part One focus on the strategic role of corporate universities. In Chapter Two, Aimee George-Leary and Ed Cohen describe how to build a holistic development framework, which they define as one that is linked to all people processes through the organization, and they use their experience at Booz Allen Hamilton as a case study. They begin their chapter with five words that effectively capture the spirit of this book: "Development is more than training."

In Chapter Three, Karen Barley, president of the consulting firm Corporate University Enterprise, looks at learning as a competitive business variable in order to explore the notion of learning as a strategic business process.

Part Two is devoted to some internal functions of corporate universities. As corporate university professionals look over the menu of possible functions of a corporate university, they need to decide what they are going to do. The next question is equally important: How are they going to do it?

One solution that many organizations have decided on is e-learning. They cite the potential cost savings and the ability to widely distribute learning products as major benefits. What they fail to see is that e-learning has frequently not lived up to its potential of helping people learn and helping organizations achieve better results.

In 2001, I attended the Virtual Corporate University Week conference. Hundreds of people descended on San Francisco to talk about how they were going to get rid of all of their classrooms and have a completely virtual corporate university. (I wondered at the time why they all needed to descend when we could, theoretically, have held the conference virtually.) Within three years, I knew of no corporate university that was completely virtual. This one-size-fits-all approach didn't work. First, different subjects lend themselves more readily to e-learning than others. For example, how to use a certain software program might be a better e-learning subject than how to conduct better face-to-face conversations. Also, not every employee in an organization has the same learning style. Some people might take very well to an online learning environment, but it just won't work for others. There is no single solution that will effectively engage everyone in an organization. The notion of a completely virtual corporate university has faded away.

Hybrid programs and *blended learning* then became the buzzwords. The idea was to blend together classroom sessions with electronic programs and presto, you've got a learning smoothie. But what organizations in fact discovered was that although they could generally get people to show up in classrooms, the e-learning piece was more problematical. People would start these programs but never quite finish.

I knew this part of the business was in trouble when I heard someone bragging that he had developed an e-learning program that was so good that it had a 60 percent completion rate. People looked at him with envy. I tried to imagine a traditional university bragging that its programs were so good that only 40 percent of its students dropped out.

It's not that e-learning didn't hold a lot of potential. It always did, and it still does. The problem is that the focus is usually on the technology (the "e"), not the learning. Although it is not impossible to truly engage people using technology, it is very difficult. Organizations have discovered that most (not all, but most) e-learning programs and blended learning programs have not delivered on their promise.

So the question remained: To e or not to e? Roger Schank provides some answers in Chapter Four. Rather than focus on classroom learning versus e-learning versus blended learning, Schank asserts that we should focus on what he refers to as "splendid learning." As the subtitle of the chapter tells us, the technology doesn't matter. First, focus on ensuring that people are learning and are learning the right things; then determine how to deliver that learning. Schank was supposed to write a chapter on technology for this book, but he cheated and instead gives us a chapter about learning (imagine that in a book on corporate education!). Nevertheless, he provides examples of how to use technology to deliver learning that is splendid.

An important but often overlooked corporate university function is branding. Annick Renaud-Coulon is the president of the Global Council of Corporate Universities and one of the leading experts on corporate universities in Europe and around the globe. In Chapter Five, she presents the case for corporate university branding as a vital function that has a direct impact on corporate university success.

As ethical scandals dominate the headlines, companies are grappling with how to promote ethical behaviors. In Chapter Six, Philip McGee and John Duncan suggest that corporate universities could take responsibility not only for delivering classes that ensure compliance with ethical requirements, but also genuinely promote an ethical culture throughout the organization. They use three very different organizations as illustrative examples.

Jack Phillips, the guru of return on investment measures for training programs and corporate universities, and Patti Phillips discuss in Chapter Seven the challenges of evaluation and offer suggestions for how evaluation can help both determine as well as add value.

You may have noted that the definition of corporate university earlier in this chapter does not use the word *corporation*. The reason is that a corporate university does not have to be housed in a corporation. In fact, many of the finest specimens are located in nonprofit organizations, governments, and other nontraditional places. In Part Three, we explore these distinctive settings.

Global companies face extra challenges in implementing corporate universities. Different languages, cultures, and time zones are among the issues that global corporate universities face. In Chapter Eight, Ed Cohen, the former Booz Allen Hamilton executive who collaborated on Chapter Two and now heads up the corporate university for Satyam Computer Services, a global company based in India, shares his insights on running a global corporate university and tells the story of what Satyam has done.

Another frequently asked question about corporate universities is how big an organization needs to be for the corporate university model to make sense.

This is a case where size clearly doesn't matter. I have worked with organizations with as few as four hundred employees that have effectively implemented a corporate university. One of them is Enclos Corp. In Chapter Nine, Lee Steffens and Shannon Novotne tell the Enclos story and offer advice on how small companies with small budgets can create corporate universities with large impacts.

The for-profit sector is not the exclusive province of corporate universities. The next two chapters are devoted to the stories of successful corporate universities in nonprofit organizations. First, Deborah Grayson Riegel offers insight into how a nonprofit can effectively implement a corporate university. Then Kevin Bruny, who started and runs the corporate university for Chesterfield County, Virginia, gives a detailed description of a government-based corporate university.

In Part Four, we examine the various functions and activities beyond traditional training that corporate universities can and do engage in. One of the most important and often overlooked aspects of organizational change is culture change. Even when organizations attempt to travel down this difficult path, they usually do not look to the corporate university as the enabler. But since cultures are a product of people and corporate universities are devoted to developing people, Laree Kiely contends in Chapter Twelve that the corporate university should lead the culture change charge. She offers step-by-step guidelines for how this might be accomplished.

Countless organizations are employing mentoring and executive coaching, occasionally as part of formalized programs, but frequently in less structured arrangements. Yet these are exactly the types of functions that can add tremendous value to both individuals and organizations if they are managed properly. In Chapter Thirteen, Lynn Slavenski describes how her organization, Equifax, has put in place a formal process managed by the corporate university to implement mentoring on a widespread basis throughout the organization. Then Merrill Anderson offers his perspective on the strategic contribution of corporate universities to leadership coaching in Chapter Fourteen.

Jack Gregg, the dean of Space University at Northrop Grumman, explores the idea of career path management in Chapter Fifteen. This is another concept that can provide tremendous value to both the individual and the organization if managed properly and is another function that is not normally thought of as residing in a corporate university.

I have long been mystified by organizations that have a corporate university but conduct succession planning activities without involving corporate university personnel. Succession planning goes beyond identifying candidates; it also entails developing people. I don't see how you can do succession planning divorced from the corporate university. In Chapter Sixteen, Lynn Schmidt goes beyond the old notion of succession planning and discusses succession management, a much more comprehensive process that goes beyond planning and into implementation and management.

In Chapter Seventeen, my eponymous colleague Mark W. Allen (who shares my name and interest in corporate universities but is not related to me) discusses an important but often maligned function: knowledge management. If you ask corporate executives if they agree with the statement, "The most valuable asset in your organization is the knowledge in the heads of the workers," most would say they do. If you then asked, "Do you do a good job managing the acquisition, sharing, and use of that knowledge?" most would say they don't. This is not mere speculation on my part; I have asked these questions of hundreds of managers and executives. Almost all agree with the first statement, and the vast majority concede that the second statement is a problem. Many dismiss knowledge management as a fad or the latest flavor of the month. Yet unless you expect the value of workers' knowledge to decrease in importance, it is unlikely that the concept of knowledge management will fade away.

Part of the reason for the dismissal of knowledge management is that many organizations misfired when they first tried to implement it. Recognizing that there was a need for knowledge to be shared among large numbers of people across great geographical distances, knowledge management promoters decided that a database was necessary. They summoned the information technology (IT) department and put them in charge of building the knowledge management database. The IT folks did what they always do: a good job of doing exactly what we asked them to do. The problem is that we asked them to do the wrong thing. They built it, but no one came.

It turns out that we made two mistakes. First, we confused knowledge with data. Computers are good at storing data, but knowledge resides in people's brains. Knowledge comes in two flavors: declarative and procedural. Declarative knowledge is facts—the kind that can be written down and stored in a database. Procedural knowledge refers to how to do something. People know how to do stuff, but it's hard to capture that in a database. And guess which type of knowledge is more important to an organization? At the risk of being a heretic, I think Peter Drucker got it wrong (slightly) when he wrote of the growing importance of knowledge workers. We don't value workers for what they know; we value people for what they know how to do. And that is harder to capture in a database.

The other problem is that one of the major issues in knowledge management is the sharing of knowledge. The organization gets much better value out of my knowledge if I share it with others rather than keep it to myself. Unfortunately, for decades, organizations have rewarded hoarding knowledge instead of sharing it. Remember knowledge is power. Whether intentional or not, there are typically organizational rewards and benefits for being the only person in an organization who knows something. Build all the databases you want, but if you're going to reward me for being the only person who knows something, I'm not going to share it with others just because we now have a database.

As it turns out, knowledge management is not at all an IT issue; it is a people issue (though one that can be aided by electronic tools provided by the IT department). This often involves a change in the reward system and frequently necessitates a major shift in culture (as discussed in Chapter Twelve). Since it is a people issue, it is a corporate university issue. Chapter Seventeen delves into the ways that a corporate university can successfully manage an organization's knowledge management function.

And while knowledge management usually focuses on acquiring, storing, and sharing knowledge, the missing link is often applying the knowledge. In Chapter Seven, Jack and Patti Phillips share some research that shows that between 60 and 90 percent of the job-related skills and knowledge acquired in a corporate education program is still not being implemented on the job. So while we might be doing a good job of getting knowledge into the heads of our workers, we have not been doing as good a job of getting them to use it in a way that benefits the organization.

The solution to this is presented in Chapter Eighteen with a topic I call wisdom management. This coda to the book serves as a reminder that all of the good ideas in this book are just that—good ideas—unless they are applied in the workplace in ways that benefit the organization. Wisdom management describes an organized process of ensuring that all of our fine development efforts are put to good use.

The book is intended as a practical, hands-on, how-to book for corporate university professionals. Just as wisdom management prescribes that we use our knowledge to improve personal or organizational performance, those of us who put this book together know you are reading it out of a desire to improve your performance, not understand more theory. The theory is at a minimum here, and the professionals who contributed chapters to this book did so out of a desire to help you by sharing their experience, successes, failures, knowledge, and even wisdom. We hope you enjoy reading about our journeys as much as we enjoyed traveling them.

References

Allen, M. *The Corporate University Handbook.* New York: AMACOM, 2002.

Thompson, G. "Unfulfilled Prophecy: The Evolution of Corporate Colleges." *Journal of Higher Education,* 2000, *71*(3), 322–341.

Mark Allen, Ph.D., is an educator, consultant, author, and speaker. He is the editor of and a contributor to *The Corporate University Handbook* (2002) and the author of numerous articles on the topic of corporate universities. An internationally recognized authority, he is a popular speaker and has published and presented research on corporate universities and nontraditional higher education throughout the world. Other research interests include the assessment of training and development programs and the evaluation of teaching and learning in postsecondary and adult education. He serves as a consultant to both new and mature corporate universities.

Allen is a participating faculty member in Organization Theory and Management at Pepperdine University's Graziadio School of Business and Management, where he also served for ten years as director of executive education. An award-winning teacher, he also teaches at Pepperdine's Graduate School of Education and Psychology.

Previously he was program director in executive education at the University of Southern California's Marshall School of Business, where he developed a variety of highly successful executive education programs. He has also held managerial positions at several organizations.

Among the organizations he has worked with are 3M, Boeing, Caesars World, the Los Angeles Police Department, Verizon, Southern California Edison, Farmers Insurance, Enclos Corp., Infonet, Safeguard, Samsung, Hughes, Kaiser Permanente, and the government of Taiwan.

Allen has a B.A. in psychology from Columbia University, an M.B.A. from Pepperdine University, and a Ph.D. in education from the University of Southern California. He can be reached at mark.allen@pepperdine.edu.

Ed Cohen is one of the most respected and innovative chief learning officers I have met. Both he and the company where he worked for many years, Booz Allen Hamilton, earned excellent reputations for people development, culminating in Booz Allen Hamilton's rank of number one in Training magazine's Training Top 100 in 2006.

I knew that Ed would be an excellent choice to contribute a chapter to this book, and he quickly agreed to write a chapter on how to build a development framework that is holistic, linking all people processes throughout the organization. This chapter discusses how to accomplish this, and it uses Booz Allen Hamilton as a case study.

Shortly after the conception of this book, Ed accepted a job at Satyam Computer Services in India. He asked Aimee George-Leary, a colleague from Booz Allen Hamilton, to collaborate on the chapter. Their story demonstrates the broad range of developmental activities that next-generation corporate universities undertake.

2

Building a Holistic Development Framework

Aimee George-Leary, Ed Cohen

DEVELOPMENT IS MORE than training. It is also more than just an investment. It is about satisfying the need for a documented process that builds value both on and off the job. A solid development framework, aligned to competencies and assessment processes, serves as a road map, specific to level, that lays out success factors, career derailers, formal training, supportive colleagues, and on-the-job or work-stretch activities. A solid development framework is key to the value proposition that an organization offers its employees.

A holistic development model is one that is linked to all people processes throughout the organization. It incorporates all on-the-job learning as well as formal and informal learning, while also documenting the people who are influential throughout an individual's career.

The development framework, as a development model, challenges current beliefs regarding development. It explicitly makes the role of the classroom experience tangential to development rather than its cornerstone. It places development closer to where most learning occurs: on the job. It shifts the role of the manager from "user of talent" to "developer of talent," making the model a shared responsibility and value proposition.

Booz Allen Hamilton, a global strategy and technology consulting firm, initiated an intensive effort to define the development needs of all staff. Booz Allen's development framework grew out of the 1998 People Strategy survey and continues to be reinforced and expanded every two years to help the firm shape its people programs. During the initial stages of the people strategy, Booz Allen enhanced the career management system, refined competencies at all levels, and developed and aligned a set of training courses to employee competencies. This multiyear effort resulted in a series of guides aligned to employee levels and different roles and competencies.

The development framework has many benefits:

- It defines and correlates success criteria with a methodology for development.
- It provides robust development tools for employees and managers that incorporate multiple learning approaches.
- It clarifies manager/supervisor and employee ownership in the development process.
- It addresses timely on-the-job performance feedback.
- It allows employees to take an active role in the feedback process.

There are five steps in building a development framework, which we explore in this chapter:

1. Create the framework.
2. Populate the framework.
3. Communicate and implement the framework.
4. Refine the framework.
5. Evaluate the framework.

Step 1: Create the Framework

The model is based on defined performance standards for the organization. Organizational performance standards are derived from the needs of the organization's stakeholders: its customers, investors, and employees. The standards are based on the following components:

- Organization-specific requirements: knowledge, skills, or abilities specific and unique to the organization. These have an impact on everyone.

- Roles and responsibilities: knowledge, skills, or abilities specific to a role within the organization. These have an impact on specific groups.

- Competencies: knowledge, skills, or abilities specific to an individual. These have an impact on each individual in distinctive ways.

- Measures: how individuals are held accountable for the specific knowledge, skills, and abilities. These have an impact on everyone.

Collective development includes all the predictable experiences and courses that anyone coming into a specific role or level requires to be successful. Individual development expands on collective development by recognizing that people learn differently and have unique needs. Identifying success factors and potential derailers allows for the deployment of the right development activities matched to specific needs.

Five factors are applied to the model to build the development framework (see Figure 2.1):

- Experiential work-stretch activities
- Formal training and education
- Career derailers
- Success factors
- Colleagues

Figure 2.1. Booz Allen Hamilton's Factors in Employee Development

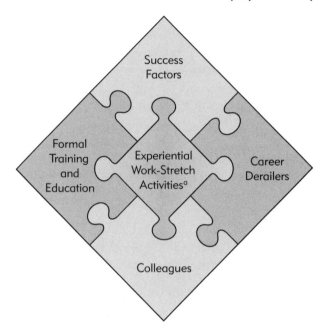

ªIncludes developmental assignments.

The development framework applies performance standards to the factors of development in order to achieve these goals:

- Broaden thinking about development.

- Foster stronger development discussions.

- Identify and define the right blend of learning, experiences, advice, and colleagues.

- Generate greater awareness of potential derailers.

- Assist with development planning.

- Centrally track development.

Experiential Work-Stretch Activities

At their core, experiential work-stretch activities, aligned to competencies by role and level, articulate the right experiences to build and demonstrate skills in the most expedient manner. Surrounding these types of activities are the supplemental yet critical additional factors. Experiential work-stretch activities and developmental assignments can help develop competency outside the classroom. For example, work-stretch activities for the competency "leadership behavior" could include these elements:

- Working with a team to develop a one-year plan for a project or program, including objectives and strategy

- Meeting regularly with a second team to review goals, business, and progress and to provide coaching and mentoring

- Participating in associations and organizations that align with the participant's area of expertise

Formal Training and Education

Formal training and education primarily articulate the collective learning that is available through classroom and online learning. A formal curriculum should be aligned by competency and level within an organization. It should also leverage and build on the other components within a development framework. The formal training should be focused; too many options aligned to competencies can create confusion.

Career Derailers

Career derailers articulate the extreme opposite of success. They identify the behaviors that prevent individual success within an organization and guidance on how to avoid them. Typical career derailers are associated with areas such as core values, relationships, impact, and business perspective. The key is to define the derailer, outline its characteristics within the context of the organization, and then provide recommendations to remedy the problem.

Success Factors

Success factors articulate what success at a particular level looks like from the point of view of leadership and others who have been promoted from that level. These factors are specific to the organization and reflect how to navigate within the system and culture—for example:

- Becoming comfortable with a collaborative work and decision-making style
- Developing a network of professional relationships
- Getting out of one's comfort zone and taking some risks

Colleagues

Colleagues represent the supportive individuals who are available to assist at that particular point in the employee's career (for example, manager, assessor, mentor). It is necessary to clearly define the roles and the impact they have on building the institution. Everyone needs to understand the expectations of the roles that these colleagues are being asked to play in the development process.

Step 2: Populate the Framework

Several steps aid in populating a development framework for the organization:

1. Analyze existing materials to fill in the framework.
2. Build a development road map.
3. Define roles in development, and build support processes and consequences.
4. Build partnerships.
5. Obtain buy-in and approval.
6. Publish the outcome as development guides.

Analyze Existing Materials

Unless an organization is brand new, it typically has documented learning and measures against existing competency models so the effort in this step is in the definition of the work-stretch activities, development assignments, derailers, and success factors. A development team, composed of learning leaders and human resource professionals, should analyze, synthesize, and interpret the existing data. Existing data could include development plans, performance reviews, performance-based objectives, role descriptions and responsibilities, existing course objectives, competency models, and exit interviews. These data become the foundational information for the framework.

Performance reviews should be divided into three categories: top performers, middle performers, and poor performers. Top performers provide excellent insight into experiential activities and success factors. Middle performers provide information on how most of the organization's members are currently developing and progressing through their careers. Reviewing poor performers provides insight into derailers as well as limitations that may result from certain employee experiences.

At Booz Allen, a team of learning professionals and business stakeholders conducted two years of research to complete the development framework. This included review of thousands of competency assessments, exit interviews, employee interviews, and focus groups to articulate how people develop, both collectively and individually.

We recommend preparing a single template useful for both collecting data and creating an employee survey. For each competency category, ask focus group participants to provide information and comments on data already collected. Hold focus groups that include a diverse sampling of participants that vary by gender, age, experience level, geographical location, and other relevant factors. Help focus group participants stay on track by encouraging them to discuss on-the-job activities that have had high impact rather than brainstorming new ideas.

Career derailers should be defined based on the areas of values, team relationships, impact, and business perspective. Exit data are an excellent resource for this information. Also, interviews with managers asking about employees who were terminated or stagnated in their career progress provide excellent information.

Build a Development Road Map

Articulation of a road map at each level within the organization results in greater understanding of the wide array of development opportunities and career progression. The development road map is a list of specific development opportunities aligned to business goals that allow individuals to build the necessary competencies, through the right experiences, to reach the next level.

Define Roles in Development

Colleagues play formal and informal roles in supporting development activities. Depending on the level of the individuals within the organization, they may be expected to play several of these roles to support the development of staff. Typical roles can include managers, mentors, coaches, peer sponsors, and project managers.

At Booz Allen, five specific colleagues were designated to support the development process: the administrative manager, assignment manager, assessor, mentor, and advocate. The expectations for each role were clearly defined, and tools (training, templates, and Web portals) were provided to assist the staff members playing these roles. For example, the administrative manager is expected to support the development process by deploying staff on the basis of skills, development needs, business needs, and employees' personal aspirations; assess performance and provide ongoing performance feedback; ensure that the assessment process is fair and equitable; assist staff in acting on their personal development plans; and make development resources available.

The development framework is the catalyst for improving managers' involvement in the development process because it:

- Defines and correlates success criteria with a methodology for development

- Provides robust development tools for employees that incorporate multiple learning approaches

- Clarifies manager/supervisor and employee ownership in the development process

- Improves performance conversations by addressing manager/supervisor inability to coach effectively and the absence of timely on-the-job performance feedback

Build Partnerships

Building a comprehensive development framework requires broad partnerships across the enterprise. From creation to implementation, human resource staff members, learning professionals, and recruiting staff need to participate to review personal development plans, identify commonly prescribed development activities, conduct focus groups to validate the effectiveness of these activities, and generate high-impact activities. Members of human resource and training teams communicate the intention of this initiative, as well as ways to implement the road map. The recruiting team uses the framework as a selling point to potential employees.

Obtain Buy-in and Approval

Support from the top is critical. Identify all stakeholders at the start, and include them in key decisions and demonstrations along the way. If possible, create the framework for the most senior people first. Once this is done, the framework sells itself.

Publish the Outcome: Development Guides

It is important to provide broad and centralized access to all the information for all employees. Create and publish guides for each level within the organization. Guides should be able to be viewed, printed, and incorporated into individual development plans within your virtual learning environment. Figure 2.2 shows an example of a personal development plan and its list of resources.

Figure 2.2. Booz Allen Hamilton Online Employee
Personal Development Plan

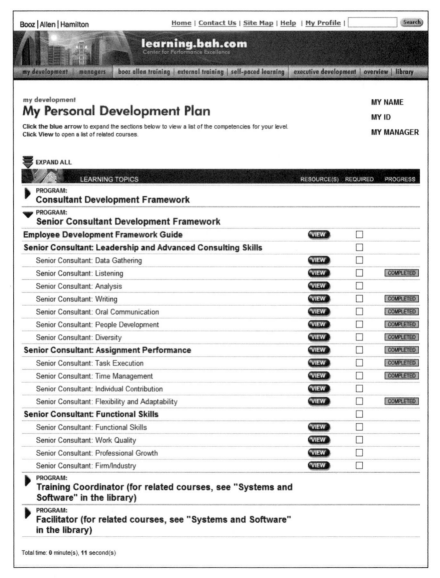

Providing accessible tools that are easy-to-read, all-in-one development road maps for employees encourages effective learning and development. Development guides should outline both collective and individual development. They should provide clear development options at each level and acknowledge that everyone has unique needs based on competency growth and experiences.

Step 3: Communicate and Implement the Framework

Development is about ensuring there is a documented process that builds value both on and off the job. Communicating the presence and usefulness of the process is central to the success of the framework. If you cannot stimulate employee participation, the arduous tasks of gaining senior management buy-in and creating a strategic learning infrastructure are a waste of time and effort.

To communicate about the framework, use posters, quick guides, announcements from the CEO, and seminars, and link the framework to all career activities. Make sure the framework is discussed in all courses and referred to in all internal employee manuals and associated materials. Figure 2.3 illustrates the Web page that gives employees access to the Employee Development Framework Guides through the Learning and Development virtual campus.

Figure 2.3. Booz Allen Hamilton Online Access to the Employee Development Framework

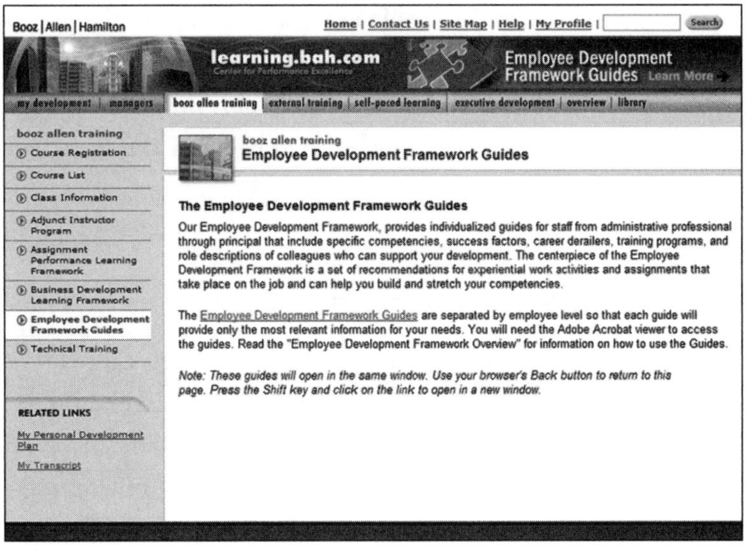

Include the framework in materials for new employees. Define development, and provide examples from the guides to showcase the importance of development and communicate that the firm has a documented road map for career success.

Integrate the framework into the assessment process. When individuals are notified regarding annual appraisals, include a link to the development guide for their level and ensure it is explicitly referenced. Include a sign-off in the appraisal for both the manager and the employee to indicate that the development guide was used as a reference for completing the appraisal.

Make sure human resource staff members use the guides to provide expert employee relations advice for career planning and development. This is especially useful when they are working with managers on completion of development plans for their employees. The guides and their use are reinforced by active use of the human resources team.

Step 4: Refine the Framework

Updating and refreshing are vital. The framework and the associated guides should be updated and refreshed annually to ensure that new activities are available for employees. This is also a good time to provide ongoing metrics and analysis reporting to senior leaders.

Usability studies should take place throughout the year to make sure competencies and activities are up-to-date with the goals and needs of the business. Continuous enhancements should take place to ensure the road maps reflect where the company wants to be in the future and not just where it is today.

Step 5: Evaluate the Framework

Evaluating the development framework is critical to attaining the desired outcome: an institutionalized method for developing knowledge assets. Determining the effectiveness of the framework involves measuring four components—awareness, penetration, effectiveness, and outcomes. Each component involves a key question, measures, and time frames. Not rushing to measure outcomes is critical; although the stimulus for positive reports begins at rollout, such reports are not maximized until at least the second year.

Awareness

- Key question: Are people aware of the framework?
- Data sources: Ongoing surveys that ask, among other questions, whether the framework was used as part of the appraisal and assessment process. The results of this measurement effort identify whether the marketing and communications of the framework are successful.
- Key measures
  - What is the level of overall awareness, as well as awareness by level, geography, and team?
  - How knowledgeable are users? Can they speak the language?
- Time frame: Six to twelve months after rollout of the framework

Penetration

- Key question: Is the framework useful?
- Data sources: Focus groups. This measurement is the first true test of the value of the framework. Up to this point, awareness and anecdotal information provide an indicator of how people perceive the framework. Now, discussions about how the information in the framework is or is not helping people to enhance development become the source for this critical measurement step. The measure here is more about perception than anything else.
- Key measures
  - How useful are the guides?
  - What is the most important aspect of the framework?
  - What aspects of the framework can be improved?
- Time frame: Twelve months after rollout of the framework

Effectiveness

- Key question: Is the framework having an impact on behaviors?

- Data sources: Reviews of development plans and appraisals as well as results of interviews, focus groups, and surveys. Analysis of development activities included in individual plans identifies whether the guides provide the right kind of activities. This analysis also serves as the basis for modification and updating of the framework at regular intervals.

- Key measures

  - Are appraisals and development plans written better than those generated prior to rollout and those developed without using the framework?

  - Do staff report that appraisals and development plans have greater value to them?

- Time frame: Twelve to twenty-four months after rollout of the framework

Outcomes

- Key question: Is the framework having an impact on overall business economics?

- Data sources: Specific surveys and extensive reviews of appraisal data trends. Analysis of promotion cycles and tenure also provides information to measure the effectiveness of the framework. If the model is working, faster career progression should be documented and measurable.

- Key measures

  - How many promotions occurred, and what are the competencies of managers?

  - What is the level of satisfaction with the overall development process?

- Is there greater awareness and clarity regarding career paths and what it takes to get promoted?
- Time frame: Twenty-four to thirty-six months after rollout of the framework

Booz Allen measured several additional benefits of the development framework, including the following:

- A culture shift. Individuals try new activities to build skills at each individual level
- A work-stretch component encourages new and creative approaches to skill building. Seventy-one percent of survey respondents said the development framework broadened the definition of development to go beyond formal training.
- A reduction in overuse of training. The focus of development activities, as identified in the framework, expands beyond the classroom. Developmental assignments and work-stretch components expose employees to deeper competency building and immediate opportunities to demonstrate abilities. The result from the framework survey indicated that 69 percent of respondents relied less on formal training as a developmental suggestion. In addition, training delivery grew at a modest 15 percent the year after the framework was rolled out, even though in that same year, the firm grew by more than 20 percent. During the five years before rollout of the framework, delivery had been growing at an annual rate of more than 50 percent.
- Benefits from more robust development plans for managers and staff. Having a holistic development framework means that development plans are easier to write, are less time-consuming, and contain more valuable information (both perceived and audited) than they would without the framework. Development plans are audited by human resource professionals on an ongoing basis.

In addition to the four key questions associated with awareness, penetration, effectiveness, and outcomes, several additional questions explore whether the framework is having the right impact:

- Although new employees continue to rely on programs, training curricula, and infrastructure to immerse themselves and ramp up, how rapidly do they shift to development driven by the work-stretch, challenge, and coaching that is supplemented by training?

- Is training seen as a supporting activity or a primary activity?

- Is development supported by appropriate training opportunities and activities, including performing pro bono or community service work?

- Is the framework having an impact on recruiting? Does the detailed information on development allow the company to hire exceptional talent and develop these people to meet future needs?

- Are staff contributing at increasing higher levels?

- Does the framework result in development activities that lead to greater potential for success that is not strictly promotion or formula driven?

- Have managers shifted from users of talent to talent developers?

If the answer to any of these questions is not yes, then establish a plan for improving the framework. If the answer to all the questions is yes, then expect positive outcomes and significant impact.

If a holistic development model is to work, measurement is the most critical component. Evaluation, measurement, and enhancement of the model must be factored into planning and conducted at least annually.

Key Success Factors for Implementing a Development Framework

Support from the top is critical. Identify all stakeholders up front, and include them in key decisions and demonstrations. Internal partnerships across sub-teams and a comprehensive communication plan for rollout are essential.

Following are some specific process-oriented recommendations for replicating the development framework:

- Do not try to make it happen overnight. Depending on organization size, it can take months or even years to conduct the research to document and create a solid framework.

- Populate the framework with information from employees. Do not have managers create on-the-job activity suggestions. Collect data from current development, and allow employees to rate the effectiveness of those suggestions for their own level.

- Collect both quantitative and qualitative data to determine the best development plan currently in use. This forms the basis for the framework. Prepare a single template for both collecting data and creating a survey.

- For each competency category, allow focus group participants to reword items or add new items.

- Hold focus groups that include a diverse sampling of employees based on gender, age, experience level, and geographical location. Help focus group participants stay on track by encouraging them to discuss on-the-job activities that have had high impact rather than brainstorming new ideas.

- Allow at least thirty minutes to discuss the do's and don'ts for success.

- Be prepared for a vast amount of data input. Dissemination, analysis, and synthesis of data are extremely important. The framework needs to contain key areas, not every detail.

- Make sure all stakeholders have access to and understand the framework. Conduct train-the-trainer sessions for those who communicate context and use of the framework and development guides. Produce a quick guide or job aid for distribution to staff. Provide multiple ways to access the development guides. Communicate extensively to all employees. Incorporate the framework in all training courses, especially programs for new employees.

Summary

A solid development framework, aligned to competencies and assessment processes, serves as a road map, specific to level, that lays out success factors, career derailers, formal training, supportive colleagues, and on-the-job or work-stretch activities. The development framework can be implemented in any organization that is prepared to do the research and invest the time and financial resources to allow it to come to life. The phases for designing and populating the framework are the same, but the data collected are unique to each organization. The entire framework should be designed to align with organizational goals and integrate high-value development activities into individual guides for staff and managers to use for successful career planning. A solid development framework is key to the value proposition that the organization offers its employees.

Aimee George-Leary is the acting director for Booz Allen Hamilton's Center for Performance Excellence. She has more than thirteen years of leadership experience in corporate learning and development and has been featured at conferences speaking on learning strategies, online resources to enhance learning, and instructional systems design.

George-Leary has focused on numerous areas, including defining competency and performance-based learning strategies, technical training, technology-based learning tools, and instructional systems design. She leads a team of over eighty experts who are responsible for full employee life cycle development at Booz Allen.

She holds a B.S. in communications media from Indiana University of Pennsylvania and an M.S. in instructional technology from Bloomsburg University of Pennsylvania.

Ed Cohen is the senior vice president for Satyam Computer Service's School of Leadership, responsible for creating the vision and strategy for leadership development and for building the school. Satyam leverages his

expertise in setting up and managing the corporate university concept. Considered a statesman in this segment, Cohen continuously explores and maintains new methodologies and programs in tune with customer expectations. He has been directing organizational, training, and employee development services for almost a quarter-century.

Prior to joining Satyam, Cohen spent eight years with Booz Allen Hamilton, where he founded and was the strategic leader of its corporate university, the Center for Performance Excellence. During his tenure as the leader of learning at Booz Allen, the Center for Performance Excellence grew from a start-up in 1998 to become one of the most widely recognized corporate universities. Under his leadership, Booz Allen climbed the Training Top 100, reaching the number one spot in 2006. During that time, Booz Allen received more than thirty Excellence in Practice recognitions from the American Society for Training and Development (ASTD).

Cohen was program chair of the 2005 ASTD Conference in May 2005, serves on the advisory board for ASTD's Learning Executive Network and the editorial advisory board of *Training* magazine, and is a member of the Conference Board Council for Education and Training. He earned a B.S. in accounting from the University of Florida and an M.S. in education from Nova Southeastern University, and he has participated in Harvard Business School's Professional Service Firms and Strategic Executive Leadership programs.

Karen Barley is a true corporate university professional. During the five years I have known her, she has built her company, Corporate University Enterprise, into a large consulting firm focusing exclusively on corporate universities. Having worked with dozens of corporate universities, Karen has gained a broad perspective. And while she has learned a great deal from her interactions with all of these corporate universities, I have no doubt that they have learned a lot more from her. In this chapter, she presents a discussion of how organizations can use learning as a source of competitive advantage. It delivers the theme that learning is more than an important tactic; it is a strategic tool.

3

Learning as a Competitive Business Variable

Karen Barley

You can change the behavior in an entire organization,
provided you treat training as a process rather than an event.
Warren G. Bennis

TEN YEARS AGO, the quest to define *corporate university* was at the forefront of the training community. Emerging chief learning officers, instructional designers, training managers, evaluation experts, training software companies, academicians, and consultants in organization development (including me) all sought to define this concept that swept through the American and later the international training community swiftly and ubiquitously. There has been only one common theme in this quest for definition: no one agrees on anything except strategy.

Thanks to Harley Colon, freelance graphic designer, who transformed the mental image of the learning landscape in Figure 3.1 into a thousand-word picture; and to Rita Smith, dean of Ingersoll-Rand University, who contributed to the concepts and ideas in the integration-versus-isolation sections of this chapter.

In the corporate training world, *strategy* has two meanings. Its first con-notation is about planning—taking deliberate and careful action for how training is organized, announced, and distributed throughout an organiza-tion. The second meaning is more about alignment and how learning posi-tions itself to support or influence achievement of larger organizational initiatives. Examine any proclaimed corporate university, and you will most likely find a strategic plan, with a clear purpose and deliberate planning, that is intertwined with the parent organization's larger goals and objectives. Every-thing else—the scope, audience, funding, approach to instructional design, formula for using external vendors, integration of technology, size of the train-ing team, and value proposition and measurement methodology—are sim-ply variables in the strategy equation.

Strategy is the common denominator. The notion that learning should be strategic, purposeful, deliberate, and connected to organizational missions is not new. In fact, this concept has been the intent of workplace learning since its birth in the early part of the twentieth century in the United States. Yet not all corporate universities (whether they call themselves such or not) solve the strategy equation successfully. Some dive in head first without a life vest and announce their accountability for sweeping cultural change. Others stick their toes in the water and shy away from the shore, worried about what risks lie in uncharted waters. The ones that attack the waters with a strong captain, a map and some navigation tools, a steady crew, skills for sailing in questionable weather, and a sound hull are those that find not only longevity but joy in the journey, not to mention the acceptance of being part of the fleet.

Being part of the whole: that's what strategic learning is, and it is what defines the next-generation corporate university. Strategic learning, as cas-caded by corporate universities, is one force in organizational change, not a sole contributor. The charge for organizational learning should be one of true integration, not isolationism. The next-generation corporate university is one that understands, and executes against, the difference between isolation and integration as well as the difference between strategy and tactics, and it posi-tions learning as a true competitive variable in the business. This chapter distinguishes between tactical training and strategic learning and prescribes stages of corporate university development to leverage learning as a competitive business variable.

Maturation of Learning Strategy

Corporate universities have typically differentiated themselves from traditional approaches to training by focusing on a variety of concepts. Although the lists vary to some degree, practitioners of corporate universities typically try to transform organizations in these ways:

- From being focused on the tactics of training to being deliberate about learning strategy
- From being completely reactive to workplace challenges to being proactive about upcoming changes
- From being focused on training individuals to placing emphasis on building the organization
- From delivering classes to providing solutions
- From thinking of training as a human resource proprietorship to considering learning as a partner in the business
- From providing tuition reimbursement to endorsing more targeted roles for higher education
- From having distributed training records to centralizing how learning is tracked
- From little to no evaluation practice to a robust system of measurement and accountability
- From a completely overhead costing model to a competitive, value-added charge-back financial system

With this expansion of scope and practice, corporate universities start to influence organizational change and become more intertwined with the performance of the business overall.

Still, corporate universities are evolutionary, not revolutionary, constructs. They do not develop and implement these differentiating features and emerge as fully grown strategic learning programs overnight. Instead, they mature and grow, adjusting as their organizations change and developing more sophisticated approaches over time. In the early stages, the term *corporate university* can be a compelling differentiator to help a problematic or challenged training department make a statement about its adjustments to become more aligned with the business. Over time, the term becomes relatively insignificant, while the nimbleness, depth, and sophistication of the differentiators become increasingly more important.

Achieving depth in these areas requires progressive development in the intent or purpose of the corporate university. Early-stage corporate universities often dedicate their resources to building and maintaining appropriate training infrastructures. Activities such as selecting and launching a learning management system, establishing a robust and engaging curriculum, integrating technology-based training, and providing one-stop access to all training events through a Web portal are common. What we often find in intent in early-stage corporate universities are output-based goals, defined by the tasks the corporate university needs to complete. An example of an output goal might be, "Select and implement a companywide learning management system" or "Launch a competency-based curriculum." These kinds of goals focus on tasks, not strategies, that have finite completion dates. They are operationally focused and result in developing individual behaviors. This approach to training and development is fine, although it will most likely not get a corporate university noticed as a contributor to bottom-line results and elevate learning to a competitive business variable.

Next-generation corporate universities are more focused on contributing to organizational performance. This demands a shift from the tactics of training to the strategies of learning. With a solid training infrastructure in place, the corporate university can broaden its intent to how learning will influence the business's performance against its larger organizational goals. Corporate universities in this position change their output goals to strategic objectives, such as, "Incubate the direction of the company" and "Generate revenue for the organization." These more strategic objectives are based not on completion of tasks but on contribution to organizational performance, and they are tightly aligned with stated organizational goals. The stakes are higher in this kind of corporate university approach; there is great accountability and risk. Evaluation becomes increasingly significant. Success, however, also results in the true alignment of learning and its position as a competitive influence on the organization's performance.

Some corporate universities choose to skip the tactical start-up phase and move right into the more strategic model. This dive-right-in approach may be influenced by senior executives who want to see learning contribute quickly. Learning teams often feel a sense of building the airplane in the air as they attempt to construct the tactical infrastructure while simultaneously influencing the bottom line. Having the time to develop and implement the tactical components in isolation is the organic way to progressively position learning as a competitive variable. Corporate expectations, and sometimes small windows of opportunity, suggest that we do build the airplane in the air. It's just important to ensure that we have the priority pieces in place—things like wings and propellers—before lifting off the ground.

Transition from Tactical Training to Strategic Learning

What I am really addressing is creating an integrated learning landscape, one that ensures that learning is as important to the overall performance of the company as the quality of the goods and services, the leadership style and vision, the technological infrastructure, the soundness of its business processes and practices, and the financial prowess. Getting past the tactics of training into real strategy and alignment can help a corporate university realize that kind of position and influence. To do that, it must consider how to move beyond the operations and services of training to strategy and evaluation. In other words, it's about providing content in context and with appropriate layers of accountability.

There are four major components at work:

- Strategic foundation, which defines the purpose and position of a corporate university. It represents the high-level overview of the organization's learning strategy. It can obviously be more tactically and output focused or more strategic and goal oriented.

- Curriculum and services, which represent the delivery offerings of the corporate university. These offerings may include courses, coaching, mentoring, a core learning program, internal certifications, college and university programs, external certificate programs, internal consulting options, and/or computer-based learning tools.

- Operations and logistics, which describe the business processes associated with launching and maintaining the corporate university.

- Evaluation and assessment, which describes the performance measures and overall evaluation plan to show the corporate university's impact on the organization, specifically aligned with the goals, whether output-based or strategically focused. It also addresses the process for assessing needs and performance gaps over time.

Visually, these four components create an interesting picture of learning in an organization as shown in Figure 3.1. The upper left section displays images that define operations and logistics: a distribution center for learning materials, hotels and other classroom-type facilities; a hand-held audio device representing electronically delivered learning; a print shop; and other hardware and software images for supporting registration processes. This is the infrastructure component of a corporate university. Right next door is a shopping mall concept that shows various approaches to curriculum and services. Kiosks representing online resource centers, an instructional design methodology depicted on the train, coaching and talents shops, a movie theater, and demonstration centers all represent the various ways that learning is designed and delivered in organizations.

Figure 3.1. An Integrated Learning Landscape

Corporate universities that are in the early stages and those that are more tactically focused often put their focus on operations and logistics and curriculum and services. It's a natural starting point as it gets product to customer. In these cases, they put their energy into the specific courses and programs they will offer and the means by which to manage customer interactions. Table 3.1 shows the specifics that a new or early-stage corporate university prioritizes. These areas are quite tactical, especially when void of a strategic foundation and assessment and evaluation role. Strategy, and its connection to effective measurements, is the differentiator between a tactically focused and a strategically focused corporate university. Therein lies the key to effectively

Table 3.1. Tactically Focused Corporate University Components

Operations and Logistics	*Curriculum and Services*
Staffing plan • Depicts the staff requirements necessary to maintain the operations of the new corporate university • Develops an organizational chart to define roles and responsibilities	Content model • Develops a pictorial image of the content areas offered • Defines internal career frameworks as correlated to learning and development • Identifies a core learning program for all employees • Focuses on the culture and the business of the organization as it should arise in learning and development • Defines tracks of learning
Marketing plan • Describes the initial and ongoing marketing campaigns • Defines the corporate university brand and message • Explains how messages about the corporate university will be distributed	Competency models • Defines competency models, if appropriate • Describes how competencies will be engaged
Workflow map • Maps the workflow processes associated with managing the corporate university • Shows the required internal alliances with marketing, information technology, and other divisions	Faculty/trainer qualification standards • Identifies that a qualification process for faculty/trainers will be developed that aligns with the professorship vision • Outlines initial criteria for faculty/professorship qualification
Budget and funding model • Outlines the budget required to launch and maintain the corporate university • Describes the funding strategy • Describes the pricing strategy for courses and services • Outlines the customer service standards	Delivery mechanisms • Capitalizes on existing technology infrastructure • Recommends possible augmentation to technology infrastructure • Describes the e-learning and blended learning plan and strategy

Table 3.1. Tactically Focused Corporate University Components, Cont'd

Operations and Logistics	Curriculum and Services
Facilities and technologies • Identifies the facilities necessary to support the corporate university • Identifies potential external partners • Outlines learning management system options and integration plans • Develops an overall technology strategy for anchoring the corporate university	Catalogue and schedules for learning opportunities • Describes the process for posting and updating learning schedules • Describes how the curriculum catalogue will be distributed
Change management plan • Develops a strategy for communicating the corporate university design to the organization • Involves instructions for socializing the new plan and gaining buy-in from various divisions and units • Includes an approach to managing change	External partners • Explains the role of external partners in the curriculum • Identifies potential external partners, especially technology vendors, to support curriculum

integrating learning as a competitive business variable: good training tactics may get you noticed; solid strategy and responsibility for risk get you valued.

In Figure 3.1, the lower two quadrants represent the strategic foundation and evaluation and assessment components. There are pictorials for items such as vision, innovation, mission, branding, and goals in the strategic foundation quadrant, the lower-left portion of the picture. The lower-right section describes the techniques and methods for data collection, along with an evaluation service station, a mountain of accountability, a data mine, and a path of analytics. These components, when layered with the right curriculum and a sound infrastructure, contribute to make learning a competitive business variable. Table 3.2 describes the visual depictions in more detail.

Table 3.2. Strategically Focused Corporate University Components

Strategic Alignment	*Evaluation and Assessment*
Vision and mission • Identifies a clear purpose or vision for the new corporate university • Identifies a mission statement for learning at the organization	Expected outcomes • Identifies expected results based on the new corporate university objectives • Considers the value or impact of the program to employees, divisions, the company overall, and the company's customers
Governance • Explains how the corporate university should be governed • Describes the functions of the governing body • Identifies the kinds of individuals (or specifies particular names) who should sit on the governing board	Evaluation plan • Shows how each expected result maps to the Kirkpatrick model of evaluation • Ensures that all four levels of evaluation are addressed • Provides an explanation of what data points will be collected • Describes how and when data will be collected • Describes how evaluation data will be reported and used, including scorecards
Goals • Specifies clear goals for the corporate university • Maps learning goals to corporate goals • Considers a phased approach to achieve those goals	Assessment plan • Identifies stakeholder groups • Describes the time line of needs assessment activities • Describes specific needs assessment activities • Describes the use and integration of key findings from needs assessment activities
Objectives • Identifies clear methods for achieving goals • Aligns with corporate business objectives	

Table 3.2. Strategically Focused Corporate University Components, Cont'd

Strategic Alignment	
Business model • Develops a pictorial business model for the corporate university • Describes the interrelationships among the various components of the new corporate university	
Placement in the corporate structure • Shows where the corporate university fits into the corporate hierarchy • Articulates reporting lines, both hard and dotted • Develops positioning strategies	

When a corporate university aligns these quadrants and gets them all firing and moving in the same direction as the organization itself, the corporate university can then have an important impact on the organization's effectiveness. It's the difference between thinking of learning as an event and considering it to be an ongoing process with all four components representing critical areas in the process. The key to success is integration—both internal integration as a learning function and external integration with the business itself.

From Training Integration to Business Integration

Integration has two layers, both of which are critical for using a corporate university to position learning as a competitive business variable. The first layer is about integrating all training functions in an organization to respond to and perform against the same strategic plan. The second layer of integration involves aligning learning with business processes and performance. One is more inward facing; the other is more outward facing.

The inward-facing integration effort does not necessarily mean that all training functions and units have to centralize and report to one person, although that is one way to approach the internal integration question.

Another way is to maintain a network or system of training units in the organization, each with distinct areas of focus and a common set of shared practices that cross functions among all training efforts, regardless of their specific areas of curriculum focus. This kind of integration manifests itself through a common learning management system, a shared and consistent approach to instructional design, a shared evaluation practice and scorecarding reporting system, and one agreed-on vision and charge. It also leads to consistency in the business processes associated with designing and delivering training. While each training unit may hold onto some individual control, the majority of the process elements involved with training is integrated to avoid redundancy. Figure 3.2 depicts the process elements that are often integrated. What remains distinct in each training unit are the topics to be trained and perhaps the audience. In other words, some control for training is still distributed, but the items that can be consolidated are integrated in a way that makes sense for everyone.

Figure 3.2. Integrating Tactical Training Elements

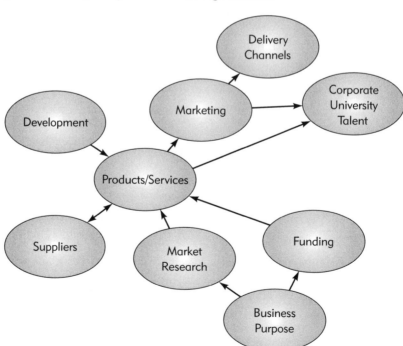

To Figure 3.2, we add an element that is critical for transforming internal integration to business alignment: business partnerships (see Figure 3.3). Techniques and processes for engaging with the business units themselves are the link between all the well-functioning internal practices and the perception of value in the organization. Without the alignments, corporate universities often find themselves struggling to prove themselves as the sole reason for a particular business result rather than making the case for what they contributed to the bottom line. It's really the difference between isolation and integration. Business partnerships, alliances, and relationships are the critical factor.

Figure 3.3. Integrating Training with the Business

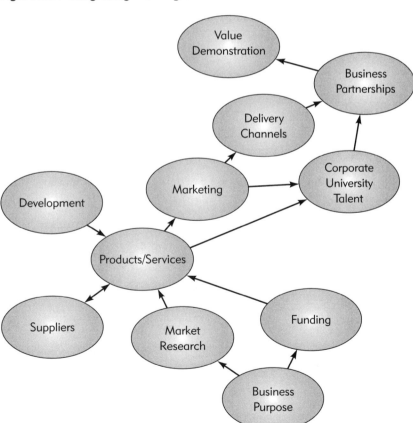

Let's consider a few best practices and techniques that some corporate universities engage to build relationships and alliances:

• *Input or advisory boards.* Some corporate universities establish input or advisory groups to maintain connection with the business. These boards meet regularly to identify emerging learning needs that are directly tied to priorities in the lines of business or as connected to organizational initiatives. Members of the advisory boards do not report to the corporate university but to their respective lines of business.

• *Account managers and internal consultants.* Another best practice is the designation of account managers who provide internal consulting with particular business areas to determine needs, scope training-related projects, and follow up with evaluation activities. Account managers report to the corporate university but spend the majority of their time in the business unit to which they are aligned. The best account managers are those who have an intimate knowledge of the business units and experience and competence in human resource development.

• *Using leaders and subject experts as instructors.* Perhaps one of the strongest alignment practices is the use of business personnel as teachers in the corporate university. Rather than hiring external trainers or carrying a lot of instructors on the corporate university organizational chart, the practice is to find subject experts internally and prepare them to facilitate courses and programs. The instructional design methodology and flow of the course still come from the corporate university; the qualified and recognized expert conducts the event. Using subject experts in this way builds credibility for the learning initiative as it places well-known and credible individuals on the platform. It also ensures that the content is vibrant and current with the way things really work in the business units themselves.

• *Coaching.* An interesting and creative way to build alliances and produce alignment is through coaching. As corporate universities work to produce behavioral change in their employees, coaches become an integral part of the process. Coaches come from the business unit and are developed in their coaching role by the corporate university. They learn how to encourage changes in behavior that align with the skills they were taught in a corporate university course or program. Because the coaches come from the business, they have perspective on real-world situations. Their understanding of new skills, as developed in learning events, however, enables them to establish an environment that fosters new behaviors.

Through these best practices, corporate universities are able to achieve greater access and alignment with the business. The result is the final component in Figure 3.3: value demonstration. Being aligned with the business will produce the results; however, the corporate university must still take responsibility for collecting data and reporting the role that it played in achieving organizational results. This responsibility makes the case for an effective evaluation methodology that shows how training programs and learning activities contributed to organizational results.

Being integrated and connected to the business blurs the lines of accountability. In other words, it becomes more difficult to isolate what role learning had as an independent variable in achieving organizational results. When we boil this down, the dilemma lies in integration versus isolation. How can learning isolate its accountability and value when the contributions for learning come from all over the organization? The truth is, it can't. Evaluation is about providing evidence of value, not proving worth. If we get the alignment and integration problem resolved through alliances and bridge building and implement an evaluation program that collects evidence of value, the perception and acceptance that learning should get credit for organizational results will follow.

Internal and external integration efforts help align learning with the business itself. This integration requires that the corporate university function and perform like other business units in the organization, with the same levels of accountability and responsibility.

Charting the Course for Integration

Corporate universities may go through several stages of development before they truly become competitive business variables. Four specific quadrants, as shown in Figure 3.4, define the stages and show a progressive movement from tactical to strategic and from an individual to an organizational focus. These four quadrants are arranged by sophistication of strategy (over tactics) and emphasis on organization development (rather than stopping at developing individuals).

Figure 3.4. Strategic Learning Maturation

3. Tactical/Organizational A learning function that focuses on building organizational efficiencies through training	**4. Strategic/Organizational** An integrated line of business to leverage learning for competitive advantage
1. Tactical/Individual A learning function that builds employee competence	**2. Strategic/Individual** A learning function that focuses on performance improvement

From an individual to an organizational orientation ↑

From a tactical to a strategic foundation →

Quadrant 1 places emphasis on the tactics of training and employees as individuals. With a focus to build employee competence, the audience is typically restricted to direct employees of the organization or some subset of the employee population. Various training functions may exist in the organization, although they are typically related to competency models or specific knowledge and skill requirements for particular job roles. This quadrant is best described as a network of training activities that are tied to skill requirements and competencies. The training units, however, are not necessarily linked or tied to each other, and an integrated companywide learning management system is most likely not in place. Evaluation activities align with individual courses and programs by individual training units.

Quadrant 2 is more strategic yet still focused on developing individuals. Internal employees remain the target audience, but the intent moves from simply building competence to improving performance. The multiple training units may still exist; however, they are now linked to performance management, not just competencies. Performance management, as established and aligned with an organization performance system, is the driver in this quadrant, which is also what makes this quadrant more strategic. Performance gaps, not just skill requirements, determine the kinds of training offered.

Quadrant 3 focuses on building organizational efficiencies through learning with a focus on training tactics and organizational strategies. The presence of the corporate university is a single, integrated approach for all development activities in the organization. The tactical focus is on the operational components, such as one common learning management system and a one-stop-shop access point for learning companywide. The kinds of delivery are more sophisticated, offering action learning and blended opportunities that blur the line between learning and work. Standardization of instructional design practices and facilitation become part of the fabric. It's internal integration at its best. Yet it is not quite strategic because the connection to other development activities, such as career development, performance management, and talent management, has not been realized, and the lines of business have not been integrated into the learning function.

That kind of integration occurs in quadrant 4, where learning truly becomes a competitive business variable. In this quadrant, alliances have been formed, and evaluation is a healthy practice in learning, not simply approached through smile sheets and posttests. Learning appears on the company scorecard and takes accountability for its role in organizational performance through both good and bad times. Moreover, learning is happening around the organization, not just in training classes. Think tanks, communities of practice, and experiential and action learning are as popular and prolific as courses and boot camps. Learning and work are interchangeable.

What we see in these quadrants is a progression toward organization performance and strategic connection to the business. As the corporate university broadens its focus to organization development, not just individual development, and from the tactics of training to the strategies of learning, it strengthens its position and contribution as a competitive business variable. In the learning landscape in Figure 3.1, the progression gets us to that sweet cityscape in the middle, the place where the business and learning come together.

Fear of Accountability

Stopping many corporate universities on the road to integration is the fear of accountability. Take a look at any instructional design course, program development model, or even corporate university design model, and you will see evaluation tacked neatly at the end of the course or the bottom of the model. The visuals give the impression that evaluation can be—and maybe even should be—considered at the end. In fact, evaluation must be considered as part of the development process, no matter how small or large the learning initiative is. The fear of accountability arises largely from our practice of trying to collect evaluation data without considering them during development. It's nearly impossible to show a contribution if you haven't prepared for it during design.

It's also wrong to try to take credit for results without addressing that trail of evidence. Consider, for instance, a corporate university that initiates a sales training program. Six months after the implementation of the program, the company posts increases in sales. The corporate university might take credit for those sales increases with a strong argument that the sales training program contributed to those results. Imagine going before senior leadership to make that case without any evidence of knowledge and skill development, as captured during the boot camp, or behavior change that occurred on the job. Practices like this one give corporate universities a bad reputation. Jumping to results is like leaping out of an airplane without a parachute. The fall may be exhilarating for the first few thousand feet, but as the ground gets closer, panic sets in and someone inevitably will get hurt.

Taking responsibility for results is risky business. It requires a solid evaluation practice and methodology based on a trail of evidence. It also demands skill in data collection, survey methodology, analytics, and data display and reporting. Making sure the talent to conduct evaluation is evident in the training team is the first step. Bringing evaluation from the bottom of the model and the end of the course to the top, right next to strategy, is the first big leap. Mitigate the risk by empowering the team with the right knowledge, skills, and abilities in evaluation, and give the team time to perform evaluation activities. It will make the difference in the corporate university's perception of value and credibility as a contributor to results, ingredients in the movement of training from tactical delivery to strategic position.

Summary

The next-generation corporate university is one that operates, delivers, and holds itself accountable, just as the rest of the business does. It's about having strategy, executing against that strategy, ensuring that the strategy aligns with organizational strategy and couples with other variables in the organization, and provides evidence of value. Training is something that is done to employees; learning is something they do for themselves. The next-generation corporate university understands and embraces this difference and brings learning to the heart of the business, following the same practices, standards, and operating principles that the employees are held accountable for every day: true alignment, true integration, true results.

Karen Barley, the president and cofounder of Corporate University Enterprise, has served clients throughout the United States, Europe, and Asia. She holds the copyright on one of the only corporate university planning models and is an international speaker on the subject.

She has created dozens of corporate universities for national and global organizations. Her work with various learning programs has been published and highlighted in the *New Corporate University Review* and *Employee Benefit News*, and she is a contributing author to Mark Allen, ed., *The Corporate University Handbook: Designing, Managing, and Growing a Successful Program.*

Barley has served on several judging panels for corporate university awards, including the National Alliance of Business Corporate University of the Year and HR Events' Corporate University Best in Class Awards.

Prior to launching Corporate University Enterprise, Barley directed the award-winning U.S. Patent and Trademark Office University. Her recent client list includes Northern Orient Lines, the Ritz-Carlton Hotel Company, Simonton Windows, and the U.S. Department of Health and Human Services.

Her undergraduate degree is from Dickinson College, and her master's is in adult and continuing education from Virginia Tech. Her graduate studies included an independent research project and thesis on conceptualizing the corporate university. Barley is also a founding member and sponsor of the Washington Area Corporate University Consortium, the first regional network of corporate university practitioners.

PART 2

Internal Corporate University Functions

Most of the activities that corporate universities engage in are focused on developing people. However, there are some functions that are internal to the corporate university—for example, measuring the effectiveness of various programs or of the corporate university itself. The chapters in Part Two concentrate on the activities that are focused on the corporate university itself as opposed to the people it serves.

One of the first questions a corporate university must answer is how it will provide learning programs to its constituents. While it is clearly not a binary choice, many practitioners view this question as primarily centering on classroom-based instruction versus electronic delivery. If a third option is considered, it's usually a hybrid of the two. Chapter Four addresses this question and concludes that the technology is far less important than the learning behind it.

Chapter Five looks at an often forgotten corporate university function: marketing in general and branding in particular. These concepts are frequently neglected, since the corporate university caters to internal clients as opposed to external paying customers, so the notion arises that selling is unnecessary. This chapter refutes that notion and provides a case study on the branding of a corporate university.

Although the leaders of most organizations would readily agree with the concept that ethical behavior is a critical issue, there would be less agreement about how to ensure it. More to the point, it is not always clear where in the organization the promotion of ethical behavior should reside and who should be responsible for it. Chapter Six addresses this issue, concluding, not surprisingly, that the corporate university should be the new keeper of the ethical flame.

Chapter Seven provides a discussion of what its authors call "next-generation evaluation." The chapter focuses on accountability and demonstrating value.

I had the pleasure of hearing Roger Schank speak on the topic of challenging convention. In the course of this inspiring hour, Roger shared his view of the world of e-learning. Among his conclusions was that most e-learning programs do not deliver the results that they are designed for.

I have long been an agnostic when it comes to e-learning. I believe it has tremendous potential, but most programs do not live up to the potential. I always find it delightful when someone agrees with me, as Roger did that day, but he went well beyond my simplistic views of e-learning. Since much of what I have seen in e-learning does not work, I have focused my career on classroom-based learning. But what I admire about Roger is that starting from the same premise, his conclusion is to create programs that do work, whether using classrooms, technology, or some combination.

I thought to myself, "This guy gets it." At that moment, I began hoping that I could persuade Roger to contribute a chapter on his views of learning—e and otherwise—to this book. To the great benefit of the readers of this book, Roger readily agreed and delivered his insightful views on the world of learning and where technology fits.

4

Splendid Learning

WHY TECHNOLOGY DOESN'T MATTER

Roger C. Schank

E-LEARNING IS NOT MY favorite subject to write about. It just makes me angry. Once upon a time, we were trying to create new learning environments that would enable students to improve their performance by trying things out. These were supposed to be enjoyable and challenging experiences. Then suddenly there was the Web, and just as suddenly every chief financial officer (CFO) seemed to determine that money could be saved by converting all paper-based training to online training.

Bye-bye, new ideas. By focusing on saving money, we stopped being creative in our learning solutions; e-learning meant the same old junk that trainers used before, but now it was available electronically. How this was supposed to be an improvement in education I don't know, but it seemed to make CFOs happy. Of course, it didn't make trainees happy. They had always hated most of the training they were forced to undergo, and now the only good part—getting out of the office to go somewhere—had been eliminated.

We tried to keep on building exciting new kinds of learning environments, but these were expensive to build and didn't save anyone immediate money, and slow, complex simulations were low on companies' agendas.

I decided to ignore what had become e-learning, but it was hard to do. Then things got worse. At first I didn't get what anyone could be talking about when they used the phrase "blended learning." But then as I looked closer, I began to see people had moved on from filming plays.

I have always used the analogy of the history of the film industry to make fun of e-learning. In the 1920s, early filmmakers filmed plays to make the first movies. It was a pretty bad idea; you can hardly bear to watch those movies today. But eventually movies became a medium in their own right, quite different from theater. In e-learning we have had the same phenomenon: those awful programmed learning workbook training manuals that everyone hated were put online with some cute graphics, and presto, we had e-learning. Yippee!

I saw that the e-learning industry had moved on from filming plays to suggesting that they film only part of the play (the dullest part presumably) and then alternate that with the actual theater production itself. To put this another way, since e-learning is dull and we already have all those classrooms and all those trainers who would be mad if we eliminated their jobs, let's keep it all and call it blended learning. Then everybody wins. There are even conference sessions on blended learning and companies that proclaim their expertise in blended learning. It is hard to know what there could be to talk about or brag about. "We use classrooms and put the stuff we don't do in a classroom online." Hot dog!

One might ask if the trainees are happy about this state of affairs. But years of experience in traditional universities have taught us that students' happiness doesn't matter much. And they don't get to vote anyhow.

Companies and corporate universities have practical issues. They can't, or don't want to, put everything online. Still it should be obvious that blended learning is a meaningless concept. What to do?

Splendid learning. (I had to call it something.)

To understand splendid learning, I need to tell you about some work Socratic Arts did for Deloitte Consulting. Each year, approximately 120 new consultants join Deloitte Consulting from business schools and other firms. Socratic Arts partnered with Deloitte Consulting to design and develop a simulation for these new employees. This training simulation, based on an actual client at Deloitte Consulting, requires participants to use Deloitte's methodologies and tools, asks them to approach a client problem in a way that is aligned with corporate market strategy, and creates an environment that allows them to experience work on project teams. New employees learn the processes and standards in the consulting field, while also engaged in team building and project management. They are also introduced to Deloitte's culture and values, with particular emphasis on the on-the-job apprenticeship model of learning encouraged at the firm.

Using the story-centered curriculum approach, Socratic Arts developed a simulated scenario where participants are teamed up in groups of four to six to develop a set of recommendations for a client's problem, which are then delivered as a formal presentation to a superior. The simulation consists of a sequence of tasks that highlight key phases in a project life cycle. Teams begin by exploring the industry background and working out their final presentation. As with any other consulting project, teams wrestle with ambiguous requests, indeterminate data, and conflicting interests. As a result, the simulation truly reflects the reality of the field the new consultants will be entering.

The Deloitte Consulting folks—students, coaches, and partners—love what we built. They feel they have learned a lot and keep asking us to build more courses like that one.

I left something important out of this story: whether what we built was delivered online or in a classroom. In fact, it doesn't make a bit of difference. Splendid learning means that whatever you deliver is the same online or offline. The medium is irrelevant. Of course, one could say the same thing for classroom lectures delivered online. The difference here is that we are not filming plays. We are designing authentic learn-by-doing experiences that are mentored apprenticeships with coaches, deliverables, and as much realism as we can muster.

Still, you really want to know if this was delivered online or in a classroom, don't you? Either way, there was a giant Web site with assignments, needed documents, coaching tips, tutorials, step-by-step guides, and so on.

Deloitte happens to deliver this course online for some folks and live for others. It really doesn't matter how they deliver it. So what is my point?

I am supposed to be the technology guy. I was a professor of computer science for thirty-five years. I ran the Institute for the Learning Sciences, which was all about inventing new kinds of educational technologies. Technology is supposed to be my answer to everything. I am sorry to disappoint. Technology is the answer to nothing in education and training. Nevertheless, it is a means to something very important.

Consider this posting I found on an American Society for Training and Development (ASTD) community discussion board:

> My company has just launched a blended learning solution to one of its existing training programs. This blended learning solution consists of three face-to-face sessions, several web-based training courses, virtual sessions using a tool called Centra, and discussion postings. (This is done over a three-week period.)
>
> We are seeing that many of the students are coming to class without completing the web-based training courses (or just reviewing them very quickly). Also, we are seeing that it is difficult to maintain the level of excitement during the virtual sessions.
>
> Is there anyone out there who could give me some tips on how to keep the learner interested over this three-week time period?

Yes, I can give some tips. Stop building e-learning that sucks, and while we are at it, stop thinking there is such a thing as a "blended learning solution." A solution to what? I hate your training, and I don't even know what your training is about. Your classes are boring, and the trainees certainly aren't going to do some boring e-learning program when you aren't sitting over them and making them do it. The writer thinks this is a question about technology. Actually it is a question about proper enforcement of regulations. We know how to make people show up in a classroom. Anything else is hard if it isn't fundamentally interesting.

So the question we must ask when building training is "What makes a learning experience interesting (or compelling, exciting, thrilling, engaging, meaningful, fun, or important—put your favorite word in here: _____)?"

Note that technology is not a part of this question. It could possibly be part of the answer, but it could also not be part of the answer. What is important is to have an answer.

Making Learning Engaging

In their heart of hearts, educators do not believe education is supposed to be exciting, compelling, interesting, and so on. Oh, they believe in having funny speakers, or team-building games where people laugh, or weird buttons that say funny things to wear on your lapel before or after you have been trained, but they don't really believe that learning is anything more than hard work.

Learning as hard work is an idea that has been around for a very long time, at least as long as my parents' generation—a generation that memorized Latin declensions and endless poems and speeches because it was good for you. That generation is dying off, but for the past twenty years, almost whenever I gave a speech about how learning should be fun, some old codger would get up and disagree vehemently, saying that learning was hard work and school shouldn't be fun and that was the trouble with my (sixties) generation: "Everything has to be fun. Harumph."

Fun is an ideological issue.

Is learning fun? Should learning be fun? What exactly is funny about it?

Well, there isn't anything funny about it, and the real issue is our definition of fun. I have a rather simple one: "*Fun* is when you are so totally engaged by something that at the moment you are doing it, you can't think of anywhere else you would rather be or anything else you would rather be doing."

Let's test it. Is math fun?

Math was fun for me when I was in school. (I was a math major in college.) I loved the mental challenge of it, the problem-solving part of it, the competitive aspect of it. (I was faster at coming up with answers than most others, and there were all those test scores to beat the other kids over the head with.) But somewhere in my second year of calculus, it became not fun. It was too theoretical for me. I couldn't see the point. Maybe others were better at it than I was. For whatever reason, math was no longer fun. Clearly, fun is an idiosyncratic affair.

But people aren't so different from one another. The elements of fun are the same for everyone. Everyone likes winning, for example. Everyone likes feeling that they are particularly good at something. Everyone likes getting the right answer.

It sounds as if computer-based training (CBT) should have been loads of fun: lots of questions and answers and lots of opportunities to beat the others and be good at it. But CBT was deadly for the most part, so maybe there are more elements that comprise fun than those that I just stated. Maybe the real issue is engagement. Do you care about what you are doing? And how much do you care?

Is reading engaging? It is for those who like to read and like to read whatever it is they are reading. It is also deadly boring if you are reading something that isn't engaging. But for the most part, Web-based training that involves a lot of reading is not a whole lot of fun.

Something is wrong here.

Fun must be defined by engagement, or more colloquially: if you are really into it, that's fun.

So what are the basic elements of engagement? Here are a few:

Fascination	Curiosity
Exhilaration	Determination
Confusion	Emotional identification
Anticipation	Excitement
Arousal	

This is enough for now. It is not my intention to give a complete list here. But what is this a list of? Are these the elements of a good novel or a good movie, for example? Sure they are. Do they apply to math? Certainly all of them don't, but most of them could for the right person or even for someone who "doesn't like math" for whom the context in which the math is needed is engaging. The trick in making learning fun is to remember the elements of engagement.

The Real Issue: Curriculum Redesign

But this is a chapter on technology, or it is supposed to be. So I should be saying that engagement is the essence of building quality e-learning, which of course it is, but this has nothing to do with technology. We have simply accepted that school is boring, and training is boring, and education is rarely engaging, but suddenly we worry when e-learning turns out to be dull as dust and something you would just as soon not do.

Start worrying about the real issue: we simply have not understood learning very well. Who cares whether that learning is on a computer or not? It is not very well designed wherever it resides. Stop asking about technology, and ask about curriculum redesign, which is the real issue, no matter what curriculum we are discussing and no matter how that curriculum is delivered.

The difficulty in designing really good learning experiences is in making something engaging for someone who is not thrilled by the subject matter in the first place. I happened to be excited by mathematics as a kid, but most people are not at all excited by math. To make engaging learning in math, one would have to get all these elements in there for those who find math to be dull as dust. This means that math would need to be exhilarating, confusing, fascinating, and so on in order for it to be anything more than drudgery for most people.

This is easy to say, but how exactly do you do that? One answer is that you don't. Somehow this answer keeps getting ignored by curriculum designers.

I am often asked how we can teach algebra, for example.

"Don't," I reply.

"What do you mean?" is the stunned response.

It is not necessarily an unreasonable question to ask in a seminar about the creation of online courses. When I discuss how to construct online courses with a group of students (typically these students are professionals), I usually invite the students to pick a subject to teach, and typically they select one that they in fact have to teach in their real lives. But when they ask how to teach particular subjects, they sometimes get surprising (to them) responses.

"But suppose you had to teach algebra?" they ask.

"Just say no."

At this point, "perplexed" would be a poor way of describing the sentiment in the room. The students are annoyed, to say the least.

I feel obligated to say something and pose some questions to the class:

"Why would a student want to learn algebra?"

"What is exciting about algebra?"

"Under what circumstances is algebra engaging?"

And naturally we wander into a discussion that goes into territory where teachers fear to tread. No one really ever asks about what students want to learn when they are designing curricula. Discussions among faculty about curriculum, if they occur at all, mention what teachers want to teach, or what state boards have decided they must teach, or try to make a determination of the subjects that every young educated person must know, or work from a list of learning objectives, or involve discussions about what subjects form the basis of good thinking, reasoning, and research skills. There are lots of words but very few of them about what students want to learn.

I hear a loud grumble: "Students have to learn algebra, and we have to teach it!"

Of course, I know that. I know that state boards of education have determined that algebra is very important. I also know they haven't the slightest idea why it is important, but that, at least to the teachers who have been told to teach it, is neither here nor there.

These discussions take place in the context of my attempts to teach adults, usually people in the training or education business, how to build online courses. And quite naturally, they want to start with the assumption that they will be teaching what they have to teach, hoping that I will tell them how to do that online in an interesting way.

But I can't start with that assumption. The online education business is a lot more like the television business than it is like the on-site education business. You don't see a lot of TV producers suggesting a TV show about algebra. If they did suggest such a show, it surely wouldn't be due to their perception that people would want to watch it. They would have to believe that for some reason, people would be forced to watch it. If viewers had a choice, they would watch the grass-growing channel before they watched an algebra show.

In school curricula, the underlying assumption is that someone higher up than you has determined what everyone must know and that a teacher's job is simply to teach what he or she was told to teach. It is not easy to survive as a teacher in a school setting if you keep questioning why you have been asked to teach whatever it is you were asked to teach. Even in a corporate university setting, questioning the curriculum can get you into hot water. Important people determine curricula, and presumably they must know.

It is not my goal here to discuss how and why curricula get decided on. I have written about that elsewhere (Schank, 2004) and have no need to go over the territory again. Suffice it to say that there usually isn't a lot of method in the madness. And, not surprisingly, online curricula usually are just on-site curricula that someone determined would now be best offered online.

It won't work.

Motivating Learners

It won't work because the online medium has the same kind of voluntary "I can turn this off anytime I want to" attitude about it that television has. Students sit in classes because they have to (or because they feel they should). If a professor is very entertaining, students actually look forward to attending his or her class, but they will still blow it off if there is something better to do, like drinking or sleeping. I was a college professor for thirty-five years. I know of what I speak.

Students want a credential, and to get that credential they will do what they have to do. When online learning provides a credential and the online learning course is required to get that credential, students will do what they have to do.

But, and this is a big BUT, many online learning courses are not required by anyone for anything. They have to succeed on their own merits. Also, and this is a big ALSO, online courses are trying to compete with other online courses and with extant on-site courses.

This means that the best online course will win. And it also means that there are people trying to build really good online courses that will stand on their own merits, like a really good movie or TV show, which will be used because the students really want to learn whatever it is the courses purport to teach.

To make matters worse (or better, depending on your perspective here), online courses actually need to compete with television (and movies and time with one's kids) because they are often done at home. They have to be at least as interesting as the other available options.

So, you don't teach algebra.

Now, at first glance this seems wrong. You don't teach algebra because it's not fun? Because it's not more interesting than *ER*? This doesn't seem like an educational philosophy, does it? Actually that is not the reason, although it is part of the reason. I am not really concerned here with whether the school system teaches algebra. I am quite concerned with that question actually, just not here (Schank, 2004). Here, I pose a more relevant question: How do we design high-quality courses? The answer starts with a simple question: What does the student want to learn? So we must first address the issue of why that question ought to be the place to start.

Think about a time when you decided you needed to learn something: how to speak Spanish, how to cook Chinese, how to drive a car, how to play the piano, how to program a VCR. In cases like those, the student directs the learning process. The student decides what he or she wants to learn. The student pays attention as long as he or she feels the goal he or she has set is becoming more attainable, as long as he or she sees progress. The students in these cases—cases where the reason they are learning is that they decided to do so—decide how things are progressing. They don't need a grade. They tell the teacher what they want to know if they can, or they teach themselves if they can. The student is in charge of his or her own learning. They stop when they feel progress is no longer being made, or if they feel they have learned what they wanted to.

Real learning is like this. It is motivated by accomplishment, and the motivation is intrinsic, not extrinsic. No one said they had to cook Chinese food. If someone had said that—a Chinese-food-loving spouse perhaps—the student would be more likely to drop out of the course than would have been the case had the future cook been the one with the craving for Chinese food. Learning is all about motivation.

The thing that most course designers forget is that when motivation disappears, the student stops learning. The reason designers forget this is that they, like everyone else, went to schools where no one much cared what they wanted to learn. Students are accustomed to being mistreated. They expect it and will put up with it. We all did.

Putting the Learner in Charge

Can you imagine a school where any student could learn whatever he or she wanted to learn and would not have to learn anything he or she didn't want to learn? I can.

That is the role of technology. That is why technology matters: it offers students the opportunity to be in charge of their own learning, and this means they will come with an attitude. Those who build e-learning had better be prepared for students with that attitude: they expect their education to be designed for their needs. That is the world you are about to enter—a world where students are in charge of their own learning. Don't be frightened. You will enjoy the ride. But some cherished assumptions about education may be challenged along the way.

The first cherished assumption to go is that you, the teacher, the course designer, the curriculum committee, the corporate university professional, will decide what is to be in the course. You will not decide. You may decide that you have the right to decide and will damn well decide. But your decision will be overridden if it was made without the student clearly in mind. Who will override your decision? Someone else who listened more carefully to what students want and who students are. Online course design is just like any other consumer product design. The best courses, designed with the consumer in mind, properly marketed, will win.

This is where online education is going. It is also where education in general is going. The education establishment just doesn't know it yet.

I hear some of you saying that is an awful state of affairs. Students don't know what they need to learn. They can't be expected to decide for themselves. That is why they are called students. They trust the faculty or whomever to determine what it is they need to know. That is why they attend school: to be educated by those who know more about what education is or ought to be. This is another one of those subjects that I have written about at length (Schank, 2004), but I will briefly engage it here anyway.

The question of what subjects are worth studying is at the bottom of any attempt to design a curriculum. My point here is simple: if you fail to take student motivation into account when you design a curriculum, you will fail to design one that works, where "works" means that students will want to take the course, will continue in it, and will feel satisfied by it.

Another reason to not teach algebra is that it has no value in and of itself. To put this another way, when we decide to teach something online, what we teach has to have some real value to the student. The new material in some way has to help a student achieve a goal that he or she already had or induce a student to have a goal that the course designers would like him or her to have.

Since motivation starts with goals, the first question to ask when designing an online course is: What are the goals of the students?

We know their goals in the abstract: a desire to be engaged in something meaningful. Meaningful is idiosyncratic: it depends on what your specific goals are. But engagement is not idiosyncratic. All people are engaged in similar ways.

Let's take a look at the list again:

Fascination	Curiosity
Exhilaration	Determination
Confusion	Emotional identification
Anticipation	Excitement
Arousal	

Are video games engaging? For some people, video games are great fun, and those people would probably say that all the above elements are present in video games. But for those who think blasting space invaders out of the TV set is not fascinating, exhilarating, or arousing, then video games are not fun. So if those aren't your goals, you won't want to play. You want to be aroused, but shooting video objects won't do it.

Let's consider two kinds of fun that have nothing to do with learning: roller-coasters and movies. Personally I hate roller-coasters. When I took my then eight-year-old son on Space Mountain (an indoor and dark roller-coaster at Disney World), he asked, after I released the crush hold I had on his chest that was intended to keep him from falling out, "What was the point?"

Indeed.

Nevertheless, we can say the following: those who like roller-coasters find them fascinating, exhilarating, and just a little bit confusing. They are excited by the anticipation of each hill and aroused by the descent. They are determined not to get sick and to make it to the end intact. They emotionally identify with those who don't make it and are basically curious about why the whole thing works.

But for me, a good movie—one where I identify with the characters and anticipate what is going to happen next and am aroused, confused, and exhilarated by the events that transpire—is fun.

So although any individual has his or her own tastes, attitudes, and predispositions—what confuses me may not confuse you; what excites me may well bore you—we all define the basic elements of fun in a similar way.

Because emotional identification is so important, it is worth spending some time on it here. I cannot tell you how many different e-learning programs I have seen that start with something like this: "You have been hired by a large company as its new sales director. You are about to go to an important meeting with your direct reports. The first thing you should say at the meeting is: a, b, c, or d."

Who cares about this character? You can tell me that I have been hired by this company and that this is my job, but I haven't and it isn't.

So how do we create emotional identification? Think about how they create it in the movies. They do not assert that you are a character. In fact, you aren't a character. But if they do their job well, you start to care about the characters and begin to believe that one of them is a lot like some aspect of you. They do this slowly, by having interesting things happen that first cause you to be confused or curious about what is going on. This confusion makes you wonder what will happen next. If the movie is done well, after a while you are excited and exhilarated by the events that transpire.

This is what e-learning must be like if it is to be fun. Your character, in this case the user, must be placed in a world that is somewhat confusing, where events are taking place, and where his goals are being thwarted in some way. He must be forced to make decisions whose effects make things better or worse for him in the scenario. In other words, it needs to seem real, and the events need to relate to concerns that he actually has in the real world. It can't be about shooting down planes because that is not his job. But it can be about people yelling at him, or emergencies that need decisions, or people who won't cooperate with his goals, or characters who are working against him. This really happens in the workplace, and it needs to happen in your e-learning program as well. And it needs to happen visually, in such a way that it looks realistic. You can't say, "You are in a room and people are laughing at you," and expect anyone to care. People need to be laughing at some decision you just made in order for you to get upset and begin to engage in what is going on. That engagement is what e-learning must be about if it is to work at all.

Fun and engagement are pretty much the same thing in my view. Engagement doesn't just happen because an e-learning designer wills it to be so, any more than good movies are made just because someone wrote a script.

So technology is irrelevant, but it is the medium of the future. Good learning designs are the real issue. Of course, they always were the issue, but students couldn't vote with their feet as easily before. When you hear that e-learning isn't doing so well, you need to realize that learning that wasn't e didn't do so well either, but you couldn't tell as easily before.

The fix for education starts with asking some hard questions. First, what is worth learning? This is a terrible question because inevitably someone says that algebra is good for the mind and literature is good for the soul, and, by the way, isn't Latin the root of English? In a jiffy, you have the same old curriculum again.

Curriculum redesign, which needs to be at the heart of any effort to reform the schools as well as any effort to think about corporate training, starts with a different question: What is it that people are having trouble doing?

No one is having trouble (in real life) doing algebra or literary analysis because no one does that outside school. Similarly, orientation and policy courses or courses in how to use software packages or schools for new managers are all based on the school-based notion that what is known ought to be taught. The real question is, What is screwed up in these areas? Are people having trouble becoming oriented? What are they failing at? How do we make sure that they don't fail at it? We can be sure that telling them not to fail or the correct way to succeed will have no effect at all.

Identifying what the real problems are, what people don't do well, and why that failure is causing trouble is the beginning and end of all curriculum design, for employees or for kids.

Corporate curricula are usually archaic and useless for the same reason that school curricula are that way. It has been a long time since people took a long, hard look at them and asked some hard questions. If you don't do this in your corporate university, you will be holding corporate spelling bees soon enough.

What should you do then? My current favorite answer is: the story-centered curriculum.

The Story-Centered Curriculum

The story-centered curriculum is a simple idea: it says that we need to design experiences that look and feel like the real thing. If we are teaching how to be a consultant, we need to make students be consultants. If we are teaching engineering, the students need to be engineers in the story, and they need to be doing real engineering, starting with simple stuff and moving up in complexity: no theories and no lectures, just assignments and projects. We need to design experiences (stories) that look and feel real, are engaging and exciting, demand performance and deliverables, and allow students to produce and try, try again to get better with help from their friends and from mentors and from whatever else we can muster. No classes. No tests. Nothing to read except stuff that helps them just in time to do what we have asked of them. We have done this for many corporate and government clients and for the West Coast campus of Carnegie Mellon University:

West Coast Campus Celebrates First Graduating Class

Carnegie Mellon's West Coast Campus in Silicon Valley held its first graduation ceremony on Friday, Aug. 29 on the grounds of Building 17 at the NASA Ames Research Park at Moffett Field, Calif. Seventeen students received master's degrees in information technology with specializations in software engineering, e-business technology, and the learning sciences.

Established in September 2001, the West Coast Campus is the university's first branch. Its programs stress the importance of learning by doing and are designed to provide an educational experience that closely simulates the real-world work environment for which students are preparing.

All of the programs involve extensive, in-depth projects that students complete as teams. This collaborative approach is one of the defining characteristics of Carnegie Mellon's West Coast Campus and has been touted by students as one of the program's most beneficial aspects.

"What I enjoyed most about my experience at the West Coast Campus were the opportunities to learn with and from my fellow students," said software engineering student Townsend Duong. "I found that being part of a close-working team of intelligent individuals who can take the initiative on accomplishing objectives and work out sound solutions is far more valuable than having industry experience or certification of any kind."

During this past semester, students completed real-world projects in several areas. One group of software engineering students worked with the SAP Corporate Research Center in Palo Alto to complete two projects—one involving two students who worked collaboratively on a project using animated interface agents for e-commerce applications, the second involving three students who worked as a team to build a next-generation multimodal future store framework and integrated it with SAP's Retail Store backend systems.

"Our project with SAP has been one of the most positive aspects of the program in that it's provided exposure and given us the opportunity to apply what we learned at an established company," said software engineering student Ju-kay Kwek. "It's an example of Carnegie Mellon making the most of its name and industry contacts to provide access and value to its students."

Other software engineering students worked on Carnegie Mellon's NASA-sponsored High-Dependability Computing Project, a $23.3 million program created to address the agency's ability to design and build highly dependable mission-critical computing systems. Here, students focused on testbeds, or collaborative environments that bring researchers together to conduct experiments related to dependability. They worked to develop a technology that will facilitate construction, deployment, and use of further testbeds.

In a project with Patroline Air Service, e-business technology students built a prototype of an automated incident reporting system. Consisting of an in-cockpit tablet PC, the system uses digital imaging, real-time GPS/GIS mapping, and workflow automation technologies to improve the effectiveness with which pilots report any observed adverse pipeline conditions to Patroline's customers. Students pilot-tested the prototype and presented an implementation plan to Patroline's management.

"The projects I completed in Carnegie Mellon's e-business program have had a direct effect on what I've been doing for Patroline," said e-business technology student Erick Tai. "This is what's so different about Carnegie Mellon's West Coast Campus, and this is what makes this project-based learning so much more fulfilling than the traditional classes that we are used to."

A learning sciences student working with RoboCamp-West, a college-credit course aimed at high school juniors and seniors, observed the activities of the seven-week program and used what she observed to make recommendations on how to translate the curriculum into an online format. A second learning sciences student developed online performance support materials and course content to help master's level students working at a distance.

After graduation from the West Coast Campus program, some students will continue their education in doctoral programs while others plan on entering the workforce.

"I have high hopes for the future, and I think that this program has offered so many options to me," said Tai. "Whereas previously I was just an electrical/computer engineer, I now feel like I can handle just about anything. Carnegie Mellon's West Coast Campus has been quite amazing for me. It's been a great program, and I don't think I'd trade it for any other" (From Carnegie Mellon's alumni magazine).

Did our students have fun? I think they did. They worked very hard, but they were engaged. At times, they were confused, but they were determined and exhilarated and excited and fascinated as well. There were no movies and no fancy e-learning videos. But what they were doing was all on the Web and all mentored online.

Was it high technology that we built? No. It was a learning environment that was in fact very low-tech. What was new was the splendid learning: the idea that students were learning by doing, finally, three thousand years after Plato first pointed out that that is the only way learning can be accomplished. Plato wouldn't have cared if that were done online and neither do I.

References

Schank, R. C. *Making Minds Less Well Educated Than Our Own.* Mahwah, N.J.: Erlbaum, 2004.

Roger C. Schank, Ph.D., is the founder of the renowned Institute for the Learning Sciences at Northwestern University, where he is John P. Evans Professor Emeritus in Computer Science, Education and Psychology. He was professor of computer science and psychology at Yale University and director of the Yale Artificial Intelligence Project. He was a visiting professor at the University of Paris VIII, an assistant professor of computer science and linguistics at Stanford University, and research fellow at the Institute for Semantics and Cognition in Switzerland. He also served as the Distinguished Career Professor in the School of Computer Science at Carnegie Mellon University. He is a fellow of the AAAI and was founder of the Cognitive Science Society and co-founder of the *Journal of Cognitive Science.*

In 1994, he founded Cognitive Arts Corporation, a company that designs and builds high-quality multimedia simulations for use in corporate training and online university-level courses. The latter were built in partnership with Columbia University. In 2002, he founded Socratic Arts, a company that is devoted to making high-quality e-learning affordable for both businesses and schools.

Schank is the author of more than twenty books on learning, language, artificial intelligence, education, memory, reading, e-learning, and storytelling. The most recent are *Virtual Learning, Coloring Outside the Lines: Raising a Smarter Kid by Breaking All the Rules, Scrooge Meets Dick and Jane, Engines for Education,* and *Designing World Class E-Learning.*

He holds a Ph.D. in linguistics from the University of Texas.

One of the best parts of working in the corporate university world is the wonderful people that you meet. One of the finest I've come across is Annick Renaud-Coulon, a Parisian who has studied and worked with corporate universities in Europe and around the world.

Annick founded the European Club of Corporate Universities several years ago to provide a forum for European corporate university professionals to get together and share best practices. Building on that, she created the Global Council of Corporate Universities.

Annick has conducted research projects on corporate universities around the globe. Among her findings is the importance to a corporate university of having a strong brand. She has shared those findings, as well as an illustrative case study, in this chapter.

5

Branding Your Corporate University

Annick Renaud-Coulon

DURING MY VISITS TO corporations in the most unexpected places in India, China, and the Middle East, two names consistently came up when speaking to people about corporate universities: GE Crotonville and Motorola University. Without really knowing what happens within these organizations, many people nevertheless knew about them. I started to wonder about the phenomenon of their reputations. Is it because of the brand name? Can branding recognition apply to the world of corporate universities other than by analogy? We have to answer these questions because many executives are wondering what exactly their corporate university brand is, and a lot of them can't even imagine that anyone could consider the name of their university as a brand. But whether they like it or not, they are concerned with and affected by branding.

Corporate university executives know that corporate branding refers to the practice of using their company's name as a product brand name. But applying this practice in their internal educational structure is another story

altogether. Even if a corporate university brand is inadvertent, it conveys the
services, the identity, the essence, the character, the inspiration, the leadership, the power, the values, and the purpose of the educational structure. It
distinguishes it from the company's different internal and external competitors, mercantile or not. Therefore, it would be beneficial if corporate university brands were not a random issue.

Corporate university directors need to gain an understanding of what a
corporate university brand is and to maximize its effectiveness. In this chapter, I present a discussion of the factors that contribute to a corporate university brand.

What Is Your Corporate University Brand?

Branding is the act of burning with a hot iron, the act of stigmatizing, the act
of marking. Beyond this definition, what does it mean for a corporate university? Is it also branded in iron like an animal? Yes and no, because the
brand of a university is not reduced to a logo that means only that it belongs
to a proprietor. It actually evolves with time as a function of a certain number of decisions and events.

A corporate university is similar to a firm and a product. It is the vehicle
of an image and a name: its own name and the name of its company. It is a
promise. Therefore, it has everything a commercial brand has except that it
has no commercial value. It can never be sold to work outside the institutional frame that gave it birth. Just imagine the brand "Defense Acquisition
University" sold to a third party. That would make no sense, and it would be
impossible. That is why the branding of an educational structure is subtle and
fragile; it cannot be treated like something you would usually brand in the
commercial world.

A corporate university brand encompasses the following characteristics:

- The idea of your corporate university that resides in your mind and
  that you create, name, and use as a resource to your organization. It
  includes materials, technologies, intellectual property, and aesthetics.

- The sum of all that is known, thought, felt, and perceived about your corporate university.

- The total addition of all human experiences, perceptions, and feelings about your corporate university.

- The addition of all its visible and invisible attributes and characteristics, intended or not.

- The idea of your corporate university that resides in the minds of your stakeholders.

In other words, a corporate university brand is a complicated entity that doesn't belong only to those who run the university. That would be too simple. It belongs to the stakeholders who observe and use it, whether users or competitors, and all those who somehow have the power of influence over its destiny. It is both functional and emotional. It is always unstable, like the corporation itself, and difficult to comprehend. In fact, the corporate university brand is not only a position but also a process. A brand needs care if it is to maintain constant visibility.

Elements of a Corporate University Brand

The primary corporate university brand elements are all visible material, supports, and facilities. These elements constitute a kind of contract that directs the structure and those who use or have the intention of using its services.

The Image

Branding is an issue for corporate universities today because we live in a civilization of images that practically invade the entire planet through television and all of the other digital miracles. Thus, despite all strategic approaches, tactics, and operations, the corporate university brand is composed of the sum total of impressions that form a puzzle, an image more or less focused, more or less beautiful, more or less attractive, more or less positive or negative. This image is composed of:

- The faces of its team. The corporate university staff is well known or not, competent or not, open to everyone or not, close to its clients or not.

- The reputation of its activities: high or low, aligning or not on real needs, funny or boring, innovative or conservative, expensive or inexpensive, intellectual or practical.

- The values emerging from its purposes, speeches, targets, facilities, and activities. Who is the heart of the university concerned with? The corporate elite? The employees? Other people? Is its setting excessively prestigious or not enough according to its corporate values? Is there a discrepancy between what it offers and the perceived quality of its activities?

- The added value and performance as perceived by its clients, consumers, and other stakeholders. It depends on the idea of its real mission and usefulness, its real power and influence, its real support from the CEO, and its beliefs around this added value.

Ultimately is its image (both within the company and outside) good or bad? Blurry or precise? What does the credibility of the structure depend on? Do the employees of the company want to become more educated? Does the CEO want to renew the budget? In short, the future of the corporate university depends on the image.

The Identity

Without a doubt, the closest aspect to the heart of the subject of branding is that of its identity. Because the corporate university is a strategic tool of a company, it is very close to the business strategies. Therefore, the corporate university carries the identity of its company. It occupies a field of responsibility intimately tied to the identity of the firm that no business school or traditional university could. And its whole challenge will be to reflect this identity while setting up its own. Remember that the identity of a corporate university goes beyond its primary administrative function. It is also a concept. Halfway between fiction and reality, each entity tells its story since its creation and reflects a projected image, and this is what we are or what we would like to be. The identity permits self-invention. It affirms that the university of an organization is unique and has nothing to do with the twenty-five hundred others that exist on the planet. The identity is founded on similarities, differences, distinction, and perpetual change. Ownership, mission, status, responsibilities, values, images, location, power, and influence are the ingredients that define the entity and allow people to fill a part of it and be recognized as a member or a beneficiary of the corporate university. There is no doubt that its identity gives a common spirit that is possible to share inside the community. From this point of view, it is interesting to compare organizations that possess a corporate university with those that don't. The same ambition does not exist in both, nor does the same ambience or spirit.

The Promise

The corporate university brand is a promise that has the precise elements that determine whether it will be highly effective. It is an expectation waiting to be fulfilled. It is a promise for the individual and the firm. For the individual, what is promised by attracting people to participate in its activities? To get skills, competencies, recognition, employability, mobility, wage growth, diplomas, certificates, honor, social networks, or possibly rest or vacation? Maybe nothing is formally promised, but what counts is what is implied and what is understood and integrated in its training approach.

For the firm, what is promised when it is asked to support the education effort? To get rich? Or is it problem resolution, business solutions, quality awards, cultural integration, change management, or transformation of the organization? Maybe it's a brand-new image or a good conscience. What is difficult with the corporate university brand promise is that it is not always fulfilled at the moment that the educational service is consumed. You need some time, possibly a lengthy period, between the moment of acquisition of knowledge and its efficient application in the work within the firm. Hence, some of the best corporate university brands are built over time.

The corporate university brand is not just some type of psychological ploy or tactic to attract new customers. It is not just words. It is the sum of expectations plus the satisfaction of stakeholders, the primary people who are able to say yes or no to the corporate university as a brand. This is a fundamental point for a director of a firm's university who might very well consent to many efforts to construct and protect the brand of his or her corporate university. He or she must understand that the promise delivered is equally made up of the values that lie at the intersection of what is deliverable by the corporate university, desired by corporate customers, and different from the competitors.

Why Brand Your Corporate University?

The necessity of branding their corporate university is far from being obvious for all corporate university directors, and for multiple reasons: modesty, limited budgets, lack of marketing competence, but mostly a lack of information regarding what is at stake. When I made my worldwide study in 2001, I asked about the key factors of success in all of the firms studied. It came out that good marketing was the top factor. I deeply believe it. A quality offering that is not well known has no chance of being understood. And to be understood, people have to know where it comes from and what to expect. That's why the branding concept needs time, money, and intelligence. In this section, I present five reasons why branding your corporate university is important: to manage your image, manage your identify, face competitors, allow your company to reinforce or rethink its own branch, and constantly sustain momentum inside and outside your firm.

To Manage Your Image

When a corporate university has created a strong identity and received sufficient equity from its stakeholders, it is armed to endure. It becomes indispensable for the organization and would be unthinkable to function without it. Of course, the product exists without the branding since it doesn't belong only to the will of the team that runs it. However, if you don't take care of your image, of your identity, of your educational promise, others will do it in your place.

They will carve out a reputation for you that will be miles away from what you wished to promote. This reputation may make false promises that risk undermining your credibility and even the survival of your university. Therefore, these are the primary reasons for branding your corporate university:

- To form a positive perception in the minds of your target audiences and internal stakeholders—the CEO, executive board, human resource director, business units, clients, customers, teachers, consultants—and in your own mind as well. This last point is essential. The more you work on the branding of your corporate university, the more you will know it and require of it and yourself. The more you will love it and so defend it.

- To get money (from your CEO, human resource director, or customers) to survive. If your image is blurred and your stakeholders do not understand what your added value is, you risk a decrease or cut in your budget.

- To explain to external stakeholders (for example, academics, politicians) what a corporate university is and demonstrate its added value. What is this unique object? The corporate university phenomenon is not at all clear for many people.

To Manage Your Identity

Despite the efforts of some firms to copy the models of other corporate universities that enjoy excellent reputations, their effort is in vain. The very existence of a corporate university is unique and nonreproducible because of its own scope of activities, its own values, its own educational infrastructures, and its own identity even more than that of its parent firm. Who am I? is the first question that a corporate university needs to answer to direct its action. What are our corporate university characteristics (values, convictions), visions and purposes (dreams, strategic positioning facing singular challenges, with evolutions), forces and resources (team, budget, facilities), uniqueness from different internal and external competitors (services and products that are only deliverable by corporate university)?

To Face Competitors

A corporate university never develops without competitors. These are visible or invisible, active or not, but they exist. They are internal training centers, internal consultants, external consultancy firms, business schools, and information technology training providers, and even self-learning, television, books, the Internet, corporate university events, and other corporate universities. Who are your corporate university's competitors? The head of a corporate university has to answer this question because he or she could believe that his or her entity is unassailable, which is surely not the case. And the most dangerous competition often comes from within the organization. There is nothing better for combating the potential or real adversaries than to affirm the brand and impose its identity, its image, its promise. A brand exclaims, "I exist, and so you must respect me! What's more, I'll show you what I can do." The brand is there to favor the practical recognition of services offered by the corporate university and at the same time its differentiation from the rest of the company.

To Allow Your Company to Reinforce or Rethink Its Own Brand

Your corporate university branding can be an exercise in corporate branding. A strong, positive corporate university brand is important for your company. It is a tremendous lever for lifting the profile of the firm in both its human and business ambitions. When the strategic position of the corporate university is well thought out, intelligent, refined, and in conformity with the goals of the firm, then its branding, if it is well done, will make your company appear at its best, and as an employer, it is at its best for attracting and retaining employees.

To Constantly Sustain Momentum Inside and Outside Your Firm

The brand of a corporate university is rooted in the history of the firm, and it becomes a reference for its stakeholders, permitting it:

- To promote the people who benefit from its services, to see who will transform their careers, or at least to reinforce their feeling of belonging to the firm

- To prepare the company and its people for challenges
- To stimulate impetus for sustained improvement, change, and growth
- To give sense, to continue, and to survive
- To develop loyal clients

How to Brand Your Corporate University

It has become essential for a corporate university that wants to be part of the next generation of corporate universities to take its brand in hand and manage it for the long term. The only question is how to make that brand a great success.

Branding a corporate university is a process of making the university itself and its products and services into brands; identifying, codifying, and articulating these products or services; and creating compelling reasons to use them. I propose four stages for a successful corporate university branding: affirm your strategic positioning, design your corporate university brand, mobilize and communicate, and evaluate your brand equity.

Stage 1: Affirm Your Strategic Positioning

This is the most important key to success. With different constraints in mind, you have to answer fundamental questions: What is your ideal university? What is your corporate university's strategic position? From this position, you will be able to answer another question: What is your corporate university's identity and its brand? In order to answer these questions, analyze the following questions and constraints:

- What do you want to do for your corporate university according to executive aspirations and customers' needs and desires?
- What do you have to do according to your environmental situation and customers' needs? (Desire often differs from real needs in many situations.)

- What are you allowed to do according to internal and external power contingencies? What about your freedom, your own power? You know how reality often runs over your dreams!

- What are you able to do according to your own and your team's competencies and available resources?

Stage 2: Design Your Corporate University Brand

Consider several components of your corporate university: dreams, visions, purposes, values, culture, resources and competencies, market positioning, competition, and products and services. Then determine the visible components of your corporate university brand and act on the invisible elements. Do it through the light of your reason and also through your senses, because your corporate university brand will be established and memorized through different means. What is it that you want each of your stakeholders to see? (Is the aesthetic refined, empty, full, modern, retro?) What do you want them to hear? (A nice noise, sounds that are a nuisance, a tiring hubbub? Will they have a chance to listen to music, and what style?) What do you want them to smell? (Nice memorable odors, or unpleasant ones?) What do you want them to touch? (What will be their sensation when they touch the tables, chairs, files and folders, the computers of the corporate university?) What do you want them to taste? Will you offer them a drink or something to eat? What will they retain as a pleasurable memory? In short, the idea of the corporate university brand will be associated with different elements, some rational, others emotional, and these components cannot be dissociated from one another.

Consider the elements that contribute to your corporate university brand:

- *The corporate university name.* Does your corporate university name exist yet? Have you chosen to use "university," or is this entity an "academy," "institute," "learning center," or something else, such as a place name, like Four Acres for Unilever in the United Kingdom or Crotonville for GE? Is it known? If so, where is it known: Inside the company, outside the company, or even abroad? Does it provide meaning for your company, your customers, or you? Be careful in choosing the name, because you cannot easily change it. A name for your corporate university is indispensable. Without a name, it does not exist; it cannot be spoken of or promoted.

• *A logo and a tagline.* Does your corporate university have its own logo and tagline? For instance, at Thales University, the tagline is, "Developing people for success; a team committed to your service to live our values together." If there is a logo, typically it uses the colors and graphics of the company logo. But a lot of corporate universities do not have their own logo, and so use the logo of their parent company. To have a logo seems to present a stronger identity, but it is not a rule. Branding professionals talk about "mother brand" and "daughter brand." The mother brand combined with the daughter brand marks an inspirational role played by the company toward its corporate university and vice versa. It proves that the spirit and involvement of the main brand give sense to all actions, for all audiences external and internal. It is an image and an address of cohesion and conviction. I believe that it is important for a corporate university to have its own logo corresponding to its own identity even if the firm's identity seeps into the university's logo. Since one is not the other, to give a logo to a corporate university allows it to act with more freedom, to affirm itself, and to make its own communications to its own stakeholders.

• *Graphics, stationery, branded learning tools, and gadgets.* To create a high-quality brand, you must have the imagination to remind everyone of the existence of the organization or product that you want to promote. All of the support material that the corporate university uses must bear signs of recognition: name, logo, colors. That means letterhead, business cards, greeting cards (some signed by the whole university team), manuals, CD-ROMs, briefcases, notebooks, golf balls, pens, caps, T-shirts, and anything else identified with the university. Each of the visible artifacts must be conceived as a small commercial representation that reminds its past and future participants of the benefits of this educational structure.

• *Music or a specific jingle.* One can obviously memorize a brand through sound. The Web site, telephone, videos, and CD-ROMs are useful means for that. During events, the corporate university will do well to reinforce its brand through sound or music that conforms with the firm's culture. I advise an original score created by a composer, along with different versions, such as long or short jingles.

- *Facilities.* Is your corporate university virtual or on campus? How luxurious or simple is it? What about odors, perfume, smoking or nonsmoking areas? What about the lifestyle on the campus? Do people dress formally or casually? Is there a sports area, a TV channel presenting world news, or TV sets in the rooms? What do the participants think about comfort and ambiance? Is it open to all of the population or only to the elite? How does distance learning affect your corporate university brand? Firms that can equip themselves with a physical campus possess the means to have a stronger corporate university brand than those without facilities, because these facilities are an obvious representation of the firm's spirit. It is possible, however, that the site could convey a counterproductive image (too distant, too sparse, not convivial enough, boring festivities). In this case the people targeted will balk at coming. The question must always be asked about the quality, conviviality, and efficient use of the facilities. And the best way to regularly ask these questions is by doing quality satisfaction surveys of participants.

- *Online presence on the firm's Web site, corporate university intranet, or dedicated extranet.* It is becoming more common for a corporate university to have its own Internet site because it's a good way to manage what it has to offer. Some have their own Web site, others reside on their firm's Web site, and some have developed an extranet. This isn't so much about the design or graphics of the corporate university, although that is very important; rather, it is the foundation of its message and image. What do these communications project in terms of professionalism, innovation, and seriousness, and what will embellish or tarnish the corporate university brand?

- *Brochures and booklets on the corporate university and on your products and services.* These printed materials are about institutional communication and marketing. From observing what is practiced, we see that all corporate universities publish information about their offerings, either electronically or in hard copy. The question is not to know whether to produce or not (because if you say nothing about yourself and what you do, you have no chance to have any clients) but to know how, and what kind, and for what target.

• *Publications: newsletters, e-newsletters, articles, books, or white papers.* The production and dissemination of knowledge, if it is originally and professionally handled, can have an important effect on the corporate university brand. Some corporate universities succeed as true publishers. They solicit authors from the corporate university team, within the firm, or outside it. They can also publish newsletters or articles.

• *The distribution of certificates, degrees, or awards.* This can have a strong impact on the brand of a corporate university. Diplomas have an importance for those who possess them. For employees who have never gone to a traditional university, in-house diplomas tend to considerably heighten, at least for them and their colleagues, their own image and the image of the corporate university. In some cultures, certificates and diplomas are regarded as sacred documents whose legitimate delivery belongs to the academic world. If you choose to issue certificates or diplomas, be sensitive to the cultural ramifications. I have observed that some of these diplomas delivered by corporate universities hold more importance for employers and employees than those from the traditional education system.

• *Testimonials from stakeholders.* These are an intelligent way to spread the word of a corporate university's success. Testimonials make the discourse credible, and these comments seem less like self-promotion. An enormous part of the art of branding consists of finding good testimonials and transcribing them in a way that helps to advance the brand. The primary testimonial to bring forward is that from the CEO. (I have lost count of the firms that have found that their top executive is their most faithful supporter.)

• *Corporate university TV.* Some universities have their own television channel. But be warned that the competition with professional TV channels is difficult, and it is necessary to invest a lot of time and money to attract a clientele accustomed to high-quality standards elsewhere.

• *Media relations plan, a press book, and TV talk shows.* More and more corporate universities communicate directly with the media and even use publicists to obtain press coverage in widely read magazines and newspapers. The idea is to promote the corporate university inside by detouring outside. I must dissuade you from this type of practice when the added value is not apparent and the message is not clear. Poorly directed communications can do more harm than good to the brand.

• *Events organized by the corporate university, such as lunches, guest speakers, or parties.* These internally developed branding aids are designed to remind stakeholders regularly that the corporate university exists and offers activities, programs, and services. One would also expect that it brings fun and fantasy, and some festive moments in the life of the corporation. Putting on events is incontestably an activity of next-generation corporate universities.

• *Awards.* There are several external awards that some corporate universities try to obtain (for example, the CUBIC Awards presented annually by the International Quality and Productivity Center and the awards for Excellence and Innovation in Corporate Learning presented by Corporate University Xchange). Again, be careful: it sends a negative message about your focus if your corporate university is better known outside the company than within. And then there are those awards that the corporate university issues itself. Obviously, awards need to be legitimate and established in order to reward the internal pedagogic approach.

• *Participation in associations, groups, and corporate university clubs.* To get involved in club communities like the club that I founded permits corporate universities to gain exposure. Of course, the primary advantage is the exchange of ideas with national or international organizations.

Stage 3: Mobilize and Communicate

It is not sufficient to work on a brand in your own little corner of the world. You need to test it with clients, participants, and other stakeholders. The ideal way is to decide on the details with all of these people, who from now on will feel like proprietors. You will have to question them, educate them, and mobilize them and ask them to be a privileged intermediary of your brand. Among these stakeholders, you have to take special care of your CEO, the operational managers, and the business unit directors. Start with them, and then display your brand everywhere, inside and outside the firm. Invest in events and the media. And don't forget to forge partnerships with other corporate universities around the world. Lean on opinion leaders in the field of corporate universities. Give a little of your time to promote the industry, speak in forums or specialized symposiums, and write articles, and you will increase by tenfold the reach of your brand. To do this, you must decide on and manage a communication plan. It is just as important as working on the design of your programs. Do it in coordination with your teams and bosses. Problems can surface when marketing too much, which turns off managers or even participants, or when marketing too little, choosing instead to be the organization's best-kept secret.

Stage 4: Evaluate Your Brand Equity

Brand equity is a way to describe and measure the total value of the corporate university brand. Try to answer (with the maximum of proof and objective criteria) the following questions relative to the stakeholders who contribute to your corporate university brand equity:

- Awareness: Do they know of you?

- Image: What do they think of you?

- Preference: Do they want to learn and change with you?

- Loyalty: How committed are they to you?

Better yet, have an evaluation of your corporate university brand done by others.

The Campus Veolia Brand: A Case Study

This case study of Veolia Environment illustrates a corporate university that has successfully branded itself. Veolia Environment is the only company in the world that can offer the whole spectrum of environmental services in water (water cycle management), waste management (waste collection, management, treatment and recycling), energy services, and transportation. The company generated 24.7 billion euros in consolidated revenue in 2004, 83 percent of it in Europe.

The Veolia Environment Campus is its own brand, with an identity, a promise, and an image that distinguishes it from the group that created it and makes it different from other educational structures inside and outside this corporation of 260,000 employees spread throughout seventy-eight countries.

The Name

The first attribute of Veolia's corporate university is its name: Campus Veolia. According to Latin etymology, a campus is a field or a university built outside the city, in the fields, in a vast space. In this case, the terminology is barely a metaphor since Veolia Environment's principal campus, in the town of Jouy-le-Moutier near Paris, is situated on fifty acres in the countryside where employees are educated. Both the name and the campus itself give the corporate university identity and legitimacy.

The corporate university has a logo that is in total conformity with the graphics of the company (see Figure 5.1). It takes the company's logo, with the word *campus* written by hand over it by someone from the operational team (see Figure 5.2). Note the symbolism: it is a human being who is at the heart of the training process at Veolia Environment. Also note that the campus chose not to have a tagline.

Figure 5.1. The Mother Brand of Veolia Environment

Figure 5.2. The Daughter Brand of Campus Veolia

The Promise

Campus Veolia is a platform for the company's competencies, a center to which Veolia has delegated development activities for its network of three thousand companies in seventy-eight countries. Campus Veolia is concerned with the four business units of Veolia Environment and concentrates on developing three essential areas:

- Business competencies within its four services: water, transportation, sanitation, and energy

- The culture of the firm's identity (its standards and the spirit of its flag)

- The promotion and support of its business

The quality promise is made to the group's employees and future employees with education and diplomas. In 2004, the campus welcomed over fourteen thousand students. In terms of formal education, it offers sixteen professional diplomas, from certificates to master's degrees, with a success rate of 95 percent. In continuing education, 450,000 internship hours are spent annually. The global operating budget was up to 30 million euros in 2005.

Campus Veolia constitutes a promise of the creation of value, a quasi-contract:

- For employees, it helps connect them to their work and gives them the feeling of belonging, of creating moral and economic value directly through their work.

- For the directors of the company and the campus operational team, it pushes them to maintain and develop the promise of Veolia as a large, international firm. It is also an educator with strong social ambitions but at the same time centered on its business (value creation and economic strategy).

- For its clients, it focuses on the quality of the promised services (the creation of economic strategic value).

- For shareholders, it is about their investments (the creation of financial value).

The Culture

The following functions and values are associated with Campus Veolia:

- It is concerned with all of Veolia Environment's constituents.

- It produces recognition for individuals and the firm.

- It produces integration across the business units: What are the cross competencies?

- Veolia educates Veolia. The process of education and management of competencies (identifying needs, evaluating competencies, and teaching) is done with managers from the company, not outside specialists. Most of the educators are from the company and then return to their primary jobs, enriched by their pedagogic experiences.

- Differences are respected. This promotes a diversity of cultures.

- The leadership support is strong (but without interference). Henri Proglio, chairman of the Veolia Environment board of directors, is a strong presence on campus and supports its activities with enthusiasm, readily responding to requests to hand out diplomas or participate in seminars. He is also involved in the Veolia Competencies program (involving seventeen thousand people in three years with recruitment, education, diplomas, and long-term contracts).

- There is an appreciation of environmental values. Those who use the campus are invited to recycle, carpool, and in other ways show their respect for the environment.

The Physical Facility

The Jouy-le-Moutier campus has some ultramodern buildings with a historic chateau in the center. This mansion from the nineteenth century has been arranged with conference rooms and a game room, a bar, and a multimedia room (connected to a Wi-Fi network) with a flat screen television that continually displays the most watched French economic information channel. In the twenty-two thousand square meters of buildings, there are very modern facilities, including fifty-two classrooms, conference rooms, and the administrative building. The technology area is a training space divided into four parts, each corresponding to the different businesses of the firm. An amphitheater with 160 seats and an auditorium with 500 seats are used for conventions (with simultaneous translations in several languages) and conferences. The resource center is open from 9:00 A.M. to 10:00 P.M. from Monday through Friday; two thousand books are available, plus more than eighty periodicals and fifteen Internet stations. A new sports facility offers a multisports room, a weightlifting room, and a squash court. The campus has two hotel residences with three thousand rooms.

The Image

When you go beyond the rational information about the brand and let your mind go, you enter into the deeper promise of Campus Veolia, one that makes you want to contribute to the educational effort for your team and yourself.

The interior architecture of the chateau, designed by the campus director, Christian Dapilly, confronts the visitor with time frames very distant one from another. The past is reassuring and conservative, and then you enter into the future with pizzazz. The four elements of earth, air, water, and fire are found within a futuristic design, with fluorescent colors, ultramodern furniture, a stairwell in the form of flames, and different lighting effects from room to room. And so you are thrown into a completely avant-garde setting, which is the center of life, the gathering place, no matter where you fit in the company's hierarchy. This environment lends itself to some interesting personal discoveries.

The other buildings, which were built more recently, have beautiful lighting on the buildings and walkways that project a surrealistic image. The campus is well thought out. Most notable, the main plaza has a single red neon sign that indicates the entrance to the restaurant, as if to say that food for the soul is important, but nourishing the body should not be forgotten. The meals are adapted to the targeted audience: attractive, well done, and delicious.

The technology area is a miniature of this gigantic multinational firm, symbolizing the four businesses of Veolia Environment. One can imagine future bus drivers learning the maneuvers of driving, plumbers putting their pipes together, sanitation workers handling trash bins, and maintenance crews maintaining heaters.

The big auditorium with an immense bay window reveals the campus's greenery and bears witness to the great gatherings of the Veolia Environment family. This is where the CEO meets the executives and where awards ceremonies are held. It is also where the culture of the group is created and generated because there is no other place of this size or with this infrastructure or this quality at the company's headquarters.

The bright classrooms are equipped with furniture and computers like that typical of a French high school. Other rooms with a very modern design are normally occupied by seminars devoted to the managers of the group or to guests. It is important that all learners feel comfortable in a setting they are familiar with.

There are no televisions or telephones in the rooms. It is possible to watch television in a community room with others.

What is seen but not described on the institutional Web site are the faces you see at Campus Veolia, the majority of them young. Also, there is a fun and festive atmosphere, with everyone friendly to others, even to strangers. There is no elitism or hierarchy in the treatment of people. Everything is uniquely set up for conviviality, efficiency, and the best use of the training space for the objectives sought.

The operational team of 120 full-time members is a big part of the success of the brand. This staff, directed with enthusiasm and passion by Christian Dapilly, form an extremely competent team. Campus Veolia is permanently open and continually challenging itself and developing good partnerships with universities and town halls throughout the world.

Finally, the CEO and the members of the executive committee are interested in the campus and take the time to meet the team. That this place is valuable is testified to by the fact that France's president has come to meet with the trainees, something he has never done with another firm.

Communication

Institutional communications use a variety of materials (as much as possible on recycled paper and cardboard): brochures; CD-ROMs (depicting awards ceremonies and executive integration days); a newsletter in French, English, and Spanish, which talks about international education; cardboard briefcases; trainee kits; pens; note pads; umbrellas; and electronic presentations. Internet communication is done principally on the site www.campus.veoliaenvironnement.com, which displays the history, geography, and key figures of the Campus Veolia.

Communication of educational offerings is made through brochures, information guides, a newsletter, the company's Web site, and the company's intranet. Campus Veolia regularly calls attention to its existence through different events. Conferences are offered on durable development, global warming, environmental reports, carbon reports, and other subjects. These events are a vehicle for the Campus Veolia brand, reinforcing its image.

The Future of the Campus Veolia Brand

Campus Veolia has existed as a name only since 2004, and while the brand has proven to have a promise and a strong identity, it has yet to be determined if it will be an enduring brand. Campus Veolia is also part of the identity of Veolia Environment, of the people who work there, and of those who come to learn or teach. It is an incontestably creative and rich brand with value that is definitely economic, but also moral and political.

Campus Veolia is eclectic and projects us into the explicit and symbolic, into the cognitive and emotional, into stability and innovation, into the one and the all, and shows the need to mix populations, professions, and educational approaches as we seek to live together and progress as one social body of 260,000 employees spread over the world.

Campus Veolia will develop a network by creating other campuses in France and other countries that will function as resource centers. The goal is to consolidate the educational efforts around identified and understood methods, a common language of production, a system of collective information, and large partnerships with training systems in different territories, whether that be national systems of education, research, or client networks of the firm. The brand that is already visible and evokes a positive image will be reinforced, cared for, used, and emphasized. Already with a very strong cohesion with the mother brand, the daughter brand must more and more serve the Veolia Environment group for the implementation of its social and business strategies.

And so as Christian Dapilly likes to say, "The Campus Veolia brand builds and advances little by little." He has understood by following the example of other heads of corporate universities: a corporate university brand is always fragile and evolving, just like its identity and image. And this proves that it is also alive.

Conclusion

The next generation of corporate universities considers corporate university brands a holistic process and not a random one. By branding your corporate university, you will generate and sustain the momentum of your corporate university inside and outside your company. Take into account your stakeholders' and clients' wants and needs. Make sure you communicate well with all of them. Be distinct and different. Be innovative yet conservative. Give character to your brand. Develop a brand that tells people what you do. Be ambitious for your corporate university. Make a myth and a legend of it. Investing in your corporate university's brand is investing in your development and your identity—in sum, in your future.

Annick Renaud-Coulon, in addition to studying law, has been a teacher, head of human resources in an industrial organization, a consultant, and head of an enterprise. She currently works as an independent consultant and conference speaker with a network of partners in France and internationally.

Among her other specialties, she consults in the area of organizational change. She conducts research and helps heads of organizations to solve problems in a wide range of situations. Renaud-Coulon also writes articles and books and conducts seminars and conferences on corporate education and related fields.

Her consulting and speaking activities have taken her to many countries, including Canada, China, Egypt, India, Japan, Morocco, Senegal, South Korea, Taiwan, the United States, and numerous European countries.

I've known some professors who quit professing to take a job in industry. Phil McGee did it backward: he worked in industry for nearly twenty years before joining the professoriate. Because of his background, Phil teaches about and studies human resource development and other workplace performance issues. He feels that corporate universities, in their role as a strategic tool regarding people issues, can help to maintain ethical behaviors in the workplace.

In this chapter, Phil and his colleague John Duncan discuss how corporate universities can be the standard-bearers for organizational ethics, and they provide three very disparate organizations as case studies.

6

Corporate Universities

THE NEW KEEPERS OF THE ETHICAL FLAME?

Philip McGee, John R. Duncan

HARDLY A MONTH GOES by that the evening news, daily paper, and weekly magazines do not report in detail the moral failings of corporate executives, politicians, clergy, and celebrities with their hands caught in the cookie jar. Beyond the failings of our leaders, unethical behavior has become rampant in our society. One need only enter into any Internet search engine the key words "unethical behavior," and page after page of newspaper and magazine articles appear.

Unfortunately, too many of us have become morally desensitized. We shrug our shoulders, adopt a stoic attitude, and rationalize that people have always been unethical. We tell ourselves that everyone lies and cheats occasionally because of our win-at-any-cost culture. Besides, who really is hurt by a few white lies, and so what if someone steals a ream of paper from the office storeroom for their home computer? Isn't it all really quite normal? It is certainly not anything anyone should get upset about. Or is it?

Consider that unethical company employees:

- Often distrust the organization and its leadership
- Feel little, if any, loyalty toward the organization or its goals
- Tend to cut corners and perform poorly
- More often than not suffer from poor morale and lack of motivation

In contrast, ethical company employees:

- Are often proud to be associated with the organization
- Are more motivated, and the quality of their work is higher
- View profitability as one of several desired outcomes or goals to be achieved
- Possess a sense of interconnectedness with society and the world

So, if being ethical has so many benefits, why are there so many instances of unethical behavior? Why are many professional organizations, consulting firms, and business organizations scrambling to provide ethics education to their managers and employees? Is there a relationship between the world of work and what we have been teaching in institutions of higher education? And if we in corporate universities and human resource development have any influence, what should we be doing?

Practitioners and academicians have both had a tremendous amount of influence on the ethical behavior displayed in our society. We are at the same time both part of the problem and part of the solution.

Trends and Driving Forces with an Impact on Organizational Ethics

Numerous trends are changing the face of global commerce and are therefore affecting how ethical behavior is practiced in business organizations.

Trust

Ultimately all human interactions are based on trust. Despite the gut-wrenching headlines of misconduct by executives and employees, societies and organizations for centuries have realized that a common set of values and attitudes, ethical beliefs, serves as the common ground for organizations and societies. While technologies and work methods may change and evolve, it is the ethics and culture that provide the foundation for the establishment and maintenance of trustworthy relationships and behaviors.

Growth of Knowledge-Based Activities

More than ever before, organizations depend on information and those who provide it. Stated succinctly, for an organization to be viewed as trustworthy, it must be truthful. Furthermore, because knowledge is of value only when it is true, people who create and distribute knowledge must be especially careful to value and practice truthfulness, that is, ethical values and behaviors. One need only look at the corporate scandals of the past five to ten years to recognize that a vast majority of these scandals can be traced back to lies and misrepresentations concerning accounting practices, financial standing, and financial holdings. Honesty and accountability are among the basic building blocks of an ethical foundation.

Growth of Multinational Organizations and Trade

Both disposable and durable goods are as often as not designed, manufactured, assembled, and shipped from different parts of the world. For example, in a car sold by an American automaker, the engine may have been designed in Japan and built in Korea, the transmission assembled in Mexico, the dozens of computer chips that control various subsystems manufactured in Singapore, the software used by these chips written in India, and everything eventually assembled in a plant located in Kentucky. Regardless of where something is designed, produced, or assembled, ethics serves as an integral component of the culture, a culture that unifies an organization and enables it to compete successfully in a global economy.

Increased Use of Technology

Despite cheap labor, all organizations are becoming more dependent on technology. Technology enables people and organizations to increase their effectiveness and efficiency and therefore their productivity. Because technology is shaping the ethics of this century, organizations must consider this driving force when developing and implementing ethical standards and practices.

Increased Concern for the Environment

Corporations are consuming an increasing amount of the earth's resources. Not only are resources being consumed, but converting raw materials into durable and disposable goods produces pollution and eventually waste once the product wears out or becomes obsolete. For this reason, being an ethical corporation requires addressing the environment and its eventual effect on people and society.

Increased Need for and Availability of Education and Training

There is a worldwide growth in budgets for educational activities and programs. Even societies that traditionally did not value education now accept the view that educated citizens are more productive. This increased productivity enables a nation or society to participate in the international economy, which increasingly relies on information and new ideas for sustainable growth. Corporations, like governments over the past fifty years, have begun to recognize the need for trained and educated employees and have invested heavily in training and corporate universities that serve employees from a broad spectrum of cultures and societies.

Growth of Democratic Societies and Decentralized Organizations

As people acquire an education, they begin to realize they have options in terms of the type of work they do and where they live. This realization creates within people a desire to have control over their lives and their future. In short, they begin to desire to work and live within democratic societies.

Philosophers from Thomas Jefferson to John Dewey cited the need for citizens to be educated. The growth of democratic societies and local decision making will be possible only when people learn to trust one another.

Immigration

The United States is often referred to as a nation of immigrants. Since its founding, our nation has been the land of opportunity for people from many countries and cultures. As a society, America has benefited greatly from their talents, ambitions, hard work, and willingness to share their traditions, thereby making us a richer and more diverse culture.

Rise of the Corporate University

The trends and driving forces described above began to intensify after World War II. During the past sixty years, training and education have grown in importance as the U.S. economy made the transition from one based on extraction (mining, timber, and other similar organizations), manufacturing, and agriculture to one based on service and information creation and implementation. This transition has forced organizations to recognize the importance of hiring and maintaining an educated workforce.

By the 1980s, the demand for highly skilled knowledge employees had grown to the point where many college-educated professionals sought and earned master's degrees in order to increase their employability and mobility. At the same time, corporations, frustrated by traditional academia's inability to respond to corporate educational needs, began to transform their training departments into mechanisms that would give them a strategic advantage in the global marketplace. The corporate university model proved so effective that the number of corporate universities grew from an estimated four hundred in 1980 to over two thousand by the year 2000 (Meister, 2001).

Although corporate universities appeared in the United States decades ago, corporations on every continent have since adopted the concept. Wherever talented, creative people are the lifeblood of an organization, corporations and organizations are establishing corporate universities as a strategy for attracting and retaining talented employees who are able to devise creative and innovative solutions and products used worldwide. It is these employees who give corporations a competitive advantage in the global marketplace.

Looking back over the past one thousand years, it becomes evident that there has been a shift in importance from church-related universities, to secular universities, to the emergence of corporate universities. This brings us to the question: What does the future hold for corporate universities, and who will carry the ethical flame?

Three Major Approaches to Ethics Training

Organizations approach the teaching or transmission of ethics in primarily one of three ways: compliance, sacred traditions, and secular ethics (also known as utilitarianism).

Compliance

Compliance is not concerned with moral issues; rather, it is legalistic in nature. It is not concerned with a narrow interpretation of what is right or wrong, but is limited to what is legal or illegal. Compliance is about playing by the rules and avoiding negative consequences or perceptions and situations that may affect the profitability or reputation of the organization. The role of managers and executives is to develop the organization by complying with the rules established by society through laws and regulations that are interpreted through legal filters.

Ethics Based on Sacred Traditions

Over the past several decades, there has been a renewal in ethical business practices based on the Christian concept of Sacred Traditions. At the core of this system of ethics is the belief that everything belongs to God and that managers and business executives are stewards responsible for the creation of organizations that care for and distribute God's bounty. Moral principles and practices are framed by a system of absolutes as defined by an infallible God.

Secular Ethics

Modern secular ethics has its roots in utilitarianism: whatever does the most good for the most people is the most ethical course of action. Originally proposed by David Hume, utilitarianism was widely popularized by Jeremy Bentham and John Stuart Mill in the 1800s. Along with rationalism and empiricism, two diametrically opposing philosophies of how people acquire knowledge, scientific thought and moral philosophy displaced the sacred as the foundation for ethical decision making. Today, either knowingly or unknowingly, many decisions makers use utilitarian concepts and principles to develop ethical policies and practices for their organizations.

What Major Organizations Are Doing

To learn what major organizations and corporate universities are doing with regard to ethics education, we interviewed top decision makers from three different types of organizations: Owen C. Gadeken, a professor with the Defense Acquisition University; Ronnie E. Jenkins, vice president for services to clubs for the Boys & Girls Clubs of America; and Dan T. Cathy, president and chief operating officer of Chick-fil-A.

In each interview, we sought to zero in on four basic questions, with occasional minor variations: (1) What is the ethical philosophy of the organization? (2) How do you teach ethics? (3) How do you measure that what is being taught is being applied? (4) What have you learned from your experiences in designing and delivering ethics education?

The following sections provide summations of these interviews.

Defense Acquisition University

The Defense Acquisition University (DAU) provides practitioner training, career management, and services to Department of Defense (DoD) acquisition, technology, and logistics personnel. Owen C. Gadeken, a professor at the Fort Belvoir Campus, offers his thoughts on ethics education at DAU.

Brief History of the Organization. Authorized by Title 10 of U.S. Code 1746 and chartered by DoD Directive 5000.57, the Defense Acquisition University (DAU) was established on August 1, 1992. Its mission is to provide practitioner training, career management, and services to enable the DoD acquisition, technology, and logistics (AT&L) community to make smart business decisions and deliver timely and affordable capabilities to the war fighter. Using the AT&L Performance Learning Model (PLM) as a template, the university coordinates education and training programs to meet the career-long training requirements of more than 134,000 DoD AT&L personnel. It provides a full range of basic, intermediate, and advanced curriculum training, as well as assignment-specific and continuous learning courses to support the career goals and professional development of the DoD AT&L workforce. But its role does not end when a student leaves the classroom. The university also fosters professional development through performance support, rapid deployment training on emerging acquisition initiatives, online knowledge-sharing tools, and continuous learning modules.

What Is the Ethical Philosophy of the Organization? We believe that to understand ethics, we must first understand what individuals and organizations share as common values. Michael Josephson, who founded and runs the nonprofit Josephson Institute of Ethics, differentiates between ethical and nonethical values. Nonethical values often relate to personal desires such as wealth, fame, happiness, health, fulfillment, or personal freedom. Ethical values are directly related to our beliefs about what is right and wrong. Josephson identifies six core ethical values as his "six pillars of character":

> *Trustworthiness:* honesty, integrity, reliability, and loyalty
>
> *Respect:* courtesy, dignity of the individual, and tolerance
>
> *Responsibility:* accountability, pursuit of excellence, and self-restraint
>
> *Fairness:* procedural fairness, impartiality, and equity
>
> *Caring:* concern for others and how they will be affected by your actions
>
> *Citizenship:* civic virtues and duties (giving back to society)

Ethics in any organization are determined by the common values shared by its members. While individuals come to an organization with a set of values developed over time, the most influential factor affecting their ethical behavior after they arrive is the way they are led. Leadership determines the organizational climate or culture, and it has a major impact on the way all of the organization's members do their work.

How Do You Teach Ethics? We do not try so much to teach ethics as to create an ethical environment. One of the most important tasks of any leader is to create an environment where ethical behavior and decision making is standard operating procedure. This can be achieved through alignment of the personal ethical values of the individual employees with those of the organization. The leader can develop this organizational climate in several ways:

- Clarifying the organization's core ethical values so all employees know what is expected of them

- Making values alignment a key part of the hiring decision for new employees

- Developing policies so employees know how to deal with foreseeable ethical issues

- Providing training and support systems to help employees build a more ethical organization

Taking these steps will increase the degree of ethical alignment or congruence in the organization. Organizations with high ethical congruence walk their talk, meaning that their day-to-day behavior matches their stated values.

How Do You Measure That What Is Being Taught Is Being Applied? We use an online assessment tool, "Metrics That Matter," that both students and faculty members complete at the end of each of our training programs. We then follow up with selected students and their supervisors after a few weeks with another survey to find out how the material they were taught is being applied on the job. Evaluation of ethics instruction is particularly difficult to assess since it is a more complex set of skills.

What Have You Learned from Your Experiences in Designing and Delivering Ethics Education? We have found that canned, prepackaged material (such as the annual standards of conduct training) does not go over well with our students. What seems to work best is to engage the students in sharing real ethical dilemmas they have observed or faced in their workplace. This leads naturally to a discussion of how such dilemmas should be handled. What also works is to spend some time getting students to examine the value sets that drive behavior in their workplace. This leads to the importance of establishing an ethical climate as a leadership responsibility.

Boys & Girls Clubs of America

Ronnie E. Jenkins is vice president of services to clubs for this youth development organization. Here, he offers his thoughts on ethics education.

Brief History of the Organization. The Boys & Girls Clubs of America is the world's largest youth service organization, with approximately four thousand clubs, 4.5 million youth, and 45,000 full- and part-time staff. It was founded in 1860 by several women in Hartford, Connecticut, who believed that boys who roamed the streets should have a positive alternative and organized the first club.

In 1906, several Boys Clubs decided to affiliate. The Federated Boys Clubs in Boston was formed with fifty-three member organizations, marking the start of a nationwide movement. By 1931, the Boys Club Federation of America became Boys Clubs of America. And in 1956, Boys Clubs of America celebrated its fiftieth anniversary. To recognize the fact that girls are part of our cause, the national organization's name was changed in 1990 to Boys & Girls Clubs of America.

Although the Boys & Girls Clubs of America does not currently have a formal corporate university, it does have a tradition of creating training materials and educational programs through its national office. It is currently working to establish a corporate university in the near future to better serve its member clubs.

What Are the Ethical Philosophy and Organizational Policies of the Organization? The Boys & Girls Clubs of America support a set of core promises that guide the actions of the professional staffs and board members of the federated movement. These core promises are divided into three areas:

Standard Practices for Tracking Membership and Participation

- A tested, well-thought-out system consistently applied throughout the organization for collecting and recording information about member participation on a daily basis

- A tested, well-thought-out consistent system at every club for collecting and recording information on youth served through community outreach on a daily basis

- Staff training in every aspect of the club's polices and practices for tracking the attendance and participation of registered members and youth served through community outreach

- A defined policy and procedures for how information is stored

- A system that ensures that all data are checked and rechecked before being presented to anyone outside the club or used in any marketing material

Standard Practices for Hiring Staff and Selecting Volunteers of High Character

- Up-to-date written policies and procedures, reviewed by counsel, that address the organization's intent to be fair, consistent, and nondiscriminatory and to meet all legal requirements; background checks, the consequences of providing false or misleading information and criminal or civil records that will automatically bar a person from employment or volunteer service; confidentiality and security of all information

- Clearly written job descriptions for each position

- Required application forms for all staff and volunteer candidates that collect information about an applicant's work history, education, and background

- A defined process to gather information needed to make informed hiring and selection decisions for staff and volunteers

- Reference checks to gain insight into the candidate's experience, skills, and character

- Background checks on all staff and volunteers conducted prior to hiring and at least every twenty-four months after hiring

- A defined system to evaluate findings about criminal records or other concerns uncovered during the hiring process

- A formal introductory period for staff and volunteers

Standard Practices for Ethics and Financial Oversight

- A board-approved ethics policy with a conflict-of-interest statement that is signed annually by all board and staff. The policy is supported by training for all staff and volunteers, an appointed ethics officer, whistle-blower protection, and a compliance, reporting, and investigation policy.

- There are clearly defined roles and responsibilities for how board and staff work together to ensure that the organization's finances meet all legal, ethical, and business requirements.

- An active board finance committee develops and monitors financial policies and practices, reviews financial statements and reports, develops an investment strategy, and ensures that the organization has a risk management plan.

- Policies, procedures, and systems are reviewed and monitored by the finance committee to ensure sound financial practices.

- A complete financial audit is conducted by a board-appointed independent auditor annually under the direction of the finance committee.

- An annual organizational budget is developed and approved by the board to ensure resources are allocated to meet organizational goals and objectives.

- The board develops and approves an investment management policy.

- There is an annual evaluation and update to the organization's overall risk management strategy.

How Do You Teach Ethics? We have a formal, structured training program offered to all new staff and to the chief board officer and chief professional of each of our more than eleven hundred organizations once a year. This two-hour facilitated training is supported by workbooks and other media.

An e-newsletter to all officers and board members provides up-to-date information concerning ethical practices. Another publication, the *Governance Guide,* is designed to share strategies with local board and staff members in the area of building public trust. In addition, financial management training materials for staff and boards are delivered using distance learning technologies in addition to field training opportunities.

How Do You Measure That What Is Being Taught Is Being Applied? We use an evaluation rubric, Standards of Organizational Effectiveness, which is a comprehensive set of benchmarks and standards organized into seven functional areas of nonprofit management: board, human resources, resource development, program, marketing, facilities, and fiscal management. Metrics are progressively aligned to reflect progress in the following levels:

- Developing (determines needs for organizational development)

- Operational (baseline performance)

- Advancing/excelling (exceeding baseline standards)

The evaluation is required to be administered every three years and reviewed annually with each organization in membership with the national organization.

What Have You Learned from Your Experiences in Designing and Delivering Ethics Education? Couch the idea in the concept that it is an opportunity to take the high road and to build trust and not to place blame or create an environment of distrust. Keep it positive. Remind the users that the ethics strategy increases return on investment by donors and investors.

Chick-fil-A

Dan T. Cathy, president and chief operating officer of this franchise restaurant chain, offers his thoughts on ethics education in this business.

Brief History of the Organization. In 1946, Truett Cathy had what seemed like a simple idea: make a sandwich using chicken. From modest beginnings in a tiny Georgia eatery sixty years ago, Chick-fil-A has grown into one of the largest privately owned restaurant chains in the nation. Yet from the beginning, the first priority for Truett and Chick-fil-A has never been just to serve chicken: it is to serve a higher calling. The official statement of corporate purpose says that Chick-fil-A exists "to glorify God by being a faithful steward of all that is entrusted to us and to have a positive influence on all who come in contact with Chick-fil-A."

Although Chick-fil-A does not currently have a formal corporate university, the executive team works diligently to ensure that ethics training is embedded within every level of the organization. At Chick-fil-A, ethics is not viewed as something that is taught, but rather as something that you live.

What Is the Ethical Philosophy of the Organization? Because of our official statement of corporate purpose, we invest in scholarships, character-building programs for kids, foster homes, and other community services. Come to think of it, it's also not a bad motive for striving to serve a really, really good sandwich.

How Do You Teach Ethics? We begin by carefully selecting our people. We like to say that it is easier to get a job with the CIA than with CFA. As a result, we have a 96 percent retention rate, which is unheard of in our industry. Our selection process is guided by the 3Cs: competence, character, and chemistry. Competence: Is the person able to do the job for which they are being hired?

Character: Does the person have the integrity and character required to be successful in our organization? Chemistry: Is there a fit between the person we are hiring and who we are? Once people are hired, we make every effort to help them become successful through training, encouragement, and appropriate opportunities and leadership. We emphasize an atmosphere and culture that place great value on integrity and modeling desirable behaviors and attitudes. In short, we take every effort to walk the talk. We believe that ethics is about what you do, not how many policies or statements you display on workplace walls.

How Do You Measure That What Is Being Taught Is Being Applied? Financial statements may be viewed as statements of ethical behaviors when viewed over time. The issue here is trust. Are you doing what you say you are going to do? A business that cannot be trusted will ultimately fail. We also use attitudinal surveys with our customers and employees. This information helps us to benchmark performance and focus on areas that need attention. We are and have been a high-performance organization, employing high-performance people who work in an optimum environment. We create this high-performance environment by asking the question: Is this an environment in which I would want to work? To achieve this goal, from the beginning, we have used biblical principles to guide us in how we treat people. We make every effort to treat people with honor, respect, and trust, and people respond with their hard work and loyalty to the organization.

What Have You Learned from Your Experiences in Designing and Delivering Ethics Education? There was a time when children watched their parents struggle to earn a living and teach their children ethical principles. However, with the breakdown of the modern family, a generation of unethical business and community leaders has emerged, and it is for this reason that we try to create a highly ethical work environment for our employees and support community activities that develop responsible young people. We feel that we have found a better way to do business, enable people to earn a living, and promote a better and more ethical life for everyone.

Summarizing the Role of the Corporate University in Ethics Training

In order to understand the proper role of corporate universities in ethics training, we must begin by recognizing that the CEO and executive team are ultimately responsible for the governance of any organization. Effective governance begins with the development of a strategic plan that, at a minimum, must define the following:

- *The organization's mission, goals, and objectives.* Why does the organization exist? What does it hope or want to accomplish? Why is the organization important or needed? These basic questions help to define where the organization is now versus where it wants or needs to be in the future.

- *Allocation of resources and operating procedures.* The primary concern of this aspect of a strategic plan is on what must be done to achieve the mission, goals, and objectives of the organization. Included in this sphere of activity may be the establishment of benchmarks and standards that allow the organization to gain feedback concerning the performance of the organization and identify gaps where improvement is needed.

- *Core values, policies, and ethical standards.* The core issue addressed by this aspect of the strategic plan is to establish by what means resources are to be acquired and what constitutes acceptable operating procedures and behaviors used to achieve desired results.

The role and mission of corporate universities is not to develop strategic plans or create corporate policy. Rather, corporate universities should be viewed as a specialized unit composed of change-oriented resources that enable the CEO and executive team to achieve the mission, goals, and objectives as defined by the strategic plan for the organization. Among these change-oriented resources are the following:

- *Analysis.* This refers to the personnel, tools, and techniques used to identify and isolate performance problems and gaps. Performance gaps are usually classified as being skill, knowledge, or attitudinal in nature. Because ethical issues may be identified as a root cause of a performance gap, appropriate strategies and resources can be identified and brought to bear only once an analysis of the situation has been conducted.

- *Identification of resources.* Once a deficiency has been identified, appropriate resources must be identified and acquired. These resources may be off-the-shelf solutions, external consultants, or solutions developed and delivered by in-house specialists. Because ethical issues are often multidimensional, several strategies and types of resources may be required to resolve a performance gap that has an ethical issue as its root cause.

- *Implementation.* Regardless of the solution strategy selected, it should be cost-effective and deliverable within a reasonable period of time. As noted, performance problems that have an ethical issue as their root cause may require a longer period of time to resolve because they often lead to a change in belief systems, attitudes, and in some instances corporate cultures.

- *Evaluation.* As with all other intervention strategies there must be an end point where the performance problem is either solved or brought under control. This determination can be accomplished only through the use of a systematic evaluation strategy that confirms that the identified performance gap has been closed to within acceptable limits. For performance problems that have an ethical root cause, this may require monitoring for an extended period of time to ensure that the problem stays under control.

Summary

Work, ethics, and education and training have been intertwined concepts for centuries. From the earliest European universities, to the establishment of medieval trade guilds, to the founding of land grant state universities, education and training have been viewed as mechanisms that benefit both the individual and society through the development of skills, knowledge, and moral codes of conduct. Over the past fifty years, a number of driving forces have emerged that have not only created a world economic system but have driven the growth of the corporate university. Within the United States, despite the growth of a variety of government agencies that regulate the workplace, ethics has become a major concern for many organizations and corporations as they attempt to maximize their reputations and standing in the eyes of their communities, nation, and the world. As a result, corporate universities today are being viewed not so much as the new keepers of the ethical flame, but rather as an enabling resource for top management. Key to this new role, corporate universities are becoming increasingly responsible for identifying performance gaps that may have an ethical problem as a root cause and, once identified, are being asked to develop strategies and solutions that will reduce or eliminate these types of problems. This expanded role will add new dimensions and challenges for the next generation of corporate universities.

Reference

Meister, J. "The Brave New World of Corporate Education." *Chronicle of Higher Education,* Feb. 9, 2001, pp. B10–B11.

Philip McGee, Ph.D., was involved in the design and implementation of instructional and organizational systems within education, government, industry, and business through his company, Instructional Designs, for seventeen years. In addition, he served as the regional program director for the doctor of business administration program offered by the School of Business and Entrepreneurship, Nova Southeastern University, and as an adjunct professor of human resource development (HRD) at Webster University. He is currently the program coordinator for the master's program in HRD at Clemson University.

John R. Duncan, with over twenty years of experience in operations and sales management, has designed, developed, and delivered a wide variety of instructional and performance improvement interventions in education, government, and multinational business settings at locations around the world.

While teaching at the graduate level in HRD, Duncan helps to close the gap between research and practice by writing research-based articles, delivering presentations at national and international conferences, and working with businesses and non-profits in the areas of leadership development and performance improvement.

Duncan has a Ph.D. in human resource education from the University of Illinois at Urbana–Champaign and is currently an assistant professor of HRD at Clemson University.

Jack Phillips is one of the true gurus in the world of corporate education. Picking up the mantle from Donald Kirkpatrick, he has done some extensive and extraordinary work in the field of measurement and evaluation and is the world's leading authority on measuring the return on investment of training and corporate education.

Jack and his collaborator Patti Phillips have contributed a chapter on next-generation evaluation to this book. The focus of this chapter is how evaluation helps you find and demonstrate the value of learning investments. The discussion goes beyond return on investment and presents Jack and Patti's most recent ideas on measurement and evaluation.

7

Next-Generation Evaluation

SEARCHING FOR VALUE

Jack J. Phillips, Patti P. Phillips

ONE OF THE MOST IMPORTANT challenges facing the corporate university is to demonstrate the success of the learning investment. For almost a decade, this topic has dominated conference agendas and professional meetings. Journals and newsletters regularly embrace the concept with increasing print space. More than twenty-five books provide significant coverage of the topic. Even top executives have stepped up their appetite for impact and return-on-investment (ROI) data.

Although interest in the topic has heightened and much progress has been made, it remains an issue that challenges even the most sophisticated and progressive learning and development professionals. Some argue that it is difficult to have a successful evaluation process, while others are quietly and deliberately implementing effective evaluation systems. The latter group is gaining tremendous support from senior management teams and is making much progress. Regardless of the position taken on the issue, the reasons for demonstrating the value of learning and evaluation are intensifying. Almost all corporate university executives share a concern that they need to link learning to the business and must eventually show results on their learning investment. Otherwise funds may be reduced or the corporate university may not be able to maintain or enhance its current status and influence in the organization.

The dilemma surrounding the value of learning is a source of frustration with many senior executives—even with the chief learning officer (CLO). Most executives realize that learning is a basic necessity when organizations are experiencing significant growth or increased competition. They intuitively sense that there is value in providing learning opportunities, logically anticipating a payoff in important bottom-line measures such as productivity improvements, quality enhancements, cost reductions, time savings, and customer service. Yet the frustration comes from lack of evidence to show that the process is working. While results are assumed and learning programs appear to be necessary, more evidence is needed; otherwise, funding may be adjusted in the future. A comprehensive measurement and evaluation process represents the most promising way to show this level of accountability in a logical, rational approach (Long, 2004).

Trends and Issues in Evaluation

This section examines the current state of evaluation, including discussions of global trends and challenges.

Global Evaluation Trends

Measurement and evaluation have been changing and evolving, in both private and public sector organizations, across organizations and cultures—not only in the United States but in all the developed countries. The following trends have been identified in our research:

- Organizations are increasing their investment in measurement and evaluation, with best practice groups spending 3 to 5 percent of the learning and development budget on measurement and evaluation.

- Learning staff are spending more time learning about effective measurement of learning.

- Organizations are moving up the value chain, away from measuring reaction and learning to measuring application, impact, and occasionally ROI.

- The increased focus on measurement and evaluation is largely driven by the needs of the clients and sponsors of learning projects, programs, initiatives, and solutions.

- A shift from a reactive approach to a more proactive approach is developing, with evaluation addressed early in the cycle, even to the point of forecasting ROI prior to program launch.

- Measurement and evaluation processes are systematic and methodical, often designed into the delivery process.

- Technology is enhancing the measurement and evaluation process, enabling large amounts of data to be collected, processed, analyzed, and integrated across programs.

- The use of ROI is emerging as an essential part of the measurement and evaluation mix. Benchmarking studies show it is a fast-growing metric: 70 to 80 percent of companies have it on their wish list.

- Many corporate universities have created internally accepted practices for demonstrating the value of learning that focus on the value, not necessarily the financial ROI.

These trends are creating demand for more information, resources, knowledge, and skills in measurement and evaluation.

Evaluation Challenges

Evaluation seems to be a popular topic, but not all organizations are doing it and the evaluation process is not always effective. The barriers to conducting meaningful evaluation can be summarized in some basic challenges.

Too Many Theories and Models. Dozens of books on evaluation have been written specifically for the learning and development community. Add to this the dozens of books on evaluation written primarily for the social sciences, education, and government organizations. Then add the more than twenty-five models and theories for evaluation offered to practitioners to help them measure the contribution of learning and development, each claiming a unique approach and a promise of calming evaluation woes along with bringing world peace.

Lack of Understanding of Evaluation. It hasn't always been easy for practitioners to learn this process. Some books on evaluation have over six hundred pages, making it impossible for a practitioner to absorb it just through reading. Not only is it essential to understand evaluation processes, but the entire learning and development staff must learn parts of the process and understand how it fits into their role. To remedy this situation, it is essential for the organization to focus on developing and disseminating expertise within the organization.

Add to this the search for statistical precision. The use of complicated statistical models is confusing and difficult for many practitioners to absorb. Statistical precision is needed when a high-stakes decision is being made and when plenty of time and resources are available. Otherwise very simple statistics are appropriate.

Inappropriate Use of Evaluation as a Postprogram Activity. When evaluation is considered an add-on activity, it loses the power to deliver the needed results. The most appropriate way to use evaluation is to consider it at the time of program conception. When this happens, an evaluation is conducted efficiently, and the quality and quantity of data improve.

Lack of Support from Key Stakeholders. Important customers who need and use evaluation data sometimes do not provide the support needed to make the process successful. Specific steps must be taken to win support and secure buy-in from key groups, including senior executives and the management team. Executives must see that evaluation produces valuable data to improve programs and validate results. When stakeholders understand what is involved, they may offer more support.

Lack of Data Senior Managers Need. Today, clients and sponsors are asking for data beyond reaction and learning. They need data on the application of new skills on the job and the corresponding impact in the business units. Sometimes they want ROI data for major programs. They are requesting data about the business impact of learning from both short- and long-term perspectives. Ultimately, these executives are the ones who must continue funding for learning and development. If the desired data are not available, future funding could be in jeopardy.

Improper Use of Evaluation Data. Improper use of evaluation data can lead to four major problems:

- Too many organizations do not use evaluation data at all. Data are collected, tabulated, catalogued, filed, and never used by any particular group other than the individual who initially collected the data. This results in wasted resources and missed opportunity to communicate success and improve the program.

- Data are not provided to the appropriate audiences. Analyzing the target audiences and determining the specific data needed for each group are important steps when communicating results.

- Data are not used to drive improvement. If evaluation is not part of the feedback cycle, it falls short of what it is intended to accomplish.

- Data are used for the wrong reasons: to take action against an individual or group or to withhold funds rather than improve processes. Sometimes the data are used in political ways to gain power or advantage over another person.

Inconsistency and Lack of Standards. For evaluation to add value and be accepted by different stakeholders, it must be consistent in its approach and methodology. Tools and templates need to be developed to support the method of choice to prevent perpetual reinvention of the wheel. Without this consistency, evaluation consumes too many resources and raises too many concerns about the quality and credibility of the process. Closely paralleled with consistency is the use of standards. Evaluation standards are rules for making evaluation consistent, stable, and equitable. Without standards, there is little credibility in processes and stability of outcomes.

Lack of Sustainability. A new evaluation model or approach often has a short life. It is not sustained. Evaluation must be integrated into the organization so that it becomes routine and lasting. To accomplish this, the evaluation process must gain the respect of key stakeholders at the outset. The process must be well documented, and stakeholders must accept their responsibilities to make it work. Without sustainability, evaluation will be on a roller-coaster ride, where data are collected only when programs are in trouble and less attention is provided when they are not.

Necessity for Evidence Linking Learning with the Business. Many corporate executives understand the value of learning. They hired corporate university managers and CLOs, developed learning functions, and have been intimately involved in creating learning strategies for their companies (Jack Welch at GE is an example). CLOs in companies with this learning commitment are not particularly concerned about evaluation systems; they already have support for learning initiatives and continue to demonstrate the value of their work through extensive linkage with the business. However, when tough economic times are encountered, these executives need more proof of the linkage with the business. Thus, measurement and evaluation are more important.

Benefits of Measurement and Evaluation

Although the benefits of measurement and evaluation may appear obvious, several distinct and important payoffs can be realized. These key benefits, inherent in almost any type of impact evaluation process, make additional measurement and evaluation an attractive challenge for the learning function.

Satisfy Client Needs. Today's executives need information about application and implementation in the workplace and the corresponding impact on key business metrics. In some cases, they are asking for ROI data. Developing a comprehensive measurement and evaluation system can be an effective strategy to meet client requests and requirements.

Justify Budgets. Some corporate universities use evaluation data to support a requested budget, while others use evaluation data to prevent the budget from being slashed or eliminated. Additional evaluation data can show where programs add value and where they fall short. This approach can lead to protecting successful programs as well as pursuing new programs.

Improve Program Designs and Processes. A comprehensive evaluation system should provide information to improve the overall design of a corporate university program, including the critical areas of learning design, content, delivery method, duration, timing, focus, and expectations. These processes may need to be adjusted to improve learning, especially during implementation of a new program. Evaluation data can determine whether the analysis was conducted properly, thereby aligning the program with the organizational needs. Additional evaluation data can indicate whether nonlearning and development interventions are needed. Finally, evaluation data can help pinpoint inadequacies in implementation systems and identify ways to improve them.

Enhance the Transfer of Learning. Learning transfer is perhaps one of the biggest challenges facing the learning and development field. Our research at the ROI Institute shows that 60 to 90 percent of job-related skills and knowledge acquired in a program are not being implemented on the job. A comprehensive evaluation system can identify specific barriers to the use of learning. Evaluation data can also highlight supportive work environments that enable learning transfer.

Determine Whether to Eliminate or Expand Programs. Evaluation processes can provide rational, credible data to help support the decision to implement a program or discontinue it. In reality, if the program cannot add value, it should be discontinued. One caveat is that eliminating programs should not be a principal motive or rationale for increasing evaluation efforts. Although it is a valid use of evaluation data, program elimination is often viewed more negatively than positively. The flip side of eliminating programs is expanding their presence or application. Positive results may signal the possibility that a program's success in one division or region can be replicated in another division if a similar need exists.

Enhance the Respect and Credibility of the Corporate University Staff. Collecting and using evaluation data, including application, impact, and ROI, builds respect for learning and for the staff. Appropriate evaluation data can enhance the credibility of the learning executive or CLO when the data reveal the value added to the organization. They can also help shift the perception of learning from a dispensable activity to an indispensable value-adding process.

Increase Support from Managers. Immediate managers of participants need convincing data about the success of learning. They often fail to support these processes because they cannot see the value in taking employees away from the job to be involved in a program with little connection to their business unit. Data showing how learning helps these managers achieve their objectives will influence their support.

Strengthen Relationships with Key Executives and Administrators. Senior executives must perceive the corporate university manager as a business partner that can be invited to the table for important decisions and meetings. A comprehensive measurement and evaluation process, showing the contribution of the learning function, can help strengthen this relationship. A comprehensive evaluation process may influence these managers to view learning as a contributing process and an excellent investment.

Set Priorities for Learning and Development. A comprehensive measurement system can help determine which programs and projects represent the highest priority. Evaluation data can show the payoff or potential payoff of important and expensive programs or those supporting strategic objectives.

Learning Value Chain

It may be helpful to examine measurement and evaluation of learning as a value chain where different types of data (levels) are collected at different times (sometimes from different sources) to generate a balanced profile of success, providing the value desired by the various stakeholders of the process. Table 7.1 shows this value chain, which is fundamental to much of the current work

Table 7.1. Learning Value Chain

Level	Measurement Focus	Key Questions
0 Input and indicators	Measures input such as volume and efficiencies	What is the number of participants, hours, and programs, and what are the costs?
1 Reaction and planned action	Measures participant satisfaction with the project and captures planned actions	Was the learning relevant, important, useful, and helpful to participants in the job environment? Did the participants plan to use the contents in the program?
2 Learning and confidence	Measures changes in knowledge, skills, and attitudes	Did participants increase or enhance their knowledge, skills, or perceptions and have confidence to use them?
3 Application and implementation	Measures changes in on-the-job behavior or action	What did the participants do differently in the job context? Was the program implemented effectively? What changes were made on the job?
4 Impact and consequences	Measures changes in business impact variables	What are the consequences of the application in terms of output, quality, cost, time, and satisfaction?
5 ROI	Compares project benefits to the costs	Did the monetary benefits of the learning program exceed the investment in the program?

in evaluation and provides the framework for corporate universities to measure the success of learning.

This concept shows how value is developed from different perspectives. Some stakeholders are interested in knowing about the inputs so that they can be managed and made more efficient. Others are interested in reaction measures so that adjustments can be made to obtain more positive reactions.

Still others are interested in learning to identify weaknesses in the learning design. More recently, clients and sponsors have been more interested in actual behavior change (application) and the corresponding impact in the work units. Finally, a few stakeholders are concerned about the ROI.

It is helpful to view the learning value chain as a chain of impact that is necessary for learning to create value from a business perspective. The chain can be broken at any point. For example, if participants have an adverse reaction to a learning program, all is lost at that point because there will be little, if any, learning. Even if there is a positive reaction, participants may not be learning new skills, gaining new knowledge, or changing their perceptions; consequently, there would be no value from the program. Also, if there is no application of skills and knowledge, there is no corresponding business impact. Without business impact, the ROI is very negative—as much as 100 percent negative. It is helpful to remind all the stakeholders that these important data sets represent a chain of impact that must exist for learning to add business value. Collecting data along the value chain provides evidence that learning is making a difference. The additional step of isolating the effects of learning provides the proof that a learning program is adding value. This issue is discussed later in the chapter.

Setting Goals

Since more organizations are moving up the value chain, it may be helpful to assess the current status at these different levels and set specific goals over a defined period to achieve desired targets. Table 7.2 lists the levels and provides space for targets. Also included are the percentages from best practice organizations—those that have developed the competency measurement and evaluation process. This target is sometimes established as part of a transition plan for moving from the current state to a desired future state. Current assessments can be estimated from the learning and development staff, or they may come from detailed information from the learning management system. Either way, it is important to take stock of the current status and set goals for improvement.

Table 7.2. Evaluation Targets

Value Level	Percentage of Programs Evaluated at This Level		
	Current	*Target*	*Best Practices*
Inputs and indicators	100%	100%	100%
Reaction and planned action			100
Learning and confidence			60–80
Application and implementation			25–30
Impact and consequences			10–25
ROI			6–10

The concept of microlevel and macrolevel scorecards should be underscored at this point. When a project or program is evaluated with all types of data, including ROI, a microlevel scorecard is developed. The six types of data are collected at different times and from different sources, and they reflect both quantitative and qualitative information. This equates to a balanced scorecard for that specific program. When there are dozens, if not hundreds, of programs, the challenge is to collect data across programs so that there is a meaningful scorecard for the overall learning contribution. This is a macrolevel scorecard and the concept is fairly simple. Whenever a program is evaluated at level 1 (reaction), for example, a few of the measures are collected for integration into the macrolevel scorecard. In each of the succeeding levels, a few measures are taken to insert into the overall macrolevel scorecard. The concept is illustrated in Figure 7.1. As this figure shows, the key is to identify the measures at each level that are important to consider in the macrolevel scorecard and integrate the data for meaningful reports monthly, quarterly, or annually. This integration can be instantaneous with a fully automated system.

Figure 7.1. Micro- and Macrolevel Scorecards

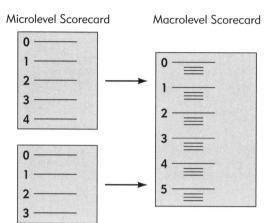

Inputs and Indicators

The most fundamental level of measurement is the capture of inputs into the system. This represents a variety of measures showing the scope, volume, and efficiencies, as well as costs. The measures in Table 7.3 represent typical benchmarking measures.

Table 7.3. Typical Inputs and Indicators

Inputs	Indicators
Participants	Total By job group
Efficiencies	Show-up rate Completion rate
Hours	Total By job group
Delivery profile	Percentage instructor-led Percentage e-learning Percentage blended Percentage on-the-job

---

Table 7.3. Typical Inputs and Indicators, Cont'd

Inputs	Indicators
Costs	Total
	Per participant
	Per employee
	Per hour instructor-led
	Per hour e-learning

Participant count is a common measure that could represent participants in different job groups and different statuses. It is usually presented in categories such as employees, suppliers, customers, and the general public. Counting hours is another issue, particularly when CLOs have a target for a certain number of learning hours per person. This accounting becomes more meaningful with extensive use of e-learning, but it also has drawbacks since hours of training is not an effective measure of what was learned.

Cost profiles are typical, reflecting costs per participant in job groups, and could include all the direct costs associated with providing learning. Some corporate universities are reporting indirect costs such as those of taking participants off the job, using average salaries for the time participants are away from normal job duties. The problem with this metric is that it assumes learning is separate from the job and is treated as an extracurricular activity instead of a job necessity.

Delivery mechanisms is an issue often presented in this level and shows how the delivery processes are changing. Categories include conventional facilitator-led learning, e-learning, and blended learning, a balanced mix often being a goal of the organization. Job rotations, on-the-job learning, coaching, and mentoring are sometimes reported. When delivery methods are reported, it is important to set goals, accept changes, and track shifts.

Efficiencies reflect a variety of measures, such as the time it takes individuals to complete programs, the percentage of learners completing programs, and the percentage of individuals who attend follow-up sessions. These measures are important to show how well the system is functioning and how data flow throughout the learning and development function.

Reaction and Planned Action

All programs are typically evaluated at this level. Direct feedback is needed from participants to capture the planned actions from the learning process. Failure to secure reaction about a program sends a message to participants that their feedback is not important and does not enable learning professionals to improve programs based on feedback. Consequently, 100 percent coverage is recommended. Typical topics covered are listed in Table 7.4.

Table 7.4. Typical Reaction Measures

Category	Examples of Data
Program design	Program objectives Program content Instructional materials Assignments
Program delivery	Method of delivery Facilitator/instructor delivery Facilities/learning environment
Potential use	Planned improvements Intent to use Relevance to job Importance to job Amount of new information Recommend to others
Overall satisfaction with program	

The measures at this level can vary significantly in the organization depending on the needs for data and the methods used to collect those data. At times, different types of methods may be used. The method is not as important as having standard approaches. Some are standardized along the intensity level. Low intensity is a quick-reaction questionnaire appropriate for e-learning or a program of short duration. Moderate intensity gets deeper into the topics listed in Table 7.4 and represents most of the programs. High intensity gets into much more detail, perhaps detailing the planned action more significantly. High-intensity feedback is needed to evaluate programs on a pilot basis where detailed feedback is required. Regardless of the set of data, it is important to be consistent and standardized and allow for integration of data across programs.

Some reaction measures tend to have more value than others. For example, some are predictive in their ability to forecast or correlate with actual use of the skills on the job. The five measures listed below have the strongest correlation to actual use based on a variety of studies in organizations and across organizations:

- This program is relevant to my current work.
- This program is very important to my job success.
- I intend to use this material on the job.
- This program contains new information.
- I would recommend this program to others in my job category.

Although planned actions cannot be summarized in a meaningful way across programs, the percentage of participants providing planned actions may be a useful measure at this level. Still, this is only reaction data, and the learning and development staff must move beyond these types of data to demonstrate other values in the value chain.

Learning and Confidence

The first measure at the learning level is the percentage of programs evaluated at this level. This measure varies not only with the needs of the organization, but with the definition of a learning measure. Some corporate universities and CLOs do not count a learning measure unless it is objective and formally structured, such as a test, demonstration, or simulation. Others consider self-assessment and facilitator assessment to be learning measures, and thus the percentage should be quite high. If the latter approach is taken, a target of 80 to 90 percent or, in some cases, 100 percent coverage is possible. Thus, it is helpful to integrate learning measures with the reaction questionnaire at the end of the program. The following measures are examples of the types of learning measures that can be integrated into the reaction instrument:

- Skill acquisition

- Knowledge acquisition

- Perception changes

- Objectives met

- Capability

- Confidence to use skills

The advantage of these measures is that they can easily be integrated across programs that ultimately appear in the overall learning and development scorecard. The disadvantage is that this is not enough detail to address issues that may surface if there are problems with a particular program's content, delivery, and learning design or the readiness of participants.

These measures must be implemented in conjunction with other learning measures that are more detailed about the program. For example, it may be common to include a role-play demonstration to measure the confidence in using a particular skill. The success of the demonstration is necessary feedback for the learner, program facilitators, and designers. Multiple-choice tests, problems, and simulations are useful to gauge skill and knowledge increases. Learning measures are meaningful at the program level only and cannot be easily included in the macrolevel scorecard.

Some organizations detail the types of learning measures in a profile on the macrolevel scorecard. Here, the learning executive's interest in learning measures may be detailed and divided into formal and informal learning methods. The trend here is twofold: first, self-assessment measures are obtained and should be taken at high percentages across programs; second, there is a move to more objective methods that can be defended when the testing is challenged.

Application and Implementation

As corporate university managers become more concerned with how behavior change, on-the-job application, guidelines, and the actions being taken by learners are connected to learning programs, this level becomes more important. The first measure at this level is the percentage of programs evaluated. Typically a best practice target is approximately 30 percent. This number involves sampling from two perspectives: (1) 30 percent of the programs are evaluated and (2) only a sample of the participants in a particular program would usually be included in the evaluation. At this level of measurement, there is both a micro- and a macroview. The microview involves measures that provide enough detail to understand how the program is driving change and how it is implemented. Specific questions, tailored to the type of program, may be relevant here. The macroview is needed to compare one program follow-up with another and be consistent with the types of issues. Typical application areas appropriate for any type of learning and development program are as follows:

- Use of skills
- Use of knowledge
- Frequency of use
- Success of use
- Programs with implementation
- Barriers
- Enablers

These measures can then be compared across programs in the macrolevel scorecard.

The barriers to the transfer of learning to the workplace are significant and must be measured. Whether labeled inhibitors, obstacles, or impediments, these measures represent serious roadblocks to application. The following list shows the barriers often collected across all programs:

- The immediate manager does not support the learning.
- The culture in the work group does not support the learning.
- There is no opportunity to use the skills.
- There is no time to use the skills.
- The employee didn't learn anything that could be applied to the job.
- The systems and processes did not support the use of the skills.
- The resources needed to use the skills are not available.
- The employee changed jobs, and the skills no longer apply.
- The skills taught are not appropriate in the work unit.
- The employee didn't see a need to apply what was learned.
- The employee could not change old habits.

These are forced-choice options and can be very powerful in understanding what the impediments are to the transfer of learning in an organization.

To complement the barriers, the enablers are often captured. Whether labeled enhancers, supporters, or enablers, these measures represent the processes that support the use of learning on the job. The combination of barriers and enablers can be very powerful to ensure that there is an adequate level of application and implementation. Without recognizing the barriers and enablers, the programs may not add significant value to the organization. Using forced-choice options, there is a possibility for roll-up across the programs, thus enabling the learning manager and executives to understand these issues on a macrolevel.

Impact and Consequences

Some learning executives and sponsors consider the impact and consequences level to contain the most important data. The first measure at this level is the percentage of programs evaluated. Best practice organizations typically measure 10 to 20 percent of their programs at this level. Sampling is used in two ways: the number of programs and number of participants in the programs. The types of data driven or influenced by a learning and development program can vary significantly and include both hard and soft data, as shown in Tables 7.5 and 7.6.

Table 7.5. Types of Hard Data

Category	Examples of Data	Category	Examples of Data
Output	Units produced	Cost	Budget variances
	Items assembled		Unit costs
	Items sold		Cost by account
	Forms processed		Variable costs
	Loans approved		Fixed costs
	Inventory turnover		Overhead costs
	Patients visited		Operating costs
	Applications processed		Number of cost reductions
	Productivity		Accident costs
	Work backlog		Sales expense
	Shipments		
	New accounts opened		
Time	Equipment downtime	Quality	Scrap
	Overtime		Rejects
	On-time shipments		Error rates
	Time to project completion		Rework
	Processing time		Shortages
	Cycle time		Deviation from standard
	Meeting schedules		Product failures
	Repair time		Inventory adjustments
	Efficiency		Percentage of tasks
	Work stoppages		completed properly
	Order response time		Number of accidents
	Late reporting		
	Lost-time days		

Table 7.6. Types of Soft Data

Category	Examples of Data
Work habits	Absenteeism
	Tardiness
	Visits to the dispensary
	First aid treatments
	Violations of safety rules
	Excessive breaks
Customer satisfaction	Churn rate
	Number of satisfied customers
	Customer satisfaction index
	Customer loyalty
	Customer complaints
Work climate	Number of grievances
	Number of discrimination charges
	Employee complaints
	Job satisfaction
	Employee turnover
	Litigation
Development/advancement	Number of promotions
	Number of pay increases
	Number of training programs attended
	Requests for transfer
	Performance appraisal ratings
	Increases in job effectiveness
Job attitudes	Job satisfaction
	Organizational commitment
	Perceptions of job responsibilities
	Employee loyalty
	Increased confidence
Initiative	Implementation of new ideas
	Successful completion of projects
	Number of suggestions implemented
	Number of goals

Data in this category are more meaningful at the microlevel where the learning program is linked to specific impact measures. This provides valuable data to make adjustments or show the contribution in a credible way.

Rolling up the data across programs becomes a bit more difficult but still possible. One potential roll-up to the macrolevel scorecard is a standard question that would appear on all follow-up questionnaires (whether at level 3 or 4). This questionnaire, shown in Exhibit 7.1 as an example, lists the most important measures in the organization. Ideally, the senior executives should identify their most critical ten or twelve measures in order of importance and have the list included in the questionnaire. Participants indicate the extent to which this program has influenced each measure, using a five-point scale. Alignment is achieved when the priorities listed by senior executives mirror the participant response. For example, if customer satisfaction is the number one measure with executives, it would be ideal if that measure was the one most influenced by learning and development programs. Rules are required to decide the depth of influence, such as obtaining a rating of 4 or 5 on a scale of 1 to 5, and deciding how to integrate the data. Ultimately, this can reveal the top ten measures influenced by the organization.

Another measure sometimes captured at this level is the method used to isolate the effects of learning on those measures. For a credible impact study, it is important to isolate the effects of learning on the impact data. When this is accomplished, it is helpful to understand which methods are being used because some methods are more credible than others. Although this information is not as easy to accumulate and compare, these are some of the most powerful data captured and communicated by the corporate university executive. (Additional information on the methods is presented later in this chapter.)

Return on Investment

ROI is calculated on a selected number of programs, and the percentage evaluated at this level is reported. Best practice companies target 5 to 10 percent of the programs. Most of the data at this level are in the microanalysis

Exhibit 7.1. Linking with Impact Measures

Indicate the extent to which you think your application of knowledge, skills, and behavior learned had a positive influence on the following business measures in your own work or your work unit. Please check the appropriate response beside each measure.

Business Measure	Not Applicable	Applies But No Influence	Some Influence	Moderate Influence	Significant Influence	Very Significant Influence
A. Work output	☐	☐	☐	☐	☐	☐
B. Quality	☐	☐	☐	☐	☐	☐
C. Cost control	☐	☐	☐	☐	☐	☐
D. Efficiency	☐	☐	☐	☐	☐	☐
E. Response time to customers	☐	☐	☐	☐	☐	☐
F. Cycle time of products	☐	☐	☐	☐	☐	☐
G. Sales	☐	☐	☐	☐	☐	☐
H. Employee turnover	☐	☐	☐	☐	☐	☐
I. Employee absenteeism	☐	☐	☐	☐	☐	☐
J. Employee satisfaction	☐	☐	☐	☐	☐	☐
K. Employee complaints	☐	☐	☐	☐	☐	☐
L. Customer satisfaction	☐	☐	☐	☐	☐	☐
M. Customer complaints	☐	☐	☐	☐	☐	☐
N. Other (please specify)	☐	☐	☐	☐	☐	☐

category. The data are meaningful only relative to the individual study and must be communicated to interested stakeholders.

When the ROI is captured, all the other data types exist as well, providing some of the most valuable data for senior executives. In a macrolevel scorecard, it may be helpful to include a summary of the studies presented in the time frame for which the scorecard is developed (annual or monthly, for example).

The issue of converting data to money is included since a monetary value is required to compare the costs to develop the ROI. This enables executives to see the financial contribution compared to the costs of the learning program. Since a variety of methods is used to convert data, it is important for executives to understand how a particular method was used to make that conversion. Consequently, the method used to convert data to monetary value is captured. For most situations, standard values will be used, but other methods are available. (This issue is covered later in the chapter.) A word of caution: it is dangerous to show an average ROI percent because sample size is small at this level and the numbers can vary significantly. It could be very misleading.

A Comprehensive Evaluation Process

We now examine the steps in the evaluation process, including planning, data collection, data analysis, isolating the effects of learning, translating the data into monetary figures, calculating the costs, and, finally, determining the return on investment.

Evaluation Planning

Figure 7.2 shows a comprehensive evaluation process labeled the ROI methodology (Phillips, 2003). The process begins with planning, overall and individually, for each program. When evaluation is conducted only at reaction levels, not much planning is involved, but as evaluation moves up the value chain, increased attention and efforts need to be placed on planning. During the typical planning cycle, it is helpful to review the purpose of evaluation for the

Figure 7.2. ROI Methodology

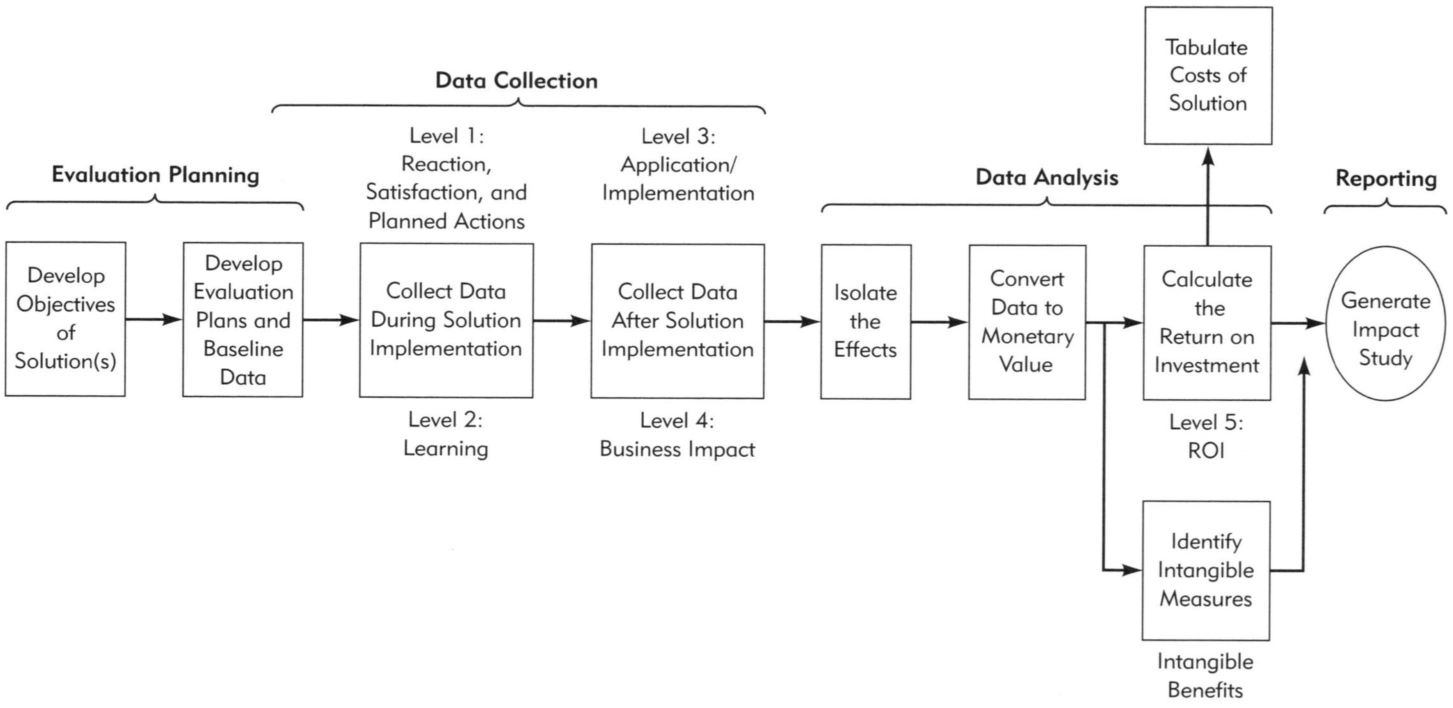

specific learning solutions and determine where the evaluation will stop on the value chain. The feasibility of evaluating at different levels is explored, and two planning documents are developed when the evaluation migrates to application, impact, and ROI: the data collection plan and the analysis plan. These documents are sometimes used in combination, but are often developed separately.

Objectives

One of the most important developments in measurement and evaluation is the creation of higher levels of objectives. Program objectives correspond to the different levels on the value chain. Ideally, the levels of objectives should be in place at the highest level desired for evaluation. The levels of objectives are:

- Input objectives (number of programs, participants, hours, and others) (level 0)
- Reaction objectives (level 1)
- Learning objectives (level 2)
- Application objectives (level 3)
- Impact objectives (level 4)
- ROI objectives (level 5)

Before an evaluation is conducted, these objectives must be identified and developed. Ideally, they should be developed early as the program is designed. If they are not readily available, they'll have to be included to take the evaluation to the desired level.

Collecting Data

Three issues must be addressed regarding data collection. First, the timing of collection must be established. In some cases, preprogram measurements are taken to compare with postprogram measures, and in a few cases, multiple measures are taken. In other situations, preprogram measurements are not available, and specific follow-ups are still taken after the program. The key issue is to determine the timing for the follow-up evaluation, which can vary from three weeks to six months.

Second, the source of data must be considered. For many of the data, the learner is the source. Other common sources are managers, direct reports, team members, external experts, and internal records and databases.

Third, the most important issue is the method used. Data are collected using the following methods:

- Surveys are taken to determine the extent to which participants are satisfied with the program, have learned skills and knowledge, and have used various aspects of the program.

- Questionnaires, usually more detailed than surveys, can be used to uncover a wide variety of data. Participants provide responses to several types of open-ended and forced-response questions.

- Tests are conducted to measure changes in knowledge and skills. Tests come in a wide variety of formal (criterion-referenced tests, performance tests and simulations, and skill practices) and informal (facilitator assessment, self-assessment, and team assessment) methods.

- On-the-job observation captures actual skill application and use. Observations are particularly useful in customer service training and are more effective when the observer is either invisible or transparent.

- Interviews are conducted with participants to determine the extent to which they have used the learning on the job.

- Focus groups are conducted to determine the degree to which a group of participants has applied the training to job situations.

- Action plans and program assignments are developed by participants during the program and implemented on the job after the program is completed. Follow-ups provide evidence of program success.

- Performance contracts are developed by the participant, the participant's supervisor, and the facilitator, who all agree on job performance outcomes.

- Business performance monitoring is useful when various performance records and operational data are examined for improvement.

The challenge is to select the method or methods appropriate for the setting and the specific program, within the constraints of the organization. There is no single way to collect the data; corporate universities need to tailor the measurement for their organizations based on the needs of the executives and employees.

Analysis

Evaluation requires analysis. Even if the evaluation stops at reaction, analysis is required, usually involving simple averages and standard deviations. As organizations progress up the value chain, additional analyses are required. In some cases, not only are the averages and standard deviations used, but simple hypothesis testing and correlations may be required; however, these are unusual situations. For the most part, analysis is simply tabulating, organizing, and integrating data and then presenting results in meaningful ways for the audience to understand and appreciate.

Isolating the Effects of Learning

An often overlooked issue in some evaluations is the process of isolating the effects of learning on output data. This step is important because many factors usually influence performance data after a learning program is conducted. Several techniques are available to determine the amount of output performance directly related to the program. These techniques pinpoint the amount of improvement directly linked to the program, resulting in increased accuracy and credibility of the evaluation data. The following techniques have been used by organizations to tackle this important issue:

- A control group arrangement is used to isolate the impact of learning. With this strategy, one group participates in a program, while another similar group does not. The difference in the performance of the two groups is attributed to the program. When properly set up and implemented, the control group arrangement is the most effective way to isolate the effects of learning and development.

- Trend lines and forecasting are used to project the values of specific output variables as if the learning program had not been undertaken. The projection is compared to the actual data after the program is conducted, and the difference represents the estimate of the impact of learning. Under certain conditions, this strategy can accurately isolate the impact of learning.

- Participants or managers estimate the amount of improvement related to the learning and development program. With this approach, participants or managers are provided with the total amount of improvement, on a pre- and postprogram basis, and are asked to indicate the percentage of the improvement that is actually related to the program.

- Other experts, such as customers, provide estimates of the impact of learning on the performance variable. Because the estimates are based on previous experience, the experts must be familiar with the type of program and the specific situation.

Converting Data to Monetary Values

To calculate ROI, business impact data collected in the evaluation are converted to monetary values and compared to program costs. This requires a value to be placed on each unit of data connected with the program. In many cases, standard values are available, as organizations have attempted to place value on measures they want to increase and develop costs for measures they want to avoid. When this is not available, internal experts can estimate the value of the measure. Several techniques are available to convert data to monetary values:

- Output data are converted to profit contribution or cost savings. With this strategy, output increases are converted to monetary value based on their unit contribution to profit or the unit of cost reduction. These values are readily available in most organizations.

- The cost of quality is calculated, and quality improvements are directly converted to cost savings. These values are available in many organizations.

- For programs where employee time is saved, the participant wages and benefits are used for the value of time. Because a variety of programs focus on improving the time required to complete projects, processes, or daily activities, the value of time becomes an important and necessary issue.

- Historical costs and current records are used when they are available for a specific variable. In this case, organizational cost data are used to establish the specific value of an improvement.

- When available, internal and external experts may be used to estimate a value for an improvement. In this situation, the credibility of the estimate hinges on the expertise and reputation of the individual.

- External databases are sometimes available to estimate the value or cost of data items. Research, government, and industry databases can provide important information for these values. The difficulty lies in finding a specific database related to the situation.

- Participants estimate the value of the data item. For this approach to be effective, participants must be capable of providing a value for the improvement.

- Supervisors of participants provide estimates when they are both willing and capable of assigning values to the improvement. This approach is especially useful when participants are not fully capable of providing this input or in situations where supervisors need to confirm or adjust the participant's estimate.

- Senior management provides estimates on the value of an improvement when they are willing to offer estimates. This approach is particularly helpful to establish values for performance measures that are very important to senior management.

- Education and training staff estimates may be used to determine a value of an output data item. In these cases, it is essential for the estimates to be provided on an unbiased basis.

This step is necessary for determining the monetary benefits from a learning program. The process is challenging, particularly with soft data, but can be methodically accomplished using one or more techniques.

Tabulating the Cost of Learning

The cost of learning is usually developed from two perspectives. For budgets, program approvals, and general information requests, the costs are often reported systematically in the organization and usually include only the direct costs. The executives and administrators are interested in the direct costs. In some cases, these reports are changing to include other indirect costs. When the actual ROI is calculated, the costs must be fully loaded to include both the direct and indirect costs. In these situations, the following cost components should be included:

- Needs assessment, design, and development, possibly prorated over the expected life of the program

- All program materials provided to each participant

- Instructor/facilitator, including preparation time as well as delivery time

- Facilities for the learning program

- Travel, lodging, and meal costs for the participants, if applicable

- Salaries, plus employee benefits of the participants who participated in the learning program

- Administrative and overhead costs of the workplace learning and performance function, allocated in some convenient way

- Evaluation, including planning, data collection, analysis, and reporting

The conservative approach is to include all of these costs so that the total is fully loaded.

Calculating the Return on Investment

The complete ROI process model for ROI development and analysis was shown in Figure 7.2. This reinforces the processes described in this chapter. When the ROI is developed, it should be calculated systematically, using standard formulas. Two formulas are available. The benefits-cost ratio is the program benefits divided by cost. In formula form it is:

$$\text{Benefit-cost ratio} = \text{Program benefits/program costs.}$$

The ROI uses the net benefits divided by program costs. The net benefits are the program benefits minus the costs. In formula form, the ROI becomes:

$$\text{ROI (\%)} = \text{Net program benefits/program costs} \times 100.$$

This is the same basic formula used in evaluating other investments where the ROI is traditionally reported as earnings divided by investment.

Identifying Intangible Benefits

In addition to tangible benefits, most learning programs influence intangible, nonmonetary benefits—for example:

- Branding of the learning center
- Increased job satisfaction
- Increased organizational commitment
- Improved teamwork
- Improved customer service
- Reduced complaints
- Reduced conflicts

During analysis, hard data such as output, quality, and time are usually converted to monetary values. The conversion of soft data is attempted; however, if the process used for conversion is too subjective or inaccurate and the resulting values lose credibility in the process, then the data are listed as an intangible benefit with the appropriate explanation. For some programs, intangible, nonmonetary benefits are extremely valuable, often carrying as much influence as the hard data items.

Reporting Data

This critical step often receives inadequate attention and planning to ensure that it is successful. It involves developing appropriate information such as impact studies, executive summaries, one-page summaries, and other brief reports. At the heart of this step are the different techniques used to communicate to a wide variety of target audiences. In most situations, several audiences are interested in and need the information. Careful planning to match the communication method with the audience is essential to ensure that the message is understood and appropriate actions follow.

Operating Standards

To ensure consistency and replication of evaluation studies, operating standards should be developed and applied in the measurement and evaluation process. It is extremely important for the results of an evaluation to stand alone and not vary depending on the individual conducting the study. The operating standards detail how each step and issue of the process will be addressed—for example:

- When a higher-level evaluation is conducted, data must be collected at lower levels.

- When an evaluation is planned for a higher level, the previous level of evaluation does not have to be comprehensive.

- When collecting and analyzing data, use only the most credible source.

- When analyzing data, choose the most conservative among the alternatives.

- If no improvement data are available for a population or from a specific source, it is assumed that little or no improvement has occurred.

- Estimates of improvements should be adjusted (discounted) for the potential error of the estimate.

- Extreme data items and unsupported claims should not be used in the analysis.

- Intangible measures are defined as measures that are purposely not converted to monetary values.

- Evaluation data must be communicated to all key stakeholders.

These specific standards not only serve as a way to consistently address each step, but also provide a much needed conservative approach to the analysis. A conservative approach will build credibility with the target audience.

Implementation Issues

A variety of organizational issues and events will influence the successful implementation of measurement and evaluation. These issues must be addressed early to ensure that evaluation is successful. Specific topics or actions may include:

- A policy statement concerning results-based learning and development

- Procedures and guidelines for different elements and techniques of the evaluation process

- Meetings and formal sessions to develop staff skills with measurement and evaluation

- Strategies to improve management commitment and support for measurement and evaluation

- Mechanisms to provide technical support for questionnaire design, data analysis, and evaluation strategy

- Specific techniques to place more attention on results

Measurement and evaluation can fail or succeed based on these implementation issues.

Final Thoughts

There is almost universal agreement that more attention is needed for measurement and evaluation. Its use is expanding, and the payoff is huge. The process is not difficult or impossible. The approaches, strategies, and techniques are not overly complex and can be useful in a variety of settings. The combined and persistent efforts of corporate universities will continue to refine the techniques and create successful applications.

References

Long, L. N. "Analytics: The CLO's Case in the CEO's Language." *Chief Learning Officer*, Sept. 2004, pp. 22–28.

Phillips, J. J. *Return on Investment in Training and Performance Improvement Programs.* (2nd ed.) Woburn, Mass.: Butterworth-Heinemann, 2003.

Jack J. Phillips, Ph.D., a world-renowned expert on measurement and evaluation, is chairman of the ROI Institute, which provides consulting services for Fortune 500 companies and workshops for major conference providers throughout the world. Phillips is also the author or editor of more than one hundred articles and over thirty books, including *Return on Investment (ROI) Basics* (2005), *ROI at Work* (2005), *Investing in Your Company's Human Capital: Strategies to Avoid Spending Too Little or Too Much* (2005), *Proving the Value of HR: How and Why to Measure ROI* (2005), *Make Training Evaluation Work* (2004), and *The Leadership Scorecard* (2004).

His expertise in measurement and evaluation is based on more than twenty-seven years of corporate experience in five industries (aerospace, textiles, metals, construction materials, and banking). Phillips has served as training and development manager at two Fortune 500 firms, senior human resource officer at two firms, president of a regional federal savings bank, and management professor at a major state university.

His background in learning and human resources led him to develop the ROI Process, a revolutionary process that provides bottom-line figures and accountability for all types of learning, performance improvement, human resources, and technology programs.

Jack Phillips has undergraduate degrees in electrical engineering, physics, and mathematics; a master's degree in decision sciences from Georgia State University; and a Ph.D. in human resource management from the University of Alabama. He can be reached at jack@roiinstitute.net.

Patti P. Phillips, Ph.D., is president of the ROI Institute, the leading source of ROI competency building, implementation support, networking, and research. She is also chairman and CEO of the Chelsea Group, an international consulting organization supporting organizations and their efforts to build accountability into their training, human resources, and performance improvement programs, with a primary focus on building accountability in public sector organizations. She helps organizations implement the ROI methodology in the United States and Canada as well as in other countries around the world, including South Africa, Singapore, Japan, New Zealand, Australia, Italy, Turkey, France, and Germany.

Her recent publications on accountability and ROI include *ROI Basics* (2005); *Proving the Value of HR: How and Why to Measure ROI* (2005); *Make Evaluation Work* (2004); *The Bottom Line on ROI* (2002), which won the 2003 ISPI Award of Excellence; *ROI at Work* (2005); the ASTD *In Action* casebooks *Measuring Return on Investment*, vol. 3 (2001), *Measuring ROI in the Public Sector* (2002), and *Retaining Your Best Employees* (2002); *Planning and Using Evaluation Data* (2003), *Mastering ROI* (1998), and *Managing Evaluation Shortcuts* (2001), all in the ASTD *Infoline* series; and *The Human Resources Scorecard: Measuring Return on Investment* (2001). Her work has also been published in a variety of journals.

Patti Phillips has a master's degree in public and private management and a Ph.D. in international development, and she frequently teaches and speaks on training evaluation. She can be reached at patti@roiinstitute.net.

PART 3

Distinctive Settings for Corporate Universities

Although the corporate university is a powerful concept for organizational advancement, it suffers from an unfortunate case of faulty nomenclature. The first word, *corporate*, is often incorrect, because corporate universities often reside in entities that are not corporations. The chapters in Part Three look at the distinctive types of organizations that may house "noncorporate" corporate universities.

The concept of the corporate university grew out of the standard American corporation, but companies headquartered outside the United States that conduct business globally are growing in number, influence, and, more to the point, in their use of corporate universities. Chapter Eight examines how a corporate university can be implemented and used effectively within a global organization.

We often think of corporate universities as dwelling in the province of large organizations; however, many small companies have embraced the concept and implemented successful corporate universities. Chapter Nine offers a discussion of how corporate universities can add value to small companies, even those with small budgets, and provides a case study of a corporate university in a company with 450 employees.

The nonprofit is another area where "noncorporate" corporate universities have proliferated. Nonprofits can be large, complex organizations, and the development of people in a nonprofit is no less important than it is in for-profit organizations. Chapter Ten is devoted to a discussion of corporate universities in the nonprofit sector and provides an in-depth look at one.

Just like nonprofits, the government sector comprises many large organizations with the same people development issues as their for-profit counterparts. The corporate university concept has been adopted by entities at the federal, state, and local levels. Like all the other chapters in Part Three, Chapter Eleven examines the concept in detail and provides a comprehensive case study.

At the beginning of Chapter Two, I introduced you to Ed Cohen. As this book was being conceived, Ed left Booz Allen Hamilton to take a job with an Indian company, Satyam Computer Services. After agreeing to write Chapter Two about holistic learning, Ed then volunteered to contribute this chapter, which describes the challenges of implementing a corporate university in a company that operates globally. Using his firsthand experience from working at Satyam, Ed discusses the challenges, successes, and lessons learned regarding a global corporate university.

8

Global Considerations for Corporate Universities

Ed Cohen

CORPORATE UNIVERSITIES WITH global responsibility must meet the learning and development needs of all constituents throughout the world. Within a global corporate university, time differences, geographical differences, escalating travel costs, opportunity cost of time, and other barriers exist. Instructor-led learning cannot be justified as the primary means for learning. Beyond actual real-time, on-the-job learning, use of virtual learning combined with alternatives, including degree and certification programs, executive coaching, performance consultancy, global learning circles, experiential learning, and self-study, needs to be a primary mechanism for learning deployment. Corporate universities are business enablers and catalysts for performance and relationship enhancement.

While many of the components of the corporate university remain the same, globalization adds unique characteristics and working principles. These characteristics are the subject of this chapter.

Satyam, a Global Company

Satyam Computer Services Ltd. is a global consulting and information technology (IT) services company, offering a wide array of customized solutions. From strategy consulting to implementing IT solutions for customers, Satyam spans the entire IT space. Its network extends over fifty-three countries and across six continents. As of February 2006, over twenty-seven thousand professionals work in development centers in India, the United States, the United Kingdom, the United Arab Emirates, Canada, Hungary, Singapore, Malaysia, China, Japan, and Australia and serve over 450 global companies, including 155 Fortune 500 corporations and alliances with over 50 business and technology leaders.

Satyam is an India-based company located in Hyderabad, India, in southern India. Over the past ten years, Hyderabad has rapidly become the high-tech home to many companies that participate in global outsourcing and development. In addition to many India-owned companies with operations in Hyderabad, Microsoft, Oracle, Tata Consulting Services, Infosys, Convergys, Deloitte Touche Tohmatsu, and IBM, among others, also have a solid presence in Hyderabad.

Satyam's Web site and the *Satyam Way Handbook* say that everyone is a leader: the company "believes its true strength lies in the potential of its Associates [employees]. Associates work in an atmosphere of trust and confidence. Every individual Associate is a leader. Leadership is demonstrated by the ways assigned tasks are implemented and by the freedom with which each Associate independently sets negotiated work styles and high standards of quality. A high degree of operational freedom helps Associates exercise their creativity and expertise in approaching tasks and achieving Customer Delight."

The Catalyst

A baby elephant does not need much room to turn around. Due to its small size, it is able to get from one place to another quickly and easily. But eventually it grows up, and when it reaches its full size, its sheer size prevents rapid movement. In addition, there are many places where the elephant can no longer fit.

The same is true for companies. In a new company, decisions are made quickly, innovation and entrepreneurship are encouraged, and the measurement of quality is simpler. As companies grow, processes are added to manage business complexities. This tends to diminish innovation and entrepreneurship and may influence quality. So how does a company hold on to the characteristics that historically have allowed for maximum success and value creation?

Satyam has achieved an environment that continues to encourage innovation and entrepreneurship, while at the same time demanding quality through the concept of full-life-cycle businesses led by empowered full-life-cycle leaders. A full-life-cycle business creates value (revenue, opportunity savings, cost savings), is logical and reasonable in size, and is led by a full-life-cycle leader.

Full-life-cycle leaders manage full-life-cycle businesses. They are empowered to make decisions as CEOs of their business, allowing rapid and decisive decision making to take place closest to the action. Innovation and entrepreneurship, risk taking, and collaboration appraisal ratings align with both promotion and compensation.

Full-life-cycle businesses are independent and interdependent. Independence allows their leaders to make rapid decisions and to be innovative and entrepreneurial. Interdependence comes from the single Satyam experience for all associates, investors, customers, and society. Solid alignment to the company's vision and a consistent set of common measures result in high stakeholder delight.

Passage to India

My passage to India began with the offer and opportunity to spearhead the launch of Satyam Computer Services Limited's School of Leadership. With the Satyam Learning Center already providing learning services for the entire firm, the School of Leadership's mission is to foster and propel distributed leadership. It has these responsibilities:

- Developing leaders to fuel Satyam's leadership engine faster and better than anyone else

- Expanding Satyam's strategic leadership capabilities by providing timely learning opportunities for full-life-cycle leaders in areas of associate, customer, investor, social, and institutional leadership

- Providing learning as the catalyst for closing leadership gaps and expanding leadership capabilities, especially in the area of strategic leadership

- Identifying and developing emerging leaders

- Tracking individual development of all leaders

Since 1991, Satyam has grown from a hundred people to more than twenty-seven thousand and from $1 million in revenue to more than $1 billion in revenue. According to Ramalinga Raju, chairman of Satyam, "Phenomenal sustained, fast and profitable growth combined with a solid commitment to growing entrepreneurial leaders holistically has led to a new paradigm for leadership at Satyam and has facilitated the launch of the Satyam School of Leadership. Satyam School of Leadership is built on the philosophy of expanding the entrepreneurial energy at Satyam, and helps us keep pace with the ever-changing business environment" (Satyam Computer Services, 2005).

Satyam's goal is to build global entrepreneurial leaders who have the capability and tools to be successful regardless of where they work. The School of Leadership seeks to identify potential leaders from the senior associate base, enhance leadership development in them through focused and holistic individualized learner interventions, and thereby develop leaders who are qualified to manage successfully in an increasingly complex business world.

When I arrived in India, I had the naive sense that my mission was to bring American leadership styles and skills to Satyam to help it be a more successful global firm. However, Satyam was already successful, growing at significant year-over-year rates. After observing the leadership for a few months, interviewing dozens of leaders, and analyzing the competencies for success, I came to realize that there is a set of universal competencies for all leaders at Satyam and leadership competencies adapted from each region of the world.

Universal competencies include business management that is proprietary to Satyam, executive presence, and business acumen. Geographical competencies include approaches to people leadership, relationship management, and specific business protocols.

Logistical and Structural Similarities and Differences

Let us look at some of the logistical and structural areas for corporate universities, comparing single-country corporate universities to global ones. Similarities include learning's vision and mission, alignment to business, support from the top, support processes, the virtual infrastructure, and implementation of measures. As shown in Table 8.1, differences include geography, languages, cultures, time zones, and learning styles.

Table 8.1. Domestic and Global Corporate University Differences

Differences	Domestic	Global
Countries	One	Many
Languages	One	Many
Cultures	One or two	Many
Time zones	A few	Many
Learning styles	Individual is considered	Individual and geographical approaches to learning must be considered

Competency Priorities

People who are working outside their geographical area or with those outside their geographical area need to understand universal competencies for being a global employee. This is even more critical for leaders and requires blending cultural definitions of leadership with geographical influences from around the globe.

As shown in Figure 8.1, today's competencies within Satyam are prioritized as follows:

- Geographical competencies: cultural differences, business protocols, and business legalities

- Corporate and proprietary competencies: internal culture, institutional business protocols, and proprietary skills; these proprietary competencies distinguish companies from each other

- Functional and market competencies: skills necessary to provide the services or products offered

Figure 8.1. Satyam's Competency Priorities

The Internet and other means of rapid communication allow diverse groups of employees to come together to learn from each other without requiring long journeys and expensive accommodations. One person might be from India working for an Indian-owned company and assigned to work in the United States. Another is from France working for an Indian-owned company and living in France. Yet another person might live in one part of the world working for a company headquartered in another part of the world and assigned to a region in yet another part of the world.

Welcome to the new global paradigm. Companies must continue to define new competencies and success factors for their employees who are doing business in a global environment. For us to be successful as global companies, our learning priorities need to shift away geographical competencies, followed by organization-specific competencies, followed by functional and market skills. As shown in Figure 8.2, the global paradigm shift requires new competency priorities:

- Universal competencies: business acumen, relationship and change leadership skills that provide the foundation for success throughout the world

- Functional and market competencies

- Geographical competencies

- Corporate and proprietary competencies

Figure 8.2. The New Global Competency Paradigm

Globalization demands that we shift development priorities. First, we need to identify universal competencies for success. These competencies break down barriers, allowing enhanced performance and relationships. Following universal competencies, our next concentration should be functional and market competencies, followed by geographical competencies. Finally, corporate and proprietary competencies are considered. For success as global organizations, we need to reduce our reliance on corporate and proprietary competencies. While it is true that these competencies distinguish organizations in a highly competitive world, they also create self-imposing barriers that diminish organization performance and strain relationships.

According to the 2004 Conference Board report, *Developing Business Leaders for 2010,* global leaders will need to be able to play four key roles:

- Master strategist
- Change manager
- Relationship builder/network manager
- Talent developer

The report concludes that fulfilling these roles successfully requires the following critical skills:

- Cognitive ability
- Strategic thinking skills
- Analytical ability
- Ability to make sound decisions
- Personal and organizational communication skills
- Influence and persuasion
- Diversity
- Delegation
- Ability to identify, attract, develop, retain talent
- Personal adaptability

I have identified these additional skills for Satyam leaders:

- Ability to have executive presence, including the ability to charm
- Ability to balance multiple tasks, behaviors, and relationships, as well as work and life

- Ability to create something from nothing

- Ability to have fun

Satyam's learning strategy addresses these skills by expanding business acumen, building strategic relationship skills, and enhancing executive presence. A variety of learning methods, including instructor-facilitated learning, virtual resources, executive coaching, performance consulting, mentoring, self-paced learning, peer learning circles, and experiential opportunities (job rotations and apprenticeships), are used to build key competencies.

Cultural Differences

Within each part of the world, learning has a different connotation and meaning. For example, in India, learning historically has focused on an academic approach, which is held in high esteem. The value that academic professionals bring to corporate learning is perceived to be very high. This is evident by the parallel structure and learning methods employed. In order to have a global corporate university that is successful, the learning methods employed in different parts of the world need to complement and supplement each other rather than make wholesale changes to force-fit learning to a one-size-fits-all model.

Training and alternative learning methods should focus on the dominant learning style for that culture as well as acceptable practices for learning. For example, certain team-building activities are not appropriate within the Indian culture but are fine elsewhere. That does not mean not having a ropes course, for example; it simply means greater awareness and local guidance when selecting activities. The same is true for conducting programs that deal with conflict, leadership, and other topics. Awareness and sensitivity to the culture are critical.

Another example is workplace harassment policies. In the United States, "comfort zone" is emphasized, and rules are established based on U.S. laws and norms. Outside the United States, the stringency of the standards can be considered either overkill or not stringent enough. Depending on where you are in the world, this one topic must be adapted to conform to local customs, standards, and laws.

Satyam uses its Crossover program to expand the cultural skills of its people. Crossover brings people from all over the globe to India and sends people from India to locations throughout the world in order to experience multiple cultures. Associates relocate for twelve to eighteen months, where they work side-by-side with local employees, learning about the local culture and at the same time sharing their culture with others. The result has been employees who are more perceptive and leaders who are capable of understanding and being successful in many different cultures.

Learning Methods: Global Considerations

Most corporate universities still rely on instructor-led learning as the primary means of teaching. Within a global corporate university, time differences, geographical differences, escalating travel costs, opportunity cost of time, and other barriers exist. Instructor-led learning cannot be justified as the primary means for learning. In addition to on-the-job learning, the use of virtual learning, degree and certification programs, executive coaching, performance consultancy, global learning circles, experiential learning, and self-study are all learning alternatives that are utilized.

Instructor-Led Learning

Instructor-led learning is best used for programs that are skill and behaviorally based and allow participants to build skills and have the opportunity to expand their personal networks and global perspective. Skill-based courses should blend multiple methods, allowing participants to prepare for the courses, attend with active learning (case studies, networking, simulations), and then have a follow-up component. Since this is the most expensive method of learning, it should always be strategically linked to the expansion of global networks and relationships.

Virtual Learning

Virtual learning provides the opportunity to reach constituents around the world at any time and anywhere. There are two types of virtual learning. Synchronous learning is delivered live over the Internet or intranet and, in many cases, is recorded for playback repeatedly. Asynchronous learning is available at any time and anywhere and includes online courses either custom developed or purchased off the shelf.

In addition to providing learning services to support teams that are co-located, a global network can be enhanced and differences appreciated. Global reach is made easy and cost-effective.

Virtual learning plays a very important role, but time differences can make it difficult to disseminate learning synchronously. When it is 9:00 A.M. in India, it is 10:30 the night before in New York City. When it is 9:00 A.M. in New York City, it is 7:30 P.M. in India. Which employee do you ask to stay up late: the one in India or the one in New York? Or which employee do you ask to get up early?

This is not always an easy decision, especially when the preponderance of population may exist in one country or the other. To reduce this conflict, multiple offerings and a stronger reliance on playback of archived sessions with access to online mentors help. It is also important to have a global footprint of learning professionals who can conduct courses live and online to meet the needs of those in various time zones. Moreover, you may need to ask trainers and presenters to teach outside normal business hours in order to respect the time zone differential.

There are some additional considerations for successful deployment of virtual learning in a global corporate university. Having mirror servers throughout the world provides more rapid access. In other words, there should be one or more redundant servers located on each continent where you wish to provide virtual learning. This comes in handy when a server fails or becomes disabled. Also, the languages in which to offer learning are a consideration that should be discussed and determined prior to rollout of any program.

Certification and Degree Programs

Today, many universities collaborate to provide seamless services across the globe. Those with a global footprint are in the best position to meet global needs. The same is true for learning providers. Certification and degree programs need to meet two distinct needs: provide validation that individuals meet specific industry standards or academic standards and assist in building the qualifications of the organization.

Since many certification programs are driven by industry standards, there may not be much difference from one region to the next. In this case, finding a provider with a strong local presence and a successful record of accomplishment is tantamount.

Geographical differences are most critical for professional skills development. Accounting standards vary from country to country, as do legal and compliance training. This is where it is critical to have the right resources.

One primary area where university relationships can consistently enhance skills is business acumen. Satyam offers a strategic business management certificate program delivered primarily online that includes key skills offered in most M.B.A. programs. This part-time program is offered over a five-month period through a global university partnership. Professors disseminate knowledge through videos and online content, supplemented by global learning teams working together on projects to strengthen their skills in organizational behavior, data analysis, operations management, strategic marketing, global finance, global and regional economics, international business, and strategic management.

Rather than customize the topics to Satyam, the developers of the program opted for a "best-in-class" approach to expand the general business knowledge of leaders. The specifics come from selecting case studies that highlight clients.

Executive Coaching

Executive coaches assist with individual development needs. Unless they are preparing someone for working in a different geographical area, executive coaches should be sourced locally. Important here is the need to have a universal set of global competencies, but they must be adapted to the local geography in order for employees to be successful. The complications of global leadership in different organizations are reduced by providing ongoing learning and updates to executive coaches who are working with leaders.

Mentoring

Mentors, who are defined as trusted counselors or guides, are useful for acclimating staff to a new company, position, or environment. They are also useful as a sounding board to test ideas, share thoughts, and assist with unfamiliar territory.

Mentoring, whether formal or informal, provides excellent learning opportunities. A formal program with individuals from different parts of the world also reduces risk. Prior to doing business in a region of the world an individual is unfamiliar with, assigning a mentor can greatly reduce business errors due to cultural and geographical differences.

Consultancy

Performance consulting looks at learning as an intervention to resolve a performance concern. Consultancy of this type has several purposes. It ensures standards of operation, enhances performance and relationships among team members, or refines and expands processes for better outcomes.

When standards are the desired outcome, performance consultants must consistently measure and monitor the culture of the organization, while regarding the geographical culture as a secondary input. For team enhancement, local performance consultants apply the cultural and geographical influences to make sure teams align to their stakeholders.

To accomplish this, we send performance consultants into the field to shadow teams. The primary customer for this service offering is the leader. The consultant spends a week with the team providing feedback and measuring the use of new skills and behaviors. This allows the leader and team to learn without loss of billability and maximizes retention because participants learn while doing.

Learning Circles

The corporate university's enhancement of global business is maximized through innovative learning opportunities. Learning circles using experiential or action learning are set up on a site-by-site basis, but have greater impact if set up virtually. Virtual teams work on an issue, research a market, or develop a strategy together with a shared space online combined with infrequent face-to-face meetings.

SAMPLE LEARNING CIRCLE ACTIVITY: UNDERSTANDING GLOBAL MARKETS

How do you get someone in Japan to understand the market in South America or someone in Europe to understand the market in India? Set up a global action learning team to perform a market analysis. Begin by selecting participants from different parts of the world. Assign the task—for example, perform a market analysis on who buys information technology consulting services in the energy sector.

Assign roles such that each team member analyzes a part of the world that he or she is not familiar with. Team members may seek advice and subject matter expertise from other team members from that part of the world, but the analysis must be completed through thorough research. The result is a broader understanding for all team members on business in different parts of the world and an excellent research document for the organization.

Experiential Learning

There is a variety of experiential learning options available, the best of which is job rotation. According to the Conference Board's *Maximizing Rotational*

Assignments (2005), "The rotational assignment—an integral component of top talent development plans at many corporations—creates an opportunity for companies to provide their executives with an accelerated learning experience that can lead to demonstrative results for both the executive and the company" (p. 2).

Job rotation allows individuals to expand their skill set, work in different regions or countries to better understand culture and business protocol differences, and take measured risks.

At Satyam, employees in the Crossover program move to India or another country, where they take on a position that allows them to become immersed in the culture for one to two years. Individuals are mentored and learn how to be successful in a variety of environments.

Apprenticeships are another excellent experiential learning opportunity. Junior leaders shadow senior leaders in order to learn how to handle complex situations that cannot be taught in the classroom. Over time, a variety of apprenticeship opportunities allows learners to expand leadership skills while at the same time developing critical thinking skills.

Self-Study

Self-study options such as audio, video, or reading materials are especially effective with a mobile global workforce. Most companies choose a single language for their business; at Satyam, all business is conducted in English. However, self-study materials can be created in multiple languages. When it comes to learning, the individual's primary language may be the best way to disseminate information.

The Right Blend

To maximize our learning investment, emphasis is being placed increasingly on virtual and alternative learning methods (see Figure 8.3). Instructor-led training is used strategically to provide a corporate headquarters experience or to bring together leaders for maximum networking opportunities.

Figure 8.3. The Blend of Learning at Satyam

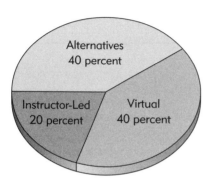

Breakdown of Alternatives

Certificate and Degree Programs,
5 percent

Executive Coaching,
5 percent

Mentoring,
5 percent

Consultancy,
5 percent

Learning Circles,
5 percent

Experiential,
10 percent

Self-study,
5 percent

Global Footprint

While it may not be feasible to have learning professionals colocated in all parts of the world, having adequate learning alliances with individual contractors, training providers, and universities is critical. Table 8.2 shows some considerations for determining a global footprint.

Table 8.2. Determining a Global Footprint

Consideration	Global footprint
Every location needs to be supported.	Every location is aligned to a region, and regional learning consultants are assigned. Where enough population exists (we use a guideline of 250 people), a full-time learning consultant is assigned. Where there are not enough people, regional learning consultants are assigned to manage multiple locations.

Table 8.2. Determining a Global Footprint, Cont'd

Consideration	Global footprint
Each location is different (reason for being, stage in life cycle, or something else).	Regional staff provide the consulting needed to assess these unique needs and provide tailored learning opportunities.
Size is not the only factor in determining support requirements.	Deployment criteria allow staff to be staged at locations based on multiple factors. Complexity, strategic direction, and market opportunities also play a role.
Needs are dynamic.	Regional learning consultants provide a conduit to the entire learning team to ensure that emerging needs are calculated into planning and service development.

Adjunct Instructors

Individual contractors and the employees of the organization can act in the capacity of adjunct instructor. The key is to have a certification process that ensures quality of content and delivery. The certification program should include content knowledge, adult learning models, presentation skills, facilitation skills, and constant monitoring. This ensures consistent quality and allows for easy adaptation to the local culture.

Travel

Should participants travel to a central site for learning programs? Should facilitators travel to local sites to conduct programs? While the latter alternative costs significantly less, there are times when bringing participants to a central location has great value.

This is especially true for programs involving senior leaders. Coming together in a residential experience helps them expand their network and expand their thinking beyond their own corner of the world. Supplementing the residential experience with virtual communities of practice and sharing of resources, tangible and intangible, helps the organization to be more successful.

Summary

Corporate universities with global responsibility must meet the learning and development needs of all constituents throughout the world. To enable success, organizations must reprioritize, emphasizing competency attainment in this order: universal, functional and market, geographical, and corporate and proprietary.

Within a global corporate university, time differences, geographical differences, escalating travel costs, opportunity cost of time, and other barriers exist. Instructor-led learning cannot be justified as the primary means for learning which is why on-the-job learning, virtual learning (including degree and certification programs), executive coaching, performance consultancy, global learning circles, experiential learning, and self-study are all used.

Mahatma Gandhi said, "Consciously or unconsciously, every one of us does render some service or another. If we cultivate the habit of doing this service deliberately, our desire for service will steadily grow stronger, and it will make not only for our own happiness, but that of the world at large." The corporate university has the opportunity to cultivate global habits, assist companies in growing stronger, and be the catalyst for teaching universal and specific competencies.

Therefore, although many of the components are the same for a global corporate university, there are unique characteristics to keep in mind. Cultures, languages, learning styles, modes of delivery, and global footprint are some of the main areas to consider. The key to a successful global corporate university is the ability to identify universal competencies, as well as to meet the unique needs of a mobile society of global citizens who need to adapt nimbly and intuitively to an abundance of differing business situations.

References

Conference Board. *Developing Business Leaders for 2010.* New York: Conference Board, 2004.

Conference Board. *Maximizing Rotational Assignments.* New York: Conference Board, 2005.

Satyam Computer Services. *Satyam Computer Services Annual Report.* Hyderabad, India: Satyam Computer Services, 2005.

Ed Cohen is the senior vice president for Satyam Computer Service's School of Leadership, responsible for creating the vision and strategy for leadership development and for building the school. Satyam leverages his expertise in setting up and managing the corporate university concept. Considered a statesman in this segment, Cohen continuously explores and maintains new methodologies and programs in tune with customer expectations. He has been directing organizational, training, and employee development services for almost a quarter-century.

Prior to joining Satyam, Cohen spent eight years with Booz Allen Hamilton, where he founded and was the strategic leader of its corporate university, the Center for Performance Excellence. During his tenure as the leader of learning at Booz Allen, the Center for Performance Excellence grew from a start-up in 1998 to become one of the most widely recognized corporate universities. Under his leadership, Booz Allen climbed the Training Top 100, reaching the number one spot in 2006. During that time, Booz Allen received more than thirty Excellence in Practice recognitions from the American Society for Training and Development (ASTD).

Cohen was program chair of the 2005 ASTD Conference in May 2005, serves on the advisory board for ASTD's Learning Executive Network and the editorial advisory board of *Training* magazine, and is a member of the Conference Board Council for Education and Training. He earned a B.S. in accounting from the University of Florida and an M.S. in education from Nova Southeastern University, and he has participated in Harvard Business School's Professional Service Firms and Strategic Executive Leadership programs.

When it came time to examine how small companies can successfully implement corporate universities, I didn't have to think twice about a choice for a case study. I had the pleasure of working with the team from Enclos when they set up their corporate university, and I knew they would succeed, even though they were a relatively small (450 employees) company. They had a firm organizational commitment to Enclos University and had the right people working on it.

Their choice for the founding director of Enclos University was Lee Steffens. Although Lee did not have a background in learning and development, he had an intimate knowledge of the company and the required competencies for its key positions. Moreover, his project management skills served him well in getting Enclos University off the ground. In this chapter, Lee and his colleague Shannon Novotne describe how they created and launched Enclos University and the successes and lessons learned along the way.

9

Corporate Universities in Small Companies

Lee E. Steffens, Shannon M. Novotne

DEFENSE ACQUISITION UNIVERSITY HAS 550 full-time employees devoted to its corporate university, which serves 134,000 employees worldwide. Caterpillar has around 100 staff members on its corporate university staff and nearly 80,000 employees within its organization. Enclos has 450 employees at regional offices across the globe and only two corporate university employees. How does this work? The example of Enclos University shows how a corporate university in a small company can work, why it can work, what can be accomplished, and what can be learned.

Background on Enclos Corp.

Enclos Corp. is a specialty contractor engaged in the design, engineering, technical drafting, procurement, and installation of curtainwall and window systems for large commercial and institutional buildings. On many commercial projects, the product used to keep the outside elements from coming inside is a curtainwall, which consists of metal framing members (usually aluminum) and glass, metal panels, or stone. Curtainwall is one of the primary components of the exterior facade of large-scale commercial buildings. With $145 million in sales, Enclos is one of the largest and most respected curtainwall contractors in the world. It focuses on projects that present design and engineering or logistical challenges. The average size of its contracts is between $15 and $20 million, with its largest contracts in the range of $100 million.

Positions at Enclos require mastery of complex competencies. From a conceptual perspective, Enclos approaches each project in the same way. However, the specifics vary greatly from project to project. Customization is Enclos's business, and the details of each project reflect this.

Enclos procures wall system components, assembles them into units at off-site locations, and then hoists these units into place on a building. Its curtainwalls are custom and unique to each project, thus requiring Enclos to build and test mock-ups of key wall types on all projects.

Enclos's customers are well-known architects, general contractors, and building owners. Typically, architects on Enclos projects are specific in the performance criteria and aesthetics of the exterior walls of buildings they have designed, but leave the development of the system details to Enclos. Enclos designs and engineers at least 50 percent of its work. The company's engineering teams are assembled by project and led by a technical project manager in the engineering department who reports to the lead operations project manager for the project. Enclos has engineering groups in Minnesota, Montreal, Manila, and New Brunswick.

Members of the operations team working on a project in a particular location do not necessarily live in or routinely work out of that location. For instance, the lead project manager on a midtown Manhattan project lives in Minneapolis. Two project managers working on a Philadelphia project live in Chicago. Another lead project manager on a different New York City project lives in the Baltimore area.

Enclos's field supervision staff is extremely mobile. The organization employs fifty union field employees who move from job to job. This group has been Enclos's most adaptable in terms of working in different locations and on different teams.

Why Corporate Universities Make Sense in a Small Company

Size has no impact on whether a company can create a corporate university. What matters are the reasons for the creation of a corporate university. Enclos University was created to achieve a specific, well-defined corporate strategy. It was then designed and implemented to fit the particular strategy, culture, and budget of Enclos.

The concept of a corporate university did not need selling to management. It was a logical outcome of the strategic planning process, which involved all upper-level management. In 2002, the strategic planning committee began to focus on three initiatives: how best to develop the workforce of the future, whether to engage in research and development, and how to make better use of the knowledge and experiences of its employees and drive best practices across all project teams.

The Link Between Strategy and Development of Enclos University

Management decided to improve on Enclos's training techniques. Up to this time, an employee's professional development came predominantly through experience. Given the changing custom nature of Enclos's work, the experiences gained from a couple of projects (which sometimes run two years each) could not possibly prepare the individual for the number of challenges he or she would face over the course of an entire career. What an Enclos employee learned through project experience was largely a matter of chance. It was often not until a project manager had worked at Enclos for twelve to fifteen years that he or she was entrusted to lead a project team on a large, complex project. This time frame was too long—much longer than it takes a graduate from medical school to become a doctor. If Enclos could discover a way to harness and share that knowledge and learning without limiting the initiative and creativity of project teams, the payback would be enormous. Through the establishment of a corporate university, Enclos felt it would be able to use e-learning, classroom learning, coaching, mentoring, and on-the-job training.

Best Practices and Knowledge Management

Because the majority of Enclos projects and employees are spread throughout the United States, sharing best practices and knowledge management was a challenge. Enclos's system of autonomously operating project teams, while beneficial in many ways, was inefficient because the same mistakes were often repeated throughout the company. Enclos employees together have over four thousand years of experience in the curtainwall industry. Management determined that by linking all that experience and knowledge together, innovation would be accelerated, efficiency would increase, and different project teams would be less likely to make the same mistakes that other teams had made.

Innovation

Enclos has prided itself on its innovation. Before Enclos University, all innovation took place in the context of individual projects. For the technical challenges Enclos faced, project-specific solutions were created by the project team facing the challenge. Enclos determined it could also benefit from a portion of its innovation being carried out by an independent R&D team, unrelated to a project. This approach would allow it to pool the learning from multiple project teams in order to optimize innovation or engage in further research around an idea that initially was considered too experimental to try on a particular project.

What Enclos Hoped to Accomplish with a University

The strategic planning committee realized that these three initiatives overlapped: all three dealt with how to identify and gather knowledge and learning and then disseminate the knowledge. It became apparent that a corporate university was part of the solution Enclos was seeking. The committee combined all three initiatives into one new initiative to create a corporate university in alignment with Enclos's mission: "To enclose the world's finest buildings with the world's finest curtainwalls." The committee endorsed the following goals to guide the creation and development of Enclos University:

- Enable Enclos to double in size without increasing risk by incorporating new employees into its system faster and decreasing development time for entry-level employees in key positions, such as project management, design, sales, and engineering.

- Build a culture of excellence and teaching. If Enclos was going to be the best, the university could help instill that value in each employee. Another key part of the Enclos culture was the value of sharing and teaching others.

- Decrease risk and write-downs of profit margins through more consistent effort and application of best practices from team to team and project to project.

- Increase efficiency through more reuse and fewer new wheels.

- Increase innovation.

- Accommodate a more decentralized workforce and geographically dispersed teams.

- Enhance its competitive advantage by building on the knowledge and learning Enclos has gained and will continue to gain.

Selecting a Leader for the University

After making the decision to establish a corporate university, the strategic planning committee realized that someone was needed to lead the effort of building and running Enclos University. The committee considered hiring an outside expert who had prior experience with corporate universities, but decided that would not be a good solution. Enclos University was going to change the company culture for most employees. Management felt there would be even greater resistance to change if the university was led by an outside expert. Moreover, much of the learning, R&D, and best practices the university would manage would be Enclos specific. The committee felt an outside expert would spend too much time learning Enclos's culture, business practices, and technical challenges before he or she could even begin to lead the university. The answer was finding an individual who could not only lead and administer, but also take an active role in developing the university's program while engaging in R&D.

After careful consideration, Enclos management selected Lee Steffens, one of its top senior project managers, as the director of Enclos University. Steffens had an impressive background in project management. The executive team felt employees would respect his opinion and that selecting him would show how serious management was in the belief that Enclos employees represent the backbone of Enclos University.

How Enclos Launched Its University

With Steffens on board, he and two other members of the strategic planning committee sought to learn more about how others designed and built their corporate universities. They met with representatives of other corporate universities and attended conferences on the subject. When the team members completed this research process, they were energized with the thought of starting a corporate university at Enclos.

Enclos University's Business Plan

As a project manager, Steffens was accustomed to creating a means and methods plan to guide him during the course of a construction project. He created a similar guide, in this case a business plan, for Enclos University that would serve as a road map for development of the university and communicate to the Enclos community the vision for the university. This purpose was critical to the university's success. Steffens's plan did not call for a large staff to conceptualize, create, and teach courses; develop the content of its knowledge management system; or conduct R&D. Although Enclos University coordinated all these efforts, Enclos employees were the primary teachers, researchers, and knowledge providers. For the university to be successful, employees had to understand its role and become motivated to play the active role expected of them. This approach had the added benefit of enabling Enclos University to operate with a limited budget; therefore, Enclos did not have to hire an extensive corporate staff or outsource the development of the university.

Enclos's business plan began with a vision that linked directly to the company mission: "Enclos University will develop the industry's finest people and the industry's finest company." In turn, this vision led to the development of Enclos University's mission statement, which linked directly to the university's strategic goals: "Enclos University gives people the knowledge, skills, and information they need to enable Enclos to grow wisely, achieve consistency in performance, and continuously innovate and improve."

The business plan had four key areas and described how each area would provide benefits to Enclos: learning management, knowledge management, wisdom management, and innovation management (R&D). A time line was created that included targeted goals for each milestone, a phased implementation plan, specific exemplary slices of the plan, a rollout plan, an evaluation plan, a best practices track, and a challenge to the company at large to support Enclos University. The business plan set up these four functional areas.

Learning Management. A curriculum was developed that would draw primarily on employees to teach, but also used some outside experts teaching courses tailored to Enclos. While many courses require attendees and the teacher to be in the same room, many smaller modules are offered by live Web presentation or prerecorded video. The learning gained from the best practice work, postproject reviews, and research influences what Enclos teaches.

Enclos's workforce is geographically dispersed. This created training challenges, knowledge management challenges, and standardization of best practice challenges. Employees who wish to progress to new levels in the company must complete course work and testing in addition to satisfying other job qualifications. Employees in established positions are also required to complete some amount of continuing education.

In the past, Enclos had done training only through live learning, which is available only when a course is offered, not necessarily when the employee needs it. An employee may not have an opportunity to use the learning in his or her job for months after the learning is delivered. For example, if a project manager takes a live course on fabrication and assembly considerations during the design process, but the project manager's current project is already beyond the design stage, he or she might have missed an opportunity to take advantage of that live instruction for a year or more.

Every employee also has an individually tailored learning development plan. This allows everyone in the company to continue to grow in their professional development not only within Enclos but also within the industry.

Knowledge Management. Knowledge management focuses on spreading learning, new information, and best practices outside formal courses. Enclos project coordinators, project managers, senior project managers, project executives, engineering personnel, and field superintendents and foremen meet annually for live training sessions taught by Enclos personnel. This also helps ensure that best practices are carried across the regions.

Enclos requires a large percentage of senior positions. The company philosophy is that as an employee progresses from junior to more senior positions, the type of knowledge he or she needs to master in order to perform at that level increasingly becomes tacit knowledge. Enclos's training and knowledge management systems need to support the transfer of tacit knowledge, such as postproject reviews or facilitating better communication.

One of the keys to Enclos's success over the years has been that the company gave its project managers, salespeople, designers, and engineers broad authority to make decisions themselves. This fostered an entrepreneurial and problem-solving culture, which has been a key factor in the company's success. The downside is that Enclos has repeated certain mistakes across projects, had large projects that lost money, at times appeared inconsistent to its customers, and often reinvented the wheel. In this culture, there has been solid teamwork and sharing of knowledge within a specific project team, but little collaboration and knowledge sharing across project teams, departments, and regions. Enclos wanted to retain the best of the old culture but change it so that collaboration across the company became the norm. In this way, employees across the company, not just the individual or team that made the mistake, could learn from past mistakes.

There are specific tasks that employees should always perform the same way and standardized documents that need to be used in a similar way. A searchable electronic library was created that includes document and best practice libraries, how-to manuals, video and photo records from all projects, product information, and technical alerts relating to products, supplier-contractor experience listing, postproject reviews, and other similar methods.

Wisdom Management. One of the university's goals was to greatly reduce the time frame it took new employees to progress to leadership positions in operations, design, and engineering. We recognized that formal learning alone would not close this gap. Wisdom that can be gained only through maturity and practical experience was also needed. At the time of the business plan's creation, the committee struggled to identify, and left for later the development of, an approach that would accelerate this wisdom attainment.

Within a year after the launch of Enclos University, the committee settled on an approach to wisdom management. The university uses a highly managed approach to job rotation, combined with the delivery of more formal learning at meaningful points at each stage in the rotation. During the course of their first two to three years at Enclos, new employees progress through six different job assignments. These job functions represent all major responsibilities Enclos typically performs, from curtainwall design to curtainwall installation. Enclos University has identified critical experiences at each stage to which new employees should be exposed and all competencies they should develop during each of the six assignments, along with learning plans for the individuals to perform that best support the development of these competencies. In addition, the delivery of many of the courses is timed to occur when the employee is engaged in a practical experience that complements the course. (Wisdom management is discussed in greater detail in Chapter Eighteen.)

Research and Development. One function Enclos wanted to include in Enclos University was research and development, or innovation management. In the past, almost all R&D at Enclos took place in the context of individual projects. Thus, innovation had always been constrained by the focus on a particular solution for a single project and by the schedule and budget for that project. While the majority of Enclos's innovation will continue to take place at the project level, Enclos benefits from some corporate-centered R&D. A large part of this new university-led R&D effort has been to improve on what the company already does, a natural extension of the university's focus on knowledge collection, sharing, and best practices. For instance, Enclos might determine as part of a post-project review that a component used within a wall system was satisfactory, but if it were redesigned slightly would have saved a specified amount in field labor costs. Within just two years of its existence, Enclos created three new products through this approach. In addition, it completed a research project that has validated a previous theoretical solution to a particular design challenge.

Making It Happen

Everyone within the company is expected not only to use the university to learn but also to contribute to it. Employees rotate through as visiting researchers or teachers. A number of Enclos employees travel a considerable amount and have high-stress jobs, and burnout is a continuing concern. One way to ameliorate this is to allow internal sabbaticals, whereby an employee can take time off between projects and develop a teaching module on a particular subject, take part in an R&D team, or assist in the development of a user-friendly approach to sharing a business practice or some sort of information with which the individual has expertise. A benefit to this approach is that it reinforces the expectation that knowledge sharing and teaching are something that all Enclos employees, not just an elite few at corporate headquarters, need to do.

Laying the Groundwork for a Successful Launch

A successful launch is important for the achievement of a thriving corporate university. Employees at many companies are skeptical of new management initiatives. It is important for employees to buy into the concept of the university at the time of the launch. For Enclos, it was even more important because Enclos employees were expected to help create courses and lead education, provide content to the knowledge management system (KMS), and actively participate in the R&D effort, while still fulfilling their regular job requirements. For these reasons, the committee wanted to be fully ready before launching the university to the Enclos community. During this time of final preparation, a learning management system (LMS) was selected and populated. Partnerships with select clients and vendors were established to make use of information and training opportunities that fit into the business plan. The LMS featured a KMS that allowed Enclos to tie its learning courses to its knowledge database. Grant proposal forms were developed for the research and development sector, and solicitations sent to employees.

In September 2004, executives joined the director of Enclos University in traveling to all Enclos offices and helped introduce the corporate university to employees. Enclos was able to showcase how the university works rather than discuss a dream.

It is important to keep positioning a corporate university in the minds of employees. After the launch, we have continued to promote and reinforce the message of the university to the Enclos community. Enclos University is also promoted throughout Enclos by its executives. The Enclos president updates employees once a year on the status of the university during his "state of the company" meeting. Enclos University is an integral part of the company newsletter and has been featured in several trade publications.

Enclos Achievements with Its Corporate University

Enclos succeeded in creating a corporate university that has four key elements: learning programs, knowledge management, wisdom management, and an R&D program.

Learning Programs

Every employee has a learning plan tied to his or her career path. The performance review process is tied to the career path and the learning plan. Enclos has over two hundred online and live training courses available for its employees, ranging from industry-specific topics to soft skills. Within the first year of the university's operation, Enclos's blended learning approach allowed employees to commit over twenty-four hundred hours toward improving their professional development. Over 25 percent of employees have taken off-site training and leadership courses. Enclos has collaborated with several of its major vendors to incorporate stronger learning opportunities on Enclos University. One of Enclos's primary vendors has developed a training course on its product that it hosts twice a year. Another major vendor has worked with Enclos to develop an electronic manual for the use of its product. A third vendor sends Enclos vignettes on different processes of fabricating glass, which has eliminated the need to send employees on plant tours and also allows clients to understand this process better without taking time out of their schedules.

Knowledge Management

The knowledge library is the place where employees seek information. The company has a backlog of information that has been shared by employees. This backlog will soon become imported into the electronic library.

Wisdom Management

Enclos has laid the groundwork for a wisdom management program that will reduce the basic training time for its operations staff by almost three years.

Research and Development

A large part of the initial R&D effort was to improve on what the company already did. Several projects have been completed that have resulted in the creation of new products for Enclos. Another research project has provided Enclos with concrete data to use in supporting one of the technical approaches it uses in the design of its curtainwall systems.

Cultural Change

Enclos University has fostered more collaboration within the company. Although it is difficult to measure if the cultural changes have been a direct result of the university, the culture of Enclos has begun to evolve, and the timing coincides with management's efforts to use Enclos University as a leader in communicating and representing this culture change. Project teams exhibit increased collaboration across regions and teams by sharing research and best practices. For example, the director of the university receives weekly questions from employees throughout the company who are seeking industry information. He puts them in contact with other employees who have this knowledge.

Another change that has taken place since the university launched is the evolution of weekly Friday meetings within the design department, where new design ideas are shared and existing designs are critiqued by the group. In addition, the design department created a new design space for better collaboration by sharing of ideas. Recruiting and career development have blossomed. Today's college graduates are interested in professional development, and Enclos University shows these graduates that Enclos cares about their career paths. The university offers not only e-courses but also live training, which has been instrumental in allowing employees to meet face-to-face in a learning environment.

Much of the knowledge and experience it took to be successful existed in the minds of Enclos employees. This information put Enclos University in the center of management's effort to change the company culture. Through the use of employees as Enclos University's teachers, researchers, and knowledge providers, Enclos has begun to create a culture that reinforces its efforts to drive consistency and a greater level of innovation throughout the organization.

Lessons Learned

Although Enclos University has had a great deal of success, not everything has gone perfectly. We have learned much along the way.

Employee Acceptance

It was hard to get complete acceptance from employees on the concept of Enclos University. Everyone has a certain level of commitment to the university, but there are people who make the university a part of their daily work life and other people who don't. Full understanding of this was something Enclos was not truly prepared to handle.

A corporate university cannot be implemented overnight. It takes patience and enough employees believing in it for the university to succeed. Enclos still struggles with the challenge of getting more employees to appreciate that contributing to Enclos University is as much a part of their job as their "real work." Employees are going to be interested in the "new deal." They will have many ideas for you. Listen.

Not everyone will be attracted to the same thing. Some employees wanted to learn new skills, while others were more interested in using the knowledge database. There were employees who were concerned with how to receive a faster promotion, while others felt more intrigued by innovation. If you are going to be a one-stop shop, you need to have a variety of products to offer customers.

Enclos learned to be unafraid to take the university into seclusion for a short period of time. Sometimes it is best to work behind the scenes with the university for a little while so that you can fine-tune the university and then bring it back into the limelight.

Building a Business Plan

An important suggestion we offer is to build a business plan. Big company or small, this is the most critical task in developing the corporate university. Without a plan, a corporate university will never meet its final objectives. Once the plan is developed and before moving forward with implementation, have the executive committee of your company accept and approve the plan. You can then move ahead confidently with support from company executives.

Setting Goals

Determine the results your corporate university program needs, and strive to achieve those goals. Conversely, ask for feedback on the programs you offer. Without feedback, you may be going in the wrong direction.

You will have to become an expert at many things. Where a large corporate university may have many trainers, e-course developers, and other staff on their payroll, Enclos found itself with one director and an assistant.

Creating a Corporate University on a Limited Budget

Small companies must be cognizant that they are on a limited budget and may not be able to do everything for everyone. Also, it is important to be aware that there are only so many hours in a day. With limited budgets, there are only a certain number of resources that can be put to the task. Therefore, avoid taking on too many tasks. Choose certain tasks, and focus on completing them. It is easier to promote completed tasks than to tell people about all the tasks you have in the works and never be able to promote completion of them.

Learn to buy, and buy hard. Enclos University couldn't do everything itself and needed to outsource certain things. Analyze your budget and the needs of your company, and then outsource those items that make sense. Enclos created a successful corporate university on a limited budget. Although company resources were more restricted than those of a larger company, Enclos found a plethora of resources internally.

Mentally prepare yourself for the task. This means that you need to realize and accept that you do not work for a company with thousands of employees. Your company has only hundreds.

Treat the corporate university like a business. You are responsible for bringing the product you wish to sell to the market within budget. You will more than likely gravitate toward a blended learning approach. On a limited budget, a company will not be able to afford to have every learning opportunity available electronically. Look at what you want employees to learn, and determine the best method of delivery. In our company, there are courses that we don't foresee developing electronically because the personal interaction required to get the context across to students is critical. You will have the same situation.

In pricing outside resources, look at pricing in context of cost per student. In large corporations, ten thousand dollars may not seem like much. For small companies, this may be a significant amount of the budget. As an example, if you find a resource that costs ten thousand dollars and you have five hundred employees, it is easier to ask for twenty dollars per employee than it is to ask for ten thousand dollars. It is much harder for the decision makers to say no to twenty dollars than it is to a lump sum of ten thousand dollars.

Determining Leadership

Find someone from within to lead your corporate university. In a small company atmosphere, you have limited latitude to increase overhead costs by employing a corporate university professional. You will find it is easier to take talented employees and educate them on the development and management of a corporate university than it is to take corporate university professionals and educate them about the nuances of your business. The employees you choose should have respect and recognition within the company that will allow them to serve the dual roles of administrator and teacher. A corporate university professional is a good choice for large companies with many staff members to manage. He or she does not need to fully understand the business, as his or her staff members can be closer to the pulse of the company happenings. In a small company, you are the staff. You need to know what is going on within the company and be ready to understand and respond to its needs.

Management

Make sure you are well represented at the executive level. Whether that is you or the person you report to, this person needs to be impassioned about the corporate university and ready to defend it and deal with tough questions that are asked.

Research

Watch what corporate universities in large companies do. There will always be a program that they do well. If the program seems to be something that your company would benefit from, come up with a plan on how you can make the approach leaner and have it work for you. Attend conferences that focus on corporate universities or training. These conferences always focus on larger companies and provide many opportunities to experience how a large corporate university works.

Technology

Use technology to your advantage. Search the Internet for sources and training opportunities. Use instant messaging and Web conferencing to do online training. Learning management systems (LMSs) can be found everywhere, and there is a system that will fit your needs. Become friends with your IT department. You will depend on technology to perform a lot of your work, so ensuring that this technology works with your IT system is critical.

Learning Management Systems

LMSs are not just for big companies. There are many companies that have LMSs designed for them. Look closely at them, and begin to understand the options each system offers. You will find an LMS that will fit your needs at a reasonable price. The original price may seem overwhelming in the beginning, but when you consider the amount of work you will need to perform in keeping track of spreadsheets and databases to manage the learning programs of your employees, the LMS will appear as an affordable option. Watch out for all the add-on packages. Do not get caught up in their frills, which may not give you the value you need.

Networking

Network within and outside your company. You will need support from department managers to help you make your corporate university a success. This support can be through the selling of the corporate university to their direct reports, providing subject matter experts, providing information for knowledge management, or providing resources for projects within the university. You will have a limited staff to discuss different ideas, so you may need to create your own "board of directors" to talk to about your situation. Professionals in this environment are willing to share their knowledge of corporate universities, and you should take full advantage of this opportunity.

When the position of corporate university director was created, Enclos didn't realize that sales was part of the job description. It is important to remember to keep your salesman's shoes polished, as selling the concept of the university internally is a critical part of the job. Prepare for the good days, the bad days, and the ugly days. They all will occur. Proper preparation will help get the university through the worst days.

Work with your company's marketing or sales staff to develop a marketing and sales approach for the corporate university to be disseminated to employees. These people are talented internal resources you can use to promote the corporate university. Make them believers in the university. You can't ask for a better group to promote the corporate university than your marketing and sales group.

Maximize the use of experts within your company, and use your internal resources whenever possible, for the people in your company are the experts in your business. They are your subject matter experts.

Using Your Company's Existing Business Relationships

Perhaps your company is small, but several companies with which you do business may have vast resources. These companies may have corporate universities. Investigate what these companies' corporate universities contain and how they operate. These companies, whether vendors or customers, may have some courses they would be willing to share with you. Most would welcome the opportunity to share training programs so they can reinforce their name in front of your students. In the same light, look at your company's client base. Do any of them have training programs of interest to you? One of the best ways to show a client that you like working with them and want to continue to do so is to say you like how they operate as a business and would like to model certain facets of your company after them.

Starting Your Own Corporate University

There is no cookie-cutter approach to creating and implementing the perfect corporate university. Not every company is meant to have one. In order for a corporate university to be successful in a small company, the company must determine its needs, its strategies, and what it is trying to accomplish with a university. Only then can it establish a corporate university that will reap benefits and become an excellent model for other businesses to replicate and modify.

Lee E. Steffens, director of Enclos University, has worked in the curtainwall industry and at Enclos Corp. for over twenty years, helping design, engineer, fabricate, and erect the exterior walls on some of the world's most prominent buildings. He has served as a project manager for Enclos on a number of projects, including the Petronas Towers in Malaysia and the Getty Center in Los Angeles. Most recently, Steffens led a project team responsible for the curtainwall on the 731 Lexington project—a fifty-five-story tower in midtown Manhattan.

As Steffens took Enclos University from concept to reality, he drew on his years of experience in project management and also on his passion for teaching, mentoring, and sharing best practices.

Steffens received his B.S. in construction management from Bradley University.

Shannon M. Novotne is a communications specialist at Enclos Corp. Her responsibilities include writing and editing *The Visible Difference* employee newsletter, advertising, internal communications, marketing, writing and designing promotional materials, public relations, video editing, photography, and Web site maintenance.

Novotne has worked in both nonprofit and for-profit industries. Her freelance writing has been featured in *Camelback Magazine* and the *SuperComm 2002 Daily News*. She received her B.A. in communication from Bethel University and her M.A. in mass communication and public relations from Arizona State University's Walter Cronkite School of Journalism and Mass Communication. Novotne is a member of the Association for Women in Communications and contributes newsletter articles to her chapter on topics such as crisis communication and public relations.

I got to know Deborah Grayson Riegel when I had the opportunity to consult for the corporate university at United Jewish Communities several years ago. Deborah worked for the corporate university and was passionate about the teaching and learning process. She now brings that passion to her work as an independent consultant, but I knew she would be perfect to discuss corporate universities in nonprofit organizations and that United Jewish Communities would be an ideal case study. Corporate universities do not have to be in corporations, and many nonprofits have successfully integrated corporate universities. In this chapter, Deborah explores the challenges and opportunities that nonprofits face when implementing a corporate university.

10

Corporate Universities in the Nonprofit Sector

Deborah Grayson Riegel

IN THE EARLY 1970s, prize-winning author and radio broadcast personality Studs Terkel told us how people felt about their jobs. In his book *Working: People Talk about What They Do All Day and How They Feel about What They Do* (1974), based on a collection of taped interviews with workers in a wide variety of jobs, Terkel captured their feelings about the daily grind. "Work," he said, "is about daily meaning as well as daily bread. For recognition as well as cash; for astonishment rather than torpor; in short, for a sort of life rather than a Monday through Friday sort of dying. . . . We have a right to ask of work that it include meaning, recognition, astonishment, and life" (p. xi).

For employees in the nonprofit sector, the quest for meaningful work seems to be a key factor for overall job satisfaction. Research indicates that public sector employees are more likely than private sector workers to strongly value the intrinsic reward of work, which they perceive to be important and provides a strong sense of accomplishment (Houston, 2000).

According to Independent Sector's 2001 publication "Employment in the Nonprofit Sector," a growing segment of America's workforce labors in the nonprofit sector. The average annual growth rate in employment for nonprofits (2.5 percent) was significantly higher than for business (1.8 percent) or government (1.6 percent), and the number of Americans working in the nonprofit sector has doubled in the past twenty-five years. Nonprofit employment represents 9.5 percent of total employment in the United States, with employees numbering 12.5 million.

With the nonprofit workforce expanding, the nonprofit workplace needs to keep pace in providing educational and professional development opportunities that reflect and reinforce the critical role that the organization's employees play in improving the human and social environment while giving them the knowledge, skills, and abilities necessary to achieve business goals.

Defining the Nonprofit Sector

According to the International Classification of Nonprofit Organizations (ICNPO), there are five basic features nonprofit organizations share:

1. "Organized, i.e., institutionalized to some extent," including a legal charter of incorporation or "some degree of internal organizational structure; relative persistence of goals, structure and activities; and meaningful organizational boundaries, i.e., some recognized difference between members and nonmembers." Excluded from this group are "purely ad hoc and temporary gatherings of people with no real structure or organizational identity" (Salamon & Anheier, 1996, pp. 2–3).

2. "Private, i.e., institutionally separate from government—'nongovernmental' in the sense of being structurally separate from the instrumentalities of government. This does not mean that they may not receive significant government support or even that government officials cannot sit on their boards" (pp. 2–3).

3. "Self-governing, i.e., equipped to control their own activities. . . . Organizations must be in a position to control their own activities to a sig-

nificant extent . . . [with] their own internal governance procedures and . . . a meaningful degree of autonomy" (pp. 2–3).

4. "Nonprofit-distributing, i.e., not returning profits generated to their owners or directors. . . . Profits must be plowed back into the basic mission of the agency, not distributed to the organizations' owners, members, founders or governing board" (pp. 2–3).

5. "Voluntary, i.e., involving some meaningful degree of voluntary participation. . . . First, the organization must engage volunteers in its operations and management, either on its board or through the use of volunteer staff and voluntary contributions. Second, 'voluntary' also carries the meaning of 'non-compulsory.' Organizations in which membership is required or otherwise stipulated by law would be excluded from the nonprofit sector. Similarly, 'voluntary' implies that contributions of time (volunteering) and money (donations) as well as contributions in kind may not be required or enforced by law, or otherwise be openly coerced" (pp. 2–3).

The ICNPO classifies twelve major groups (as well as subgroups, which will not be listed here) of nonprofit organizations: culture and recreation; education and research; health; social services; environment; development and housing; law, advocacy, and politics; philanthropic intermediaries and voluntarism promotion; international; religion; business/professional associations and unions; and those not elsewhere classified.

The depth and breadth of the sector's focus means that just as in the for-profit sector, each nonprofit corporate university will need to concentrate its activities on the particular learning needs of its employees to meet constituent-specific business goals.

A Tale of Two Workforces

As government-supported human service programs decline in number, the clients who must turn to private nonprofit human service programs increase in number. This trend, known as devolution, creates several areas of tension that have an impact on the training and education of nonprofit employees.

First, as more nonprofit organizations emerge in response to growing or changing social needs, the fundraising environment becomes increasingly competitive. Staff need to take on new or augmented fundraising responsibilities and yield increased results. Second, in response to this changing philanthropic milieu, these organizations will need to demonstrate organizational success in meeting goals and deliverables to validate donors' interests and investments. Staff may need to engage in more formal or rigorous needs assessments, strategic planning, program implementation, and evaluation, all of which require skills training and education. Third, as the demands for dollars and donors increase, so do the demands for volunteers to help carry out the work of the organization. In fact, the voluntary nature of nonprofits creates a number of unique training and educational needs. While volunteer workers can, to a varying extent, decrease some of the task burden that nonprofit employees shoulder, professionals take on the added challenge of learning to manage both a paid and a volunteer workforce.

Why is this so significant? While Diana Aviv, president and CEO of Independent Sector, admits, "It is a challenge to place a dollar value on the important work volunteers do for millions of charitable organizations and communities across the country," her organization has attempted to do just that. According to a March 2006 press release, "The estimated value of a volunteer hour in 2005 is $18.04," which is up from 2004's estimate of $17.55. Aviv confirms: "This number can help put into perspective the enormous contributions provided by our nation's volunteers."

In fact, the U.S. Bureau of Labor Statistics reported in December 2005 that about 65.4 million people volunteered through or for an organization at least once between September 2004 and September 2005. In sum, almost 30 percent of Americans volunteer.

With these statistics in view, it seems increasingly important that nonprofit professionals know how to recruit and engage volunteer workers, manage the volunteer–professional partnership, prevent the seemingly inevitable burnout of overworked volunteers, evaluate and upgrade the skill levels of volunteer workers, and ultimately help the overall organization meet its business goals to attract, keep, and reward volunteer talent.

"Noncorporate" Universities

The concept of a corporate university as an entity that undertakes a wide range of activities that an organization uses to develop its professionals in service of its mission (from gap assessments and design and delivery of training programs to creating university partnerships and succession planning) is seemingly not widely used by organization development, human resource, or training professionals. Several explanations for this come to mind. First, the very term *corporate* seems to imply commercial business objectives, which by definition defies the very nature of a nonprofit institution. Therefore, "corporate university" would not be the term of choice for a nonprofit organization looking to encapsulate its professional development activities. And because the term is neither used nor well recognized, and there is no universally used label in its place in the nonprofit sector, research into existing models is quite challenging.

Second, most nonprofits are challenged by how to quantifiably measure organizational success (especially with limited resources) and would therefore struggle to demonstrate how professional development activities and initiatives contribute to organizational success. According to a 2004 survey conducted by the nonprofit organization TechFoundation, "Many nonprofit managers find it hard to convince their staff and boards of the importance of organizational performance measurement, and establishing a place for it within the organization presents a particularly significant challenge." Of course, an effective corporate university could facilitate this measurement process.

A third possibility addresses the many hats that nonprofit professionals often play, especially in smaller nonprofit organizations. Because resources are limited (a recurring theme in nonprofits and therefore in this chapter), many organizations may not have a department, or even the equivalent of one full-time employee, solely devoted to the activities in which a corporate university might engage. (The "many hats" theory plays into my own rationalization of why very few nonprofit human resource and training professionals returned my calls in my research for this chapter.) Of course, the lack of a dedicated staff person or department in this area is often indicative of a vicious cycle in the nonprofit sector discussed above: if institutions cannot quantify or even demonstrate the value of professional development in helping to meet business goals, especially because nonprofit business goals themselves are so challenging to measure, then it is increasingly difficult to justify the allocation of already limited resources for corporate university staff and activities.

There is an additional consideration in the already complicated nonprofit fiscal environment: the vital role that volunteers play in the nonprofit workforce as hands-on workers, donors, and organizational decision makers (none of which are mutually exclusive). According to the National Center for Charitable Statistics (2004), "For better or worse, the percentage of total expenses going to program costs is the most common measure of nonprofit organizational efficiency" and in fact, research indicates that "donors expect worthy organizations to have low fundraising and administrative costs." Furthermore, few donors or funders will specifically support staff training and development because it is viewed as an administrative expense.

In order for money to be allocated to training, nonprofit organizations need to demonstrate how it serves as a strategic lever toward helping the organization achieve its mission. Donors give money to support organizations that have a positive impact on the issues important to them, not to support the needs of floundering organizations. Boards of directors must understand the connection between internal education and training for paid staff, as well as for themselves as members of the volunteer workforce, and the development or maintenance of a well-run organization.

In addition, nonprofits may need to educate board members, especially those with strong business roots in the for-profit arena, to seek the value of investment for training dollars rather than a return on investment. Professional and volunteer leadership should seek mutual understanding (thought not necessarily consensus) about the importance of investing the organization's resources internally on professional education and training, as well as how to assess, rather than quantify, impact on outcomes. As key decision makers in organizational strategic planning, resource development, and funding allocations, volunteers should be collaborators in the corporate university's planning and activities.

"Nonprofit Darwinism"

According to the National Center for Charitable Statistics (2004), the number of nonprofit organizations in the United States grew dramatically between 1996 and 2004, with an increase of 28.8 percent (from 1.1 million nonprofit organizations in 1996 to 1.4 million in 2004).

As in the for-profit sector, nonprofits are subject to the laws of supply and demand. Gary Bass, executive director of OMB Watch in Washington, D.C., comments that "those that are serving a real need float and those that don't, sink" in a demonstration of "nonprofit Darwinism" (Cohen, 2005).

United Jewish Communities Story

In 1999, in anticipation of—or perhaps in response to—this evolutionary trend, three major Jewish institutions merged (the United Jewish Appeal, United Israel Appeal, and the Council of Jewish Federations) to form United Jewish Communities (UJC). This represented one of the largest mergers in the American nonprofit sector and resulted in the most significant consolidation of Jewish communal resources ever. UJC currently represents and serves the Jewish Federation movement: 155 local Jewish Federations and 360 smaller independent Jewish communities across North America.

These local federations and communities serve as the primary instruments for planning, coordinating, and fundraising for their partner and beneficiary agencies through the UJA Federation Campaign. Through the monies raised by the campaign, UJC provides life-saving and life-enhancing humanitarian assistance to millions of Jews in hundreds of communities in North America, throughout Israel, in the former Soviet Union, and in sixty other countries around the world. The funds are allocated to support local, national, and international services and institutions in the areas of human welfare, health care, rescue and resettlement, Jewish education and identity, culture, and community.

The October 27, 2005, issue of the *Chronicle of Philanthropy* featured its annual focus on the "Philanthropy 400," a listing of the "nation's biggest charities"; UJC was listed at number forty-two, maintaining its ranking as the top Jewish charity, based on the amount raised from private sources, including individuals, foundations, and corporations (Hall, Kerkman, and Moore, 2005). Reports indicate that had UJC provided complete fundraising data on all Jewish federations, it would have ranked second on the list, behind only the United Way of America, since it estimated that the system raised $2 billion in 2004. Instead, it is listed as having raised just under $252 million, which does not include money raised by federations. In addition to UJC, a dozen Jewish federations raised enough money to get on the list on their own, including the UJA-Federation of New York and the Jewish Federation/Jewish United Fund of Metropolitan Chicago.

To support the work of the federations, UJC provides local communities with consultation, programs, tools, materials, and other resources to support fundraising, strategic planning, technology, community building, professional and volunteer leadership development, and a global partnership with Jews around the world.

According to its training materials, *An Introduction to Jewish Caring,* UJC focuses on three clear action areas:

- Serving as the vehicle and spokesperson to enable timely and strategic action on domestic and global issues of concern to the Jewish people;

- Generating new and innovative ideas that help local federations and the system as a whole secure the future of the Jewish people; and

- Providing resources and support services that will strengthen Jewish federations and the Jewish people [2006].

UJC currently employs approximately 230 staff located in New York City (its headquarters), Washington, D.C., Atlanta, Israel, Los Angeles, and several remote locations.

Evolution of UJC University

In the spring of 2002, UJC established a new department, Professional and Volunteer Development (PVD, which was soon renamed the Mandel Center for Leadership Excellence), to provide consultation and tools to the federations on issues of human resource development for both staff and volunteers.

Even before the merger that resulted in UJC, the national system had offered federation professionals learning opportunities through its continuing professional education program. These programs were aimed at knowledge acquisition and skill building for both new and seasoned professionals in areas related to fundraising, planning, marketing, and others. Nevertheless, there had not been a formalized, substantive ongoing program of education and training for the internal staff at UJC—those who provide service to the federations.

In 2002, at the initiative of UJC's new CEO/president who had successfully spearheaded an in-service training program for the staff at the Jewish Community Federation of Cleveland (where he had served as its executive director), professional staff from the Mandel Center for Leadership Excellence began developing its own staff training program. Internally referred to as "in-service training," this program was to be used as an educational mechanism, an interdepartmental collaboration tool, and an interpersonal development vehicle. In addition, a tacit objective was to help a somewhat fractured organization unite in a postmerger environment.

Building Support and Assessing Needs

The first step in the process included identifying and convening a committee of UJC staff members to build consensus on training needs, collaborate on curriculum development, and explore training delivery methods (such as instructor-led training, distance learning, etc.). The committee consisted of representatives from each department, with a careful balance of gender, religion, age, number and years in the organization (counting from premerger), and professional level (administrative, professional and senior management).

The committee developed a mission statement for the training program: "The UJC in-service training program is committed to supporting the personal growth of each and every employee, as well as helping the organization achieve its business goals. Our goal is to help the UJC staff access the training they need in order to grow in their positions." Among the program goals that the committee identified were the following:

- Provide opportunities for employees to learn, including on-site courses, off-site courses, online courses, distance learning, and field trips.

- Develop time-sensitive training courses that are aligned with current events so staff will be properly informed.

- Provide an orientation program for new professionals that will focus on curriculum related directly to the inner workings of UJC and the federation system.

- Recruit the highest-quality faculty of scholars, teachers, trainers, and Jewish communal professionals to educate UJC staff.

- Increase the overall satisfaction of UJC staff members in the workplace.

Two committee-developed needs assessments were distributed to the staff: one designated for most professional and administrative staff and the other for department heads. Both surveys asked staff to reflect on a substantial list of topics, including business skills (for example, computer training, program planning, meeting management), management skills (for example, budgeting and finance, strategic planning, supervision), personal development (for example, stress management, work/life balance, effective communication), Jewish/religious/spiritual development (bible, comparative religions, Hebrew reading), and UJC and the federation system (for example, fundraising skills, understanding the federation system, the worldwide Jewish community).

Respondents were asked to reflect on the potential offerings and indicate which of these courses would be beneficial to them and which they thought could benefit their colleagues. In addition, they were surveyed as to how often they would like to participate in training, what times of day might work best (including after work), their interest in distance learning, and whether they felt they could serve as an instructor for a course. The department heads were also asked to indicate which topics would be of most benefit to their department.

The needs assessment, important to curriculum development, also initiated the buy-in process for all staff levels and generated early brand awareness. Furthermore, the use of this methodology was noteworthy to the significant number of UJC staff who held master's degrees in social work and had undoubtedly been taught that a needs assessment is the first step in effective program planning.

The committee tallied responses, and a committee subgroup met to analyze results. The registrar tallied up all of the responses from both surveys. The offerings for Phase One consisted of the four or five top-requested courses in each of four categories:

- *Management skills:* Supervision Level I (for supervisors with fewer than three years of experience or no formal training); Supervision Level II (for supervisors with more than three years' experience); Strategic Planning; and Budgeting and Finance

- *Professional skills:* Business Writing; Public Speaking; Customer Service; and Computer Skills (Outlook, Excel, and File Management, offered in partnership with New Horizons, the largest independent information technology training company worldwide)

- *UJC and the Worldwide Jewish Community:* Understanding the Federation System; UJC 101 Internal Workings; Jewish Philanthropy; What Every Professional Needs to Know About the Arab–Israeli Conflict; and Rebuilding Community

- *Jewish learning:* Ethics of the Fathers; Hebrew Reading; World of Jewish Music; and Jewish Values and Morals

In addition to these offerings, several additional online courses offered by the Jewish Theological Seminary were made available to UJC employees, ranging from Talmud to Finding Spirituality in Prayer.

A curriculum development subcommittee convened to create course objectives and some key learning points to share with potential faculty, with the recommendation that instructors develop the primary curriculum for each course. Once faculty were identified and secured, the committee would partner with them on making sure that the course content would be customized for UJC and that the learning objectives would be met. Each member of the curriculum committee was assigned three or four courses for which they would secure instructors, create the session's description for the course catalogue, and set the dates for each course.

Faculty were recruited from UJC's senior-level staff, as well as local trainers, rabbis, and teachers. Computer training was outsourced to New Horizons, offering courses in a variety of locations. Several weeks later, committee members reconvened to review faculty, scheduling, and materials, and the program rollout got under way.

Challenge 1: Requirements Meet with Resistance

Anticipating opposition from overworked staff and from department heads who did not yet buy in to the value of workplace learning (especially in comparison to attention to workload), the in-service training program was launched with an e-mail articulating that participation would be mandatory for all staff (with the exception of those in the Israel office and those in remote one-person locations). Professional staff were required to take one course in either Management Skills, Professional Skills, or UJC and the Worldwide Jewish Community, and one course in the Jewish Learning category. Administrative staff were exempt from the Jewish Learning requirement (considering that a large proportion were not Jewish, unlike professional staff) but were required to take two courses as well. The human resource department took on the challenging role of monitoring requirements, registration, and class attendance so that the professional and volunteer development department could focus on course development, delivery, and program evaluation.

Although program participation was good, the compliance model was immediately fraught with challenges. Inevitably some employees had conflicts with course dates; new employees with supervisory responsibilities, who were required to take both Supervision Level I and UJC 101 Internal Workings, couldn't then fulfill their Jewish Learning requirement. Those who participated in the Jewish Theological Seminary's distance learning courses reported that they were using many more course hours than their colleagues who were involved in classroom learning. Staff became concerned about what would happen if they didn't or couldn't attend their required courses. Would their absence have a negative impact on their performance reviews? Would attendance be rewarded? What if a department head excused them from attending? What if senior management didn't fulfill their own requirements? What would the ramifications be for administrative union staff, who at that time did not receive performance reviews or merit-based raises? It became clear that employees at all levels were more concerned about the mechanics and consequences of compliance than the significance of gaining the requisite knowledge, skills, and abilities to help the organization meet its goals.

One particular conflict arose when, in response to a comprehensive client research project, an organization-wide customer service training initiative was prescribed for all staff. Clearly, customer service training would meet one of the organization's primary business goals in delivering superior service to the federation system. Offering customer service training through the in-service training program would have been both efficacious and appropriate, since it was so clearly connected to a critical business goal. However, adding further requirements within the existing compliance structure was problematic. Therefore, while PVD staff spearheaded the design and development of organization-wide customer service training, it was delivered outside the formal structure of the in-service training program so that employees would participate as well as meet their other training requirements.

Challenge 2: Technological Learning Curve

In partnership with the IT department, PVD was able to offer an online course listing and registration. Both effective and well received, the in-service training intranet site gave each employee a customized page, reflecting his or her individual training requirements where appropriate (such as supervision courses). Staff could read the course book either online or in paper format and then use the online registration process. Course confirmations were sent by e-mail one week before the start of each course, reminding employees about the dates, times, and locations for each session.

As with any other new endeavor, there were unanticipated technical difficulties. Employees could register themselves only from their own computer, but some staff members, such as those who worked in the mailroom, didn't have their own computers. This meant that the IT staff had to manually input their registrations. Many members of senior management asked their administrative staff to register them for courses, but this was possible only if the support staff logged into their supervisor's computer and registered them there, which created potential security issues. Furthermore, the online registration function didn't automatically indicate a conflict if someone registered for two courses that met at the same time, thereby allowing the registration to proceed. In addition, employees were not able to change their course selections past the initial registration deadline.

Over time, major glitches to the technological processes were worked out, and a more consistently user-friendly registration process became the new standard.

Challenge 3: Distance Learning Creates Interpersonal Distance

When the in-service training program began, field staff were working in UJC offices located in Atlanta, Los Angeles, Washington, D.C., and Israel, as well as in home offices and remote locations. With the exception of Washington, D.C., and Israel, each office employed both administrative and professional staff from among various departments. This meant, for the most part, that learning needs were as diverse within each office as they were in the New York office, but with limited access to learning opportunities.

In a well-meaning effort to accommodate the instructional and interpersonal needs of field staff, several courses were available by videoconference from New York. Field staff were invited and encouraged to coordinate their business-related travel to New York with in-service training courses. However, most courses were offered over four sessions, making regular in-person attendance unlikely. And since field staff were not exempt from the program's requirements (lest they feel like part of a marginalized population), frustrations surfaced. Although the effort to include field staff in the organization's learning initiative was not intended to be a symbolic one, the challenges that arose became symbolic of core issues in managing and engaging remote employees.

Some quick repair was needed to mend fences, both interpersonally and to help field staff meet learning needs. While staff in Atlanta and Los Angeles were divided across discipline, they were encouraged to work together within their office location to make recommendations about officewide professional training needs. PVD would then partner with them to locate local resources to deliver training and provide funding, within reason. A survey of the training needs for the Washington, D.C., office was developed, and on-site and local training was offered in response to those needs. Because the quality and reliability of the videoconferenced courses were inconsistent, most of the budget allotted to this was reallocated to provide local learning opportunities. Delivery solutions for field staff and the Israel Office clearly required additional thought.

Reenvisioning UJC University

Beginning with Phase I of the In-Service Training Program offered in fall 2002 and through the next several semesters (during which the program was renamed "UJC University"), course offerings varied minimally. Overall, employees evaluated courses favorably, and many indicated that the classes helped them to do their job better in the context of their department's role in advancing UJC's business goals.

Supervision courses, offered at various experience levels, were an example of how UJC University helped employees meet organizational objectives. UJC's "Agenda for the Future" declared that "upgrading the quality of personnel throughout the system" is a step toward strengthening the federations. Good staff supervision drives employee performance and yields high retention rates.

UJC University's supervision courses helped existing personnel improve the quality of their supervision, which should enhance their ability to address the professional development and retention of those whom they supervise.

Nevertheless, some classes did not directly relate to employee performance or UJC's business goals. In many instances, classes were geared to personal growth and work-life enhancement to help facilitate staff compliance. In other courses, there was no concerted effort to link classroom learning to the employee's work at UJC, within the federation system, or to the Jewish world. In each semester, several employees noted in their class evaluations that they took a particular class because it was a requirement and no other class fit into their schedule.

It became increasingly clear that UJC University was not strategically using its well-articulated goals as the driving factor in making curriculum choices.

In spring 2004, PVD staff engaged in a reassessment and reenvisioning of UJC University with the help of a consultant, Mark Allen, the editor of *The Corporate University Handbook* (2002) and of this book. The goal was to help UJC University make the transition toward a true corporate university model. Its new program mission statement that resulted from that meeting states, "UJC University enhances the knowledge, skills, and abilities of our staff to do their jobs more effectively, create community, and gain professional satisfaction. We provide Jewish learning to contextualize our work, which is rooted in Jewish heritage and Jewish life. This will assist UJC in attracting, developing, and retaining staff who can better serve the federation system and the worldwide Jewish community."

This new mission statement crystallized a much clearer understanding of the purpose of a corporate university. The previous mission statement regarded "helping the organization achieve its business goals" as secondary to facilitating employees' personal growth and highlighted helping "the UJC staff access the training they need in order to grow in their positions" rather than providing them with the professional development tools they need in order to help the organization fulfill its mission better.

To that end, the reenvisioning process established the following initiatives to expand the organizational learning capacity of United Jewish Communities by ensuring that UJC University's offerings and delivery methods would be in sync with UJC's strategic business goals, objectives, and vision for the future:

- Promote learning as an organizational necessity.
- Tap into employees' commitment and capacity to learn.
- Make learning a vital and valued tactic toward improving work quality.
- Link learning to strategic business goals and objectives for each department.
- Measure and evaluate progress of learning.

Improvements in Process: UJC University Today

As a result of the meeting, staff from the PVD department began a series of departmental conversations to gather critical information about the knowledge, skills, and abilities employees needed to help each division drive the organization's mission and begin to reeducate department heads about UJC University's evolving role in facilitating that process. The human resource department and key members of the senior management team participated in the process to help develop a more holistic and strategic picture of the organization's needs.

One important step in changing the way that UJC University operated was the elimination of course requirements for all employees. Beginning in the spring of 2006, employees were informed that they should partner with their supervisors in choosing the classes that best supported their performance goals and that, in fact, their managers would create personalized requirements for each employee. These requirements would be tailored to performance needs, not to any other organizational compliance standard. One e-mail clarified the new standard: "In short, the requirement is for managers and employees to maximize UJC U[niversity] '06 as a resource for professional growth."

As a result of this new "nonmandate" mandate, employees and managers began having much-needed conversations about performance expectations and learning needs outside the formal evaluation process. This marked a key shift in the rhythm of UJC's performance reviews, which were an annual event rather than an ongoing process. Like so many other organizations, many of UJC's performance reviews were focused primarily on tasks, had superficial employee involvement, and were often viewed by staff as punitive. Despite the fact that UJC had offered training for supervisors on how to conduct performance evaluations that specifically reinforced the value of ongoing performance management conversations, overworked supervisors often put these important tasks aside to deal with more pressing matters. The performance management process provides an opportunity for the employee and supervisor to discuss development goals and jointly create a development plan that contributes to organizational goals and the professional growth of the employee. As UJC moves toward a performance management model, UJC University serves as both its initiator and facilitator.

Current offerings reflect cross-departmental educational and performance needs and, where possible, geographical needs. While administrative staff are invited and encouraged to participate in UJC University courses, they will be offered their own personal and professional development courses aimed at addressing their specific learning needs.

In the course catalogue, each class description specifies its target audience, and many listings offer recommendations for how departments and work teams can maximize the class's impact by participating together. In addition, courses are now conducted in classroom settings, online, through one-on-one coaching, field trips, and other ways to appeal to a variety of learning styles and needs:

Business Skills

- Developing Client Relationships: A Consultative Approach, offered in New York City for all executive/professional staff

- Franklin Covey FOCUS: Achieving Your Highest Priorities, offered in New York City and in Franklin Covey classrooms in Los Angeles, Washington, D.C., and Atlanta for all staff

- Nonprofit Project Management Fundamentals, offered in New York City for all staff, with work groups encouraged to attend together

- The Oz Principle Advanced Management Workshop, offered in New York City; open to senior and managing directors, associate vice presidents, and all members of the senior management team; work groups are encouraged to attend together to encourage collaboration in planning and consistency in implementation

Communication Skills

- Advanced Business Writing: Improving Style and Clarity, offered in New York City, Los Angeles, Washington, D.C., and Atlanta for all executive and professional staff

- Executive Business Writing: Getting Results, offered in New York City, Los Angeles, Washington, D.C., and Atlanta for executive and professional staff

- Executive Communication Coaching, offered in New York City and Washington, D.C., for executive and professional staff

- Informal Speaking Workshop: Making Your Point, offered in New York City for all staff

Computer Skills and Applications

- Navigating UJC's MS Office Online Library, offered for all locations for all staff

- UJC's MS Office Online Library, delivered online and self-directed for all staff

- Microsoft Software Applications Skill Building, offered in New Horizons Learning Centers located in New York City, Washington, D.C., Atlanta, and Los Angeles for all staff

Jewish Learning

- Jewish Models of Leadership, offered in New York City with videoconferencing for all staff

- Talmud and Tzedakah, offered in New York City for all staff

- Tikkun Olam: Fixing the World, Fixing Ourselves, offered in Atlanta and Washington, D.C., for all staff

- UJC and the Global Jewish Community: A Day in the Life of a Federation, offered in any location for new executive and professional staff with no prior federation work experience

- An Introduction to the Jewish Federation Movement, offered online, with self-directed learning for new staff

- Engaging the Next Generation of Jews, offered in New York City with videoconferencing for all staff

- Israeli Politics Today, offered in New York City with videoconferencing for all staff

Next Steps

UJC University has evolved over four years from a compliance-driven training program toward a truer corporate university by identifying, facilitating, developing, and delivering educational activities that help UJC achieve its mission.

As it continues to develop, UJC University should take a more active and strategic role in developing a fuller range of activities that support the mission of the organization, including these areas:

- Improving the existing orientation and on-boarding process

- Providing training that supports UJC's staff–volunteer partnerships

- Developing core competencies for UJC staff

- Facilitating informal educational opportunities that focus on key experiences, such as specific work settings, assignments, or accomplishments required for professional growth and development

- Anticipating both immediate professional development needs (related to current responsibilities) and long-term needs (related to future responsibilities)

- Developing gap assessments

- Providing coaching, mentoring, and shadowing opportunities

- Formalizing a performance management process in collaboration with human resources

- Partnering with schools of Jewish communal service and nonprofit management to develop additional educational modules

- Partnering with managers in developing career paths and succession planning for direct reports

- Helping employees plan and sequence appropriate career development activities and take personal responsibility for their own development and advancement

The Quest for Meaningful Work Revisited

In his research paper, "Relational Job Design and the Motivation to Make a Pro-Social Difference" (in press, 2007), University of Michigan doctoral candidate Adam Grant writes that "impactful jobs can be characterized in terms of how often they provide opportunities to make a difference, how enduring the difference is in beneficiaries' lives, how many beneficiaries are affected, and whether the job prevents harm or promotes gains in different aspects of beneficiaries' lives."

Volunteer workers in nonprofit organizations often have opportunities to engage with program and service beneficiaries and may even count themselves among them. Federation volunteers have many avenues for increased involvement and commitment through hands-on volunteer work, site visits to local federation-supported agencies, or even missions to Israel, the former Soviet Union, or other worldwide Jewish communities. In fact, UJC and the federation system intentionally provide these opportunities to connect donors and volunteers with beneficiaries to inspire them to give even more generously of their time and money.

While select UJC staff members are invited to participate in missions, most UJC employees rarely connect with beneficiaries. UJC University and other corporate universities (both for-profit and nonprofit) should regularly provide opportunities for staff at all levels to see the impact of their jobs on beneficiaries as a critical learning, professional development, and retention mechanism.

Traditionally, beneficiaries of nonprofits tend to be the recipients of the programs and services funded, developed, or provided by the organization. As part of its annual staff campaign aimed at soliciting donations from staff in support of the UJA Federation Annual Campaign, UJC takes employees on a selection of federation-sponsored site visits to meet people whose lives have been touched by the monies raised. Staff members have the opportunity to meet senior citizens who get social programming and meals funded by the UJA Federation Annual Campaign, children who participate in summer camp funded by the UJA Federation Annual Campaign, or Russian immigrants who get Russian- or English-language counseling, job training, and housing support services funded by the UJA Federation Annual Campaign. For many UJC staff, this is their only opportunity to engage with people whose lives are enriched by the work that UJC and the federation system do. It is a powerful and rare opportunity for employees to come together across department, religion, race, and socioeconomic status to share in celebrating the impact of their work. Notably, the 2005 staff campaign garnered 92 percent participation, an impressive statistic considering that most of the administrative staff members are not Jewish.

Additional research by Grant (in press, 2007) highlights an experiment in which callers in a fundraising organization spent a few minutes reading about a beneficiary of their work, followed by a respectful interaction with that beneficiary. The results were dramatic: callers' "persistence and performance increased significantly as a function of the intervention." It is evident that contact with beneficiaries can positively and significantly strengthen employee motivation.

Among its other activities, the corporate university should facilitate ongoing connections between beneficiaries and employees. Although site visits can have a strong impact, they are not practical or economical for frequent use for UJC. Local beneficiaries can be invited to UJC offices for a few hours to meet with staff and talk about the impact of employees' work. Staff members might be given the names and telephone numbers of beneficiaries to contact during work hours—perhaps an elderly person who receives federation-funded Meals-on-Wheels who might also be in need of a friendly telephone call. For each organization, there may be multiple ways to engage with beneficiaries, but there are not many substitutes for the impact it can have on job passion and productivity.

Every job, regardless of sector, has its beneficiaries, and beneficiaries can be both external and internal. The construction worker counts new building tenants as beneficiaries, while the human resource professional counts internal staff as beneficiaries. UJC professionals can count the federation professionals to whom they deliver information, resources, and services among their beneficiaries. Corporate universities can play an important role in facilitating staff–beneficiary connections as an educational tool to increase motivation, productivity, and satisfaction in support of the organization's mission.

References

Allen, M. (ed.). *The Corporate University Handbook.* New York: AMA-COM, 2002.

Cohen, T. "Each 501(c)(3) Is Now." *Non Profit Times,* May 1, 2005, p. 3.

Grant, A. M. "Relational Job Design and the Motivation to Make a Pro-Social Difference." *Academy of Management Review, 32*(2), in press, 2007.

Hall, H., Kerkman, L., and Moore, C. "Giving Bounces Back: Donations to the Biggest Charities Increased by 11.6 Percent Last Year." *Chronicle of Philanthropy,* Oct. 27, 2005. http://philanthropy.com/free/articles/v18/102/0200081.htm

Houston, D. "Public Service Motivation: A Multivariate Test." *Journal of Public Administration Research and Theory,* 2000, *10*(4), 713–728.

Independent Sector. "Employment in the Nonprofit Sector." *Nonprofit Almanac Facts and Findings.* 2001. http://www.independentsector.org/PDFs/npemployment.pdf.

Independent Sector. "Independent Sector Announces New Calculation for the Value of Volunteer Time." March 2006. http://www.independentsector.org/media/20060306_volunteer_time.html.

National Center for Charitable Statistics. "Number of Nonprofit Organizations in the United States, 1996–2004." 2004. http://nccsdataweb.urban.org/PubApps/profile1.php?state=US.

Salamon, L., and Anheier, H. "The International Classification of Non-profit Organizations: ICNPO-Revision 1, 1996." Baltimore: Johns Hopkins Institute for Policy Studies, 1996.

TechFoundation. "TechFoundation and Blackbaud Look Inside Nonprofits to Reveal Key Elements of Success or Failure." Sept. 7, 2004. http://www.techfoundation.org/index.cfm?objectID=7ED90669-B60E-4420–8785DEC8F087C984&navid=7CB1E711-F249–56B2–856B2EF69DB4E21A].

Terkel, S. *Working: People Talk about What They Do All Day and How They Feel about What They Do.* New York: Pantheon Books, 1974.

United Jewish Communities. *An Introduction to Jewish Caring.* New York: United Jewish Communities, 2006.

U.S. Department of Labor, Bureau of Labor Statistics. "Volunteering in the United States, 2005." Economic News release, 2005.

Deborah Grayson Riegel, M.S.W., is the president of Elevated Training, a consulting company dedicated to helping clients identify and implement core behavior changes that lead to individual, interpersonal, and organizational success through interactive workshops, executive coaching, and curriculum and instructional design services. Clients span the nonprofit and for-profit sectors, including trade associations, health care, philanthropic organizations, advertising, publishing, and legal services. Prior to starting Elevated Training, Riegel served as the director of education and training for United Jewish Communities (UJC), where she spear-headed the development of a range of innovative and engaging training solutions for professionals and volunteer leadership. Her role as a copy-writer on UJC's interactive solicitation training e-learning Web site contributed to UJC's four consecutive Web Marketing Association WebAwards. Riegel is also a prolific author of multimedia training programs, materials, and educational review books.

Riegel was recently invited to join the faculty of the American Management Association and is a conference speaker for the American Society of Training and Development. She was awarded membership in the National Speakers Association and is a member of the International Association of Facilitators. In addition, she is a Certified Senior Professional in Corporate Universities from the International Quality and Productivity Center, as well as a conference speaker on facilitating the transition of the training function into enterprisewide learning.

Riegel earned her bachelor's degree from the University of Michigan–Ann Arbor and her master's degree in social work from Columbia University.

Kevin Bruny has proven himself to be one of the brightest and most innovative chief learning officers despite the fact that he doesn't work for a for-profit corporation. Kevin is extremely knowledgeable about the teaching and learning process and is very thoughtful in his approach.

Just as the preceding chapter demonstrated that the corporate university model can be successfully implemented in a nonprofit organization, this chapter shows how government entities can benefit from a corporate university. In fact, the single largest corporate university that I know of, Defense Acquisition University, is part of a government entity. Of course you don't have to be as large as the U.S. Department of Defense to have a corporate university. All sorts of government entities from the U.S. government down to municipalities have implemented successful corporate universities. In this chapter, Kevin describes how a government entity can develop and benefit from a corporate university, using the corporate university at Chesterfield County, Virginia, as his case study.

11

Corporate Universities in Government

Kevin W. Bruny

IN TODAY'S FAST-CHANGING business environment, the shorter shelf life of knowledge is forcing organizations to continuously update the knowledge and skills of their employees in order to remain competitive. While one might not immediately think of local governments as competitive organizations, maintaining a well-informed and well-educated workforce is a necessity at the local level of government in the twenty-first century. As county citizens become more accustomed to the service standards and delivery systems of corporate America, they have come to expect the same conveniences in service delivery from their county or city government. In response to these expectations, local governments are being challenged to attract and retain workers who can innovate and create comparable services standards to meet citizen expectations. Realizing that compensation structures, benefits plans, and work environments are often differentiators for public sector organizations, learning and employee education have become strong elements in attracting and retaining employees. With the employment turbulence of the private sector, many workers seek stability and opportunities to contribute to society even if it means a little less in salary and benefits. The upside of a more stable work environment with opportunities to engage meaningful issues that are important to society often outweighs the stress and pressure placed on workers to meet this quarter's profit projection. To this end, local governments are realizing that providing employees with opportunities to develop and advance their careers are critical elements for attracting and retaining employee talent.

The government of Chesterfield County, Virginia, has embraced this competitive advantage by creating a corporate university tied to the county's seven strategic goals, its business strategy, and its eight core competencies. For well over a decade, senior county leaders have realized that employee development and personal growth are critical and differentiating factors to fulfilling the organization's vision and mission. Supporting the creation of Chesterfield University was a natural step in executing a strategy the organization had come to value over time.

Having served Chesterfield County in several roles for over twelve years and currently as the county's first chief learning officer, I've witnessed much of the organization's growth and acceptance of learning. In this chapter, I share some of the insights of the development process, the university's current efforts in supporting organizational effectiveness, and where we anticipate future impact.

Where Is Chesterfield County, Virginia?

Chesterfield County is a local government located in the heart of the Commonwealth of Virginia, adjacent to the capital city of Richmond, and encompasses 446 square miles. In this suburban county of 291,000, there is room to grow, as two-thirds of the land is undeveloped. The county, with an adopted fiscal year 2006 budget of $912 million, provides a full range of award-winning municipal programs and services, including public safety, health and welfare, parks and recreation, cultural activities, community development, water and wastewater services, and public health. Programs and services are delivered in a variety of ways: in person, online, by telephone and mail, through print and electronic media, as well as physical facilities (parks, libraries, and an airport, among them).

The county's vision "is to be the recognized leader in local government across the commonwealth and the nation—the standard by which others measure their progress and success." Our mission is to "provide a FIRST CHOICE community through excellence in public service," and our organization has corporately and individually embraced the values of customer focus, ethical behavior, teamwork, leadership, continuous improvement, open communications, employee involvement, progressive thinking, and data-driven decisions.

The county has a committed, highly productive staff of 3,184 full-time and 986 part-time employees, with a ratio of one full-time employee for every 91 citizens. The county benefits from many employees with long tenure, adding depth and breadth to organizational knowledge. The average full-time county employee is forty-two years old and has ten years of service. The county has approximately 550 job classifications that include accountants, engineers, chemists, psychiatrists, police officers, firefighters, system programmers, clerical workers, and a variety of technical and trades positions. With such a diverse workforce in both age and profession, creating relevant and accessible learning is a challenge and one that Chesterfield County has embraced over the past decade.

Chesterfield County's Quality Journey

Our journey in creating Chesterfield University began many years before it was trendy to have a corporate university as the learning arm of an organization. For Chesterfield County, it began in the early 1990s as a component of our Total Quality Improvement (TQI) initiative. The county administrator had been directed by a member of the board of supervisors to explore the concepts of quality and determine if there was applicability in local government. Looking back, this request was putting a new spin to local government management, as we found ourselves to be early implementers and explorers of these concepts to service delivery in local governments.

Initial training brought new concepts, processes, and suggestions to the many departments of the county. With a top-down process of training delivery, a core group of employees and leaders became the engine behind this effort. With a consultant's off-the-shelf training being modified to fit government services, employees were questioning its application and intended outcomes for a government organization. With a slow ascent, TQI soon became the organization's focus. Process management was an early concept, along with statistical process control, benchmarking strategies, and meeting management. Leaders were encouraged to attend training on these principles and explore the possibilities of application to their departmental business. As with any other new initiative where change is required, there were early initiators and some not-so-eager implementers of these principles.

As the organization grew in its application of quality principles, so did its training needs. In response to those needs, TQI University was established in partnership with John Tyler Community College in 1996, offering nine core quality courses and four electives. These courses provided the basis for a certificate in quality improvement from TQI University with accompanying continuing education credits from the community college. This partnership and certificate offering provided a needed boost to embracing the quality movement and was a pivotal milestone for organizational learning. From its inception, 628 employees graduated from TQI University and proudly displayed a unique quality medallion awarded by the county administrator. Since becoming the School of Quality and Continuous Improvement of Chesterfield University, 858 additional employees have attained this same recognition.

Creating Chesterfield University

In 1999, after several years of quality training through TQI University, two training professionals brought forth the idea of a corporate university in relationship to the already established TQI University. These women had learned of the concept at a conference and returned with the thought of its possibility for Chesterfield County. From what they had learned, it seemed that many aspects of a corporate university were already in place with TQI University and that, if expanded, it could further the ideas of consolidation, efficiencies, and possible savings for the county.

The corporate university concept was presented to key leaders and supported with interest. Later that year, a steering committee was established to set the initial direction and lay the foundation for what was to become

Chesterfield University. The fifteen members of the committee were department directors, assistant directors, members of the learning and development staff, and other individuals from across the county who were interested in organizational learning. Member selection was strategic: the intent was to build partnerships with departments that had tended their turf and typically created solutions for their own learning needs. In local government, these departments tend to be public safety areas, such as fire, police, sheriff, and emergency communications, since they are always of high priority for citizen satisfaction.

The Corporate University Steering Committee, as it became known, met monthly and together read and discussed the only relevant book available at that time: Jeanne Meister's *Corporate Universities: Lessons in Building a World-Class Work Force* (1998). As is typical with most other new Chesterfield County initiatives, this creation process followed a structured, methodical, and organized evolution. Foundational elements were identified and built concurrently before the university opened for business. Unlike many other early corporate universities, the county did not give an executive mandate to quickly create and execute this new initiative to increase profits for the year. Our strategy was to build on an already successful TQI University and further explore organizational learning as a means of identifying efficiencies and improving service delivery.

It was quickly recognized that by creating a broader learning organization, several key organizational issues might be addressed as well:

- Attracting and retaining employees is a key contributor to maintaining a competitive edge. If employees see that the county offers them further education and career development, they may be more inclined to stay.

- By embracing current technology, learning would no longer be just a classroom activity, but would address scheduling challenges and unique learning needs that employees often raised.

- Communication issues would improve through a greater focus on learning by encouraging employees to share information and experiences with others across departmental boundaries with the hope of creating communities of practice.

- Involving organizational leaders as learners and faculty would ensure that key organizational information would be shared with the leaders of tomorrow.

The steering committee laid out initial plans and strategies to ensure that what was being created met organizational, departmental, and individual learning needs. An initial organizational training needs assessment, completed to support this strategy, revealed duplication of county training efforts and opportunities to pool learning resources. Assessment results also revealed that several departments had developed and were delivering customer service and leadership training with little or no internal collaboration. This raised questions on curriculum content, delivery models, and performance expectations following course completion. It seemed logical that a county-wide model for service delivery and leadership could be created with the addition of a flexible module to address specific departmental needs. After this initial assessment and further discussion, it was clear that by creating a unified delivery model focused on the county's service strategy, Chesterfield County would see greater impact and rewards in many areas of organizational life. Today, Chesterfield University has centralized much of the county's learning content and design so that consistent curriculum is delivered across the enterprise.

Applying the quality improvement principle of benchmarking, an extensive effort produced successful implementation strategies and lessons learned that would help build the foundational elements of Chesterfield University. Chesterfield County benchmarked with many learning organizations in the private and public sectors, including Motorola, First Union Financial Corporation, Tennessee Valley Authority, the Royal Canadian Mounted Police, and the Bureau of Printing and Engraving, to name just a few. Santa Barbara County, California, was a strong partner in sharing its success and university components as another locality that had entered the corporate university segment. These benchmarking efforts produced various models, organizational structures, funding channels, and critical components to successful learning organizations. The steering committee was quick to review each and determine its applicability to Chesterfield County.

As the benchmarking efforts concluded, it became overwhelmingly clear that much needed to be done to make this learning initiative applicable to and appropriate for Chesterfield County and its employees. Members realized that not all findings would fit our culture or organizational structure but that some key components needed initial attention. The benchmarking findings presented us with opportunities to create core competencies, define a measurement strategy, craft curriculum standards, assess learning styles, identify technology possibilities and desires, formulate an instructor certificate process, name schools of learning, and determine a possible e-learning solution, which was nonexistent at the time for Chesterfield County. (See Figure 11.1 for a model of the university.) It soon became clear that many hands would be needed to complete each of these in a timely manner.

Figure 11.1. The Chesterfield University Model

© 2000, Chesterfield County, Virginia.

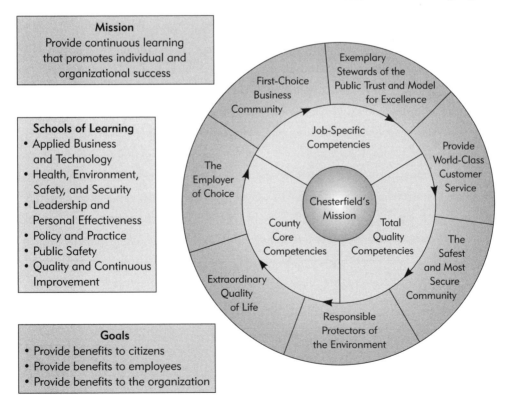

Mission
Provide continuous learning that promotes individual and organizational success

Schools of Learning
• Applied Business and Technology
• Health, Environment, Safety, and Security
• Leadership and Personal Effectiveness
• Policy and Practice
• Public Safety
• Quality and Continuous Improvement

Goals
• Provide benefits to citizens
• Provide benefits to employees
• Provide benefits to the organization

First-Choice Business Community

Exemplary Stewards of the Public Trust and Model for Excellence

Job-Specific Competencies

The Employer of Choice

Provide World-Class Customer Service

Chesterfield's Mission

County Core Competencies

Total Quality Competencies

The Safest and Most Secure Community

Extraordinary Quality of Life

Responsible Protectors of the Environment

Creating Ambassadors Through Teams

The application of cross-functional teams, a common occurrence for county employees, provided the capacity to gain quicker results and involve more employees. They could offer their knowledge and assistance, learn about Chesterfield University, and become ambassadors to others about this new initiative. To that end, tactical teams were proposed and empowered to concurrently complete the many identified tasks. Teams were formed to create a communications and marketing strategy, a measurement model, a curriculum standards model, and an instructor development model and to identify desired learning technologies. Each team was led by a learning and development professional who had knowledge of the issues and the ability to bring departmental representatives together from across the county to develop a countywide solution. While each tactical team has a detailed story, the process of internally creating the county's eight core competencies is frequently requested.

Core Competency Development

A foundational element of any successful corporate university is the competency model on which the curriculum is built. Like other necessary components, a cross-functional team was identified to drive and oversee this foundational initiative. An easier way to accomplish such a task would have been to hire a consultant to guide and execute the necessary steps to full competency development. However, in typical Chesterfield County practice, we chose to develop competencies internally using existing staff and teach ourselves along the way. One member of the training team had competency development experience and felt confident to oversee and guide the process. The selected team studied the book *Building Robust Competencies: Linking Human Resource Systems to Organizational Strategies* (1999) by Paul C. Green to learn the foundational elements and understanding of the process that was about to unfold.

Efforts initially focused on reviewing the benchmarking data from organizations that had successfully identified competencies and were known for their identification process. The Royal Canadian Mounted Police had an impressive set of competencies and willingly shared their experience with the team. It became immediately clear that many of their competencies were applicable to Chesterfield County since they too were a government service organization.

Further communication and sharing with the Mounties proved beneficial to our effort. Once sufficient benchmarking data were obtained on organizational competencies and their creation, efforts turned to identifying those applicable to Chesterfield County government.

Through a survey questionnaire, we asked department directors, "When you hire new employees, what general skills or abilities do you seek to obtain beyond the specific job skills?" We wanted to hear directly from directors what basic skills they desired and sought during the recruitment and employment process. The survey results provided the team with a wide variety of competencies. After consolidating, categorizing, and naming the suggested competencies, energy was directed toward narrowing the list to a manageable number. Again, through a survey, directors were asked to rank the list of competencies from most to least important in their area of responsibility. The results of this ranking allowed the team to narrow the number and attain approval for the county's current eight competencies: communication, continuous learning, leadership, planning and organizing, interpersonal skills, flexibility, reasoning, and customer-focused service.

Once identified, it was time to define. What did these words mean for Chesterfield County? In an attempt to define each competency, the team reviewed the relevant benchmarking information and created draft definitions that were cycled through the department directors for feedback. The results of this round of feedback provided many hours of discussion and additional editing by the team. Next, efforts turned to creating behavioral statements on which employees could be measured. Directors were asked to identify one or two employees from their department who best exemplified each competency on a daily basis. Those employees became members of a focus group for that competency. Over several months, each competency focus group convened, and employees were asked to describe their behaviors or actions for that competency. Getting employees to open up and talk about their performance took time, but once the conversation was set in motion, it was fascinating to watch the behavioral statements take shape.

To create competencies for all county employees, the team recommended that behavioral statements be identified at the frontline, supervisory, manager, and executive levels of the organization. With eight competencies, that equaled the convening of thirty-two focus groups to create the needed behavioral statements.

This seemingly simple task had quickly become a huge undertaking for the organization. When the competency team initially convened, one of the members announced that she thought the process "should only take a few hours." In fact, the competency development process took between eighteen months and two years to complete. Following the focus groups, the proposed competencies and behavioral statements were presented and approved by the county's leadership group as the core competencies expected for all county employees.

Due to this team's dedication, the university's curriculum would provide learning opportunities to assist employees in becoming successful in these eight areas of competence for four levels of the organization. In addition, four 360-degree assessment instruments were created using the behavioral statements at each of the four levels to assess an individual's competence. These online assessments are accessible to employees through a third-party vendor, Edge Training Systems. County leaders are expected to complete an assessment every other year as part of their individual development plan.

Core Competencies and Performance Management

With competencies created at four levels, it seemed natural to incorporate them into the county's performance management system, the Employee Development Program (EDP), since they were already the foundation of the university's curriculum. Changes had occurred several years earlier to align the EDP with the county's quality initiative. That change focused on teamwork, customer service, and application of quality tools and processes to departmental business. While the quality competencies are part of our business strategy and required of all employees, moving to core competencies caused county leaders to pause and question clear connections to quality competencies that had been the basic component of performance management for several years. A solution of mapping the core competencies to the county's quality competencies and values provided the needed assurance that quality gains would not be lost with this new system.

In partnership with human resource management (HRM), Chesterfield University led an effort to update the EDP with the eight core competencies and any needed position-specific competencies for each employee. Employees were given one full year to make the transition to the new format and select specific behavioral statements for each competency. An enhanced individual development plan became a standard requirement, with the intent to drive development and lifelong learning in each employee. The transition has been positive for the organization. Now, in year two, the university has measured an increase in university classes and requests for specific learning, demonstrating the connection that managers and supervisors are making to competency-driven learning opportunities.

Branding Chesterfield University

Establishing a brand was important to the steering committee as the county made the transition from the existing TQI University to an expanded learning initiative. A team of marketing and communication professionals created a countywide contest that invited employees to submit suggested names for the new university. Over ninety suggestions were received and reviewed before "Chesterfield University" was selected on the merits of clearly identifying our locality and the breadth of learning opportunity that a university provides. With over 550 position classifications, it has never been the intent for Chesterfield University to meet all employee learning needs. However, allowing for future development and growth, it was felt that the university name would permit that to happen over time.

With the name identified, efforts turned to branding the university. A graphic artist from the county's public affairs department was tasked with creating several logos for selection by county employees. Three were created, and one took top honors by county employees. The selected logo (see Figure 11.2) was modern and unique in comparison to the standard county seals that are often found in local governments. Its play on a combined *C* and *U* was the most often mentioned aspect of the selected logo. As the university later defined its schools of learning, further branding was created to identify the content of each school (see Figure 11.3). With this additional branding came guidelines on logo placement as well as stationery and slide templates for use by each school. These efforts ensure the integrity of the branding and consistent application of guidelines within the six schools.

Figure 11.2. Employee-Selected Logo for Chesterfield University

Figure 11.3. Logo for Each School of Learning

Chesterfield University's Structure and Governance

Chesterfield University comprises six schools of learning: School of Leadership and Personal Effectiveness; School of Health, Safety, and Security; School of Quality and Continuous Improvement; School of Policies and Practices; School of Public Safety; and School of Applied Business Skills and Technology. Each is led by a dean and governed by a board of advisers that oversees the creation and delivery of curriculum while monitoring student registrations, course evaluations, and overall performance standards. Boards meet regularly to evaluate curricula and ensure that learning continues to be aligned with county goals and business initiatives. Proposals for new curricula are reviewed by board members, who decide their appropriateness. Quarterly and annual metrics and measures are used to monitor learning and school performance.

The overall governance of the university is achieved through the Council of Learning, a fifteen-member body of executive and director-level leaders who, working in conjunction with the chief learning officer and university dean, oversee the operations and effectiveness of Chesterfield University and organizational learning. This council maintains representation from all divisions of county government, including public safety and the county's school system, and includes the deans of each school of learning. The council meets monthly to review strategic issues related to organizational learning and identifies areas where consolidation, partnerships, and efficiencies can be obtained. The overall structure is shown in Figure 11.4.

Figure 11.4. Chesterfield University's Organizational Structure

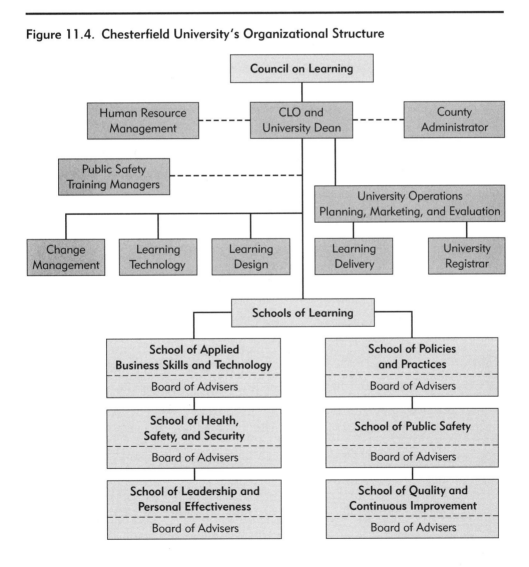

The deans and boards of adviser members are employees from across the county who are interested in learning, are subject matter experts, or have learning responsibilities associated with their specific job. They serve voluntarily in these roles in addition to maintaining their positional responsibilities. Deans are department directors who are selected based on their subject matter areas, willingness to serve, and identification as high-potential leaders within the organization. The county administrator believes that for a future leader, time spent in leading enterprise initiatives and people from across the organization is important for development. Dean succession is closely linked to the county's talent management initiative.

Once developed, Chesterfield University was positioned to be a county-wide resource that would support the many diverse learning needs of all departments. As with many other corporate universities, it was created while housed in the HRM department. The steering committee deliberated on whether it should become a department of its own or stay in HRM. In March 2003, with the full support of HRM's director, it was recommended and championed by the county administrator that Chesterfield University would become a separate department and be led by a chief learning officer. Since that time, Chesterfield University has operated as a separate department, managing its own budget and a staff of six learning consultants and four support staff.

The chief learning officer and university dean work directly with the Council on Learning and organizational leaders to implement the strategic direction that has been established for organizational learning. The CLO also has dotted-line relationships with the county administrator and the HRM director for purposes of oversight of talent management and organizational programs where learning and development have an impact on employees' performance. The university's operations manager oversees the day-to-day activities, which focus on planning, delivery, measuring, and marketing learning to employees. A curriculum coordinator oversees curriculum design and development by introducing new methods of delivery and enhancing learning through technology. A university registrar is a key position for ensuring that employees are registered appropriately and transcripts remain current. Six full-time and part-time learning consultants provide instruction, needs assessment, and program management for the university. In addition to the university's staff, the county has fifteen to twenty volunteer employee instructors who have completed an instructor certification course and provide two to three days of instruction each quarter.

Curriculum Development and Learning Tools

Prior to the launch of Chesterfield University, curriculum was developed in a hit-or-miss fashion throughout the organization. When something was needed, learning professionals or subject matter experts would create a curriculum to best meet the need without much consideration of the elements of solid curriculum design. To remedy this, a curriculum standards model and review form were created to bring consistency and uniformity to learning offered by the university. As a result of this model and review process, curriculum requests are reviewed by knowledgeable professionals to ensure competency support, a connection to one or more of the strategic goals, the inclusion of an evaluation method, clearly defined objectives, and the articulation of performance gaps that the instruction is intended to close.

Although this model is strongly aligned to the ADDIE model of instructional design (analysis, design, development, implementation, evaluation), it nevertheless offers the opportunity for any county employee to suggest new curricula. An employee who believes that additional learning would support his or her performance is encouraged to complete a curriculum development review form and submit it for consideration. Once reviewed by the curriculum coordinator, it is passed to the council on learning for school placement. Once assigned, it is up to that school's board of advisers to determine whether the requested curriculum is relevant to their mission, whether a similar curriculum already exists, and, if created, whether it will be developed by a subject matter expert of the school or be returned to the university staff for this work. If it is developed by a subject matter expert, a final review and approval is required by the curriculum coordinator prior to delivery. This ensures that a variety of learning methods are included in each class, along with an appropriate mix of lecture and activities.

Since 2003, 36 of the university's 350 courses have been suggested by county employees. Often these suggested courses are taught by a subject matter expert or leader from within the county. A recent example is an Associated Press (AP)–style writing class designed to improve employees' ability to write within the AP style—the one used for external communication with our citizens and public by our public affairs office—which was created and is currently taught by the director and a writer in the department of public affairs. This strategy also supports the goal of involving leaders in organizational learning by having them enter the classroom as an instructor as well as a participant.

With 98 percent of all county learning being instructor-led, as stated in the university's fiscal year 2005 annual report, it remains a goal of the university to diversify its delivery methods. Efforts have been made during the past few years to create new tools that will draw employees to learn outside the classroom. Early deliverables included self-study courses for sexual harassment and the employee development program for supervisors, both required courses for county supervisors. That they are CD-ROM courses allows the newly promoted supervisor flexibility in completing the course outside the scheduled instructor-led course. Simple job aids helped to diversify delivery methods when the EDP was changed to include core competencies. These assisted supervisors in preparing employees for the new program and remained easy reference materials.

A learning community that was created to support the county's strategic planning efforts offers a new learning forum for leaders. Although it is expected that each department will create a strategic plan clearly linked to the county's strategic plan, mapping a department's strategy to budget requests and ensuring that goals, objectives, and performance measures are appropriately created and tracked can be challenging. To assist in this effort, a learning community was created for sharing information, collaborating across departments, and strengthening measurement efforts within the organization. This community will use a variety of tools, such as blogs, MP3 files, chatrooms, and formalized learning events to encourage conversations and collaboration among its members.

The Chesterfield University Virtual Book Club was established through the use of existing technology. In partnership with Chesterfield County Libraries, the university has structured a traditional book club in which members come together to discuss a book's concepts and how those concepts can be applied in the workplace. However, unlike traditional book clubs, members meet online in a librarian-facilitated chatroom, provided through Skill-Soft's learning platform, SkillPort. The book club, now in its second year, has shown increased growth and employee interest.

Unlike many resource-rich organizations, Chesterfield University has been creative with its existing tools and technology. While it is exciting to purchase and apply the latest technologies, funding sources are usually scarce, and it often takes several budget cycles to see results. Seeking ways to be creative with existing resources adds another level of challenge and reward for learning professionals at the local level.

Technology and Learning in Local Government

Early in the university's development, a technology needs assessment was deployed to determine which learning media employees preferred, which curricula could be delivered electronically, and if existing computer hardware and software could support electronic delivery methods. This countywide assessment also sought to learn what impact work schedules and numerous locations would have on the learning environment and any other demographic information that would be important to future technology decisions. Because several departments have 24/7 coverage, learning had to be offered outside the traditional work hours of 8:30 A.M. to 5:00 P.M. The most startling outcome of the assessment indicated that just over half of the county employees had access to a county-assigned personal computer. Although many county jobs are office based, a considerable number of employees work out in the community delivering services and are unable to link directly to county Web sites and electronic tools during work hours for learning purposes. This information led to the decision that a blended approach to course development and delivery would best meet employees' learning needs while building a culture that would accept new ways of learning. To date, a blended strategy has prevailed, although with a slower-than-expected acceptance in establishing an online learning culture.

Changing the county's culture from one that has viewed learning as a classroom event to one that enables 24/7 access has presented challenges with such a diverse workforce. Local governments have a greater challenge than companies comprising predominantly knowledge workers in convincing service providers and laborers to consider the computer as an acceptable learning tool. Businesses filled with computer-savvy employees who are comfortable with Web-based technologies have an advantage over organizations that have a broad mix of proficiency in the use of technology. We have found that older and more tenured workers may not have an interest in mastering new skills or an opportunity to access a personal computer.

Intent on creating a blended learning strategy, the university requested money to procure a catalogue of online courses that would map to our core competencies and support organizational learning needs. This catalogue of 350 courses, produced by SkillSoft, has been a positive addition to our curriculum. As online learning was introduced, a "learning online" campaign was launched, and several contests were held to drive employees to this new learning option. Early users indicated they liked the flexibility to learn on their own time and at their own pace and enjoyed the content. Others returned the SkillSoft license, indicating that an online learning experience didn't meet their needs. They preferred interaction with peers and a classroom setting. Although the county's number of licenses is limited, we have been pleased with the results since introducing this new strategy to county employees in 2003. With more than 220 users, we have recorded as many as 1,766 hours of learning completed annually since introducing this option.

No one should underestimate the importance of continued marketing, alignment to business needs, and the impact that learning contests have on employee participation. To our surprise, yearly course completion rates of 70 and 60 percent, respectively, have greatly exceeded our expectations against the industry average of 35 percent. These results, while good, nevertheless leave us seeking greater use and adoption by employees to establish an online learning culture. Efforts continue to increase participation by including courses as pre- and postwork for instructor-led courses, which creates that desired blended strategy.

Technology was introduced throughout the development and operation of Chesterfield University. A new training registration system provides employees Web-based registration and course approval while putting learning information and individual training history reports at employees' fingertips. This new system introduced the concept of work flow to the organization and was a critical element in centralizing learning information in one location. An effort to acquire a learning management system was initiated but soon halted as the county concurrently procured an enterprise resource system (ERP). With the realization that several areas overlapped in these two systems, it became apparent that to avoid duplication, the university needed to wait and see which ERP the county would select. In the interim, TrainingRegister would serve as a registration system and the repository for learning metrics.

With this delay and maturing of the university, efforts are currently under way to select a "human capital" or "talent management" system that is capable of tracking learning, performance, and succession planning data. Implementing this system will enhance the current manual measurement strategy and allow greater metrics for enterprisewide reporting of learning and performance. While progress has been made in obtaining enterprisewide learning metrics, departments are eager to partner through a uniform process and system. Such a system will allow the university to better automate training effectiveness measures and performance management, which are currently paper-intensive processes.

Talent Management and the University

Now that the university is in place and providing competency-based learning opportunities tied to the county's service delivery strategy, what additional role can it play for the county? Chesterfield University has positioned itself as an influential force and partner for organizational and leadership development through the coordination of the county's talent management initiative.

The county's executive leadership group identified the issue of succession management for an off-site retreat in October 2002. Through an organizational review, a snapshot of the county's workforce produced some alarming trends. At that time, 58 percent of the workforce was over the age of forty, and 8 percent of employees grade 40 and above (supervisors through directors) were eligible to retire in 2003. Taking a broader look, 28 percent of those identified would be eligible to retire by 2008, and 52 percent would be eligible to retire by 2013. The possibility that over half of the current organizational leaders could retire in ten years was alarming, and the chief learning officer was asked to create a process to better prepare future leaders for the projected vacancies. After further research, a talent management model and training program was internally developed for the organization to biennially assess and develop individuals for advancement within the county. This program, modeled on McKinsey's 1997 and 2000 studies, "The War for Talent," was created with the intent of obtaining an inventory of leaders' education, work history, strengths and weaknesses, and career desires that could be used to better prepare for future workforce changes. The talent management program also intended to increase performance conversations within the organization. These individual performance conversations are fueled by the completion of individual talent profiles by a leader's supervisor. Each profile documents the leader's core competency strengths, weaknesses, and future potential, along with a retention risk assessment. The assessments provide the information needed to ensure that succession strategies are in place and leader development remains a high priority. The results of the initial State of Talent report provided a performance benchmark and opportunities to create specific learning programs targeted to mid- to upper-level managers. The university, while managing this program, has also taken the information gleaned from the assessments and created new learning programs for employees in the program's scope.

In one such program, Learning with Lane, Lane Ramsey, the county administrator, invites six county leaders to join him for an informal breakfast conversation. Invited guests are requested to bring the topics of conversation to the session. This program is in response to an identified need of increasing contact with the county administrator and also allows him an opportunity to test ideas on a small group of county leaders. The program has been in place for a year and has been well received by both participants and the county administrator. The county has also strengthened its relationship with the University of Virginia's Weldon Cooper Center for Public Service to place high-potential leaders in a week-long program entitled Leading, Educating, and Developing (LEAD). The opportunity provides leaders with exposure to peer government leaders from across the United States while introducing a high-performance organization model. While many aspects of the model have been implemented in Chesterfield County, this experience is intended to strengthen individual leaders to enhance a culture of efficiency, flexibility, and empowering of others.

The talent management initiative has provided information to assist in leader identification for unique countywide efforts such as creating and communicating a county bond referendum and identifying key positional leaders to support the county's new Baldrige-based quality model. The talent assessment database is used to provide strategic information to leaders in identifying desired opportunities as well as developmental needs. When key positions are vacated, managers are encouraged to seek information about possible candidates as part of their recruitment strategies.

Change Management and the University

Chesterfield University has broadened itself beyond being a provider of employee learning. It has established and positioned itself with the competency of change management through the addition of a change management professional. The county, in implementing an ERP system, will redesign and change most of the organization's financial and human resource systems while eliminating manual departmental processes. This system will introduce a great deal of operational change in core departments such as accounting, budget and management, purchasing, information systems technology, and human resource management. It will also have an impact on the operation of the county's fifty-two departments and create uncertainty and work process changes for key positions. Chesterfield University partnered with the project leader and established the change management lead position as a key contributor to the overall implementation effort. This position has been critical in assessing departmental readiness, identifying barriers to change and implementation, and being a key contributor to communicating the new system to the entire organization.

While this project has an extended implementation period, the benefits of the change management lead have been recognized and acknowledged by other divisions of the county. Such an acknowledgment has allowed the university to establish another partnership where change management will be critical to changing business processes and improving the efficiency of service delivery. The division of community development, which houses the services of building inspection, planning, utilities, transportation, and environmental engineering, is constructing a new building where these services will be available in an accelerated format. Creating this unique customer service center will require individual departments and employees to work in a collaborative environment to serve citizens efficiently. The change management lead will assist individuals and departments in identifying barriers to service delivery and facilitating conversations for change. As Chesterfield County continues to expand services to meet growing county needs, possessing the internal capacity to assist departments with change management is a valuable competency.

Impact of Learning on Chesterfield County

Creating and supporting a learning environment has truly been an enjoyable journey for me and the many others who have been involved. Much of our success is due to the ongoing support of county leaders, particularly Lane B. Ramsey, the county administrator, who have been open to new and often uncharacteristic suggestions for local government. Through a willingness to seek new and different ways of operating, Chesterfield County has identified itself as an innovative government in many service areas. That value for innovation has proven true for organizational learning as well. No longer can HRM professionals successfully identify the organization's learning needs and set direction without involving leaders and employees.

In the few years that it has been in existence, Chesterfield University has assessed the learning needs of the organization and introduced technological improvements that allow greater access to learning and information by employees. It has also brought independent departmental training units into one cohesive university partnership and tied all learning to core competencies and the strategic goals of the county. This has been accomplished by involving over two hundred employees at all levels of the organization in creating, participating in, and leading learning events, which creates a shared leadership and accountability for learning. Much of our success has been due to the collaborative culture of this county government.

Holding a strong belief that by engaging employees, better solutions can be identified to meet service delivery challenges of our citizenry, Chesterfield County has received numerous awards and gained considerable recognition over the years, the highest being the first and only locality to win Virginia's Senate Productivity and Quality Award Board's top honor, the Award for Continuing Excellence twice. This acknowledges that identifying improved service delivery is a priority for the county. To accomplish this achievement, Chesterfield County has demonstrated that it values employee contribution and created a learning environment supported by Chesterfield University. Through shared resources and partnerships, Chesterfield University will continue to serve as a model for local government committed to creating service efficiencies through learning by recruiting, developing, and retaining loyal employees who provide satisfying services to our citizens.

References

Green, P. C. *Building Robust Competencies: Linking Human Resource Systems to Organizational Strategies.* (1999). San Francisco: Jossey-Bass.

Meister, J. *Corporate Universities: Lessons in Building a World-Class Work Force.* New York: McGraw-Hill, 1998.

Michaels, E., Handfield-Jones, H., and Axelrod, B. *The War for Talent.* Boston: Harvard Business School Publishing, 2001.

Kevin W. Bruny, SPHR, is chief learning officer and university dean for Chesterfield County Government, Chesterfield, Virginia, where he connects employee learning and talent development with the county's service strategy. Previously, he was assistant director of human resource management and the manager of employee relations and development, where he led the training strategy of a total quality improvement initiative for the county, which resulted in its being a finalist in 1994 and winning the U.S. Senate Productivity and Quality Award Medallion for Virginia in 1995 and a second Award for Continuing Excellence in 2004. Prior to returning to Chesterfield County in 2000, Bruny was vice president and organizational development consultant with Crestar Financial Corporation, now SunTrust Financial Corporation.

Bruny holds a bachelor's degree in psychology from West Virginia Wesleyan College and a master's degree in adult education/human resource development from Virginia Commonwealth University. He is a member of the Society of Human Resource Management Association and has obtained the Senior Professional in Human Resources (SPHR) designation from the Human Resource Certification Institute. He also holds memberships with the American Society for Training and Development, Washington Area Consortium for Corporate Universities, and International Public Management Association for Human Resources. He serves as a judge for the CUBIC (Corporate University Best in Class) Awards and is a frequent speaker at conferences. Bruny holds adjunct instructor positions at the University of Richmond and Virginia Commonwealth University. He is president of the alumni association and a trustee for West Virginia Wesleyan College.

Next-Generation Corporate University Functions

At the heart of the concept of next-generation corporate universities is the idea that corporate universities can do much more than traditional training to develop people and expand organizational capabilities. This part examines many of these nontraditional functions and looks at corporate universities that are using them with great success.

Part Four starts with a look at one of the greatest organizational challenges: culture change. Chapter Twelve argues that corporate universities are well suited to be agents of culture change.

The concepts of mentoring and executive coaching are not new, but having these functions reside in the corporate university is a relatively new idea. Managing these processes in the department responsible for the development of people is a good way to maximize value. Chapters Thirteen and Fourteen address these issues and provide case studies containing road maps for how to manage these functions.

Developing people has benefits for both individuals and the organization. The purpose of development efforts is to benefit the organization, but helping people in their careers is not incidental to the process. Chapter Fifteen concentrates on career path management as a corporate university function. The related concept of succession planning is addressed in Chapter Sixteen. Here, the corporate university manages a process that is better termed "succession management" and is designed to develop people for future jobs and to meet organizational needs.

Like some of the other functions addressed in this part, knowledge management is not a new idea, but housing it in the corporate university is. Chapter Seventeen discusses the role of corporate universities in the knowledge management process and in knowledge-sharing networks. Wisdom management is a new topic. It is the connective tissue linking workplace learning with on-the-job performance and organizational results. If the process is managed properly by the corporate university, it can add tremendous value to the organization. A discussion of this concept is presented in Chapter Eighteen.

I have known Laree Kiely since 1993, when we both worked at the University of Southern California. I have seen her operate in a variety of settings, and I never cease to be impressed with the quality of her work. In baseball, the best prospects are called "five-tool players"—this means that they can hit, hit with power, run, field, and throw. In her world, Laree is definitely a five-tool player: she does outstanding work as an organizational consultant, curriculum designer, teacher, researcher, and writer. Beyond that, she is a great friend. And it wouldn't surprise me if she could also hit a curveball.

In this chapter, Laree addresses one of her favorite topics: culture change. We all know that culture change isn't easy, but it is possible. Changing an organization's structure can be comparatively easy, but culture change encompasses much more. If an organization is brave enough to attempt to change, or at least shape, its culture, it has to know that culture is above all a people issue. And since it's a people issue, its place is in the corporate university. In this chapter, Laree not only argues that culture change belongs in the corporate university, but contends that assessing, understanding, and changing an organization's culture is a necessary function of the corporate university.

12

Corporate Universities as Shapers of Culture

Laree Kiely

A S CORPORATE UNIVERSITIES and partners of corporate universities, we have at best underestimated, and at worst misunderstood, our mission. When it comes to corporate education interventions, there is an elephant in the living room. We dance around it, make vague references to it, are inconvenienced and even paralyzed by it, but nobody wants to say out loud, "There is an elephant in here!"

How the Elephant Got In Here In the First Place

Before we get into the description of the elephant and the solution to what to do with it, let's look at how it got in here in the first place. Because we have been focused on what Einstein called "a perfection of means and a confusion of ends," the problem is inherent in our choice of solutions. There are several possibilities.

Perhaps it is the borrowing of the academic model that has caused us to go astray. The academic model leaves it to individuals (or their supervisors) to choose a path and go to a catalogue of courses to determine what education to obtain. Often driven by schedule and faculty, the "students" choose what is most convenient, most exciting, or what will most likely get them the degree they want or the job they covet. We have seen many corporate universities slowly erode from an employee-centric model to a catalogue-centric model, unintentionally taking the path of least resistance over time because the alternative was too difficult and the offerings too many.

Or it might have been something nobler that we borrowed from the academic model: the belief that competencies make the individual. If I give you enough tools, you will surely be effective. Perhaps it was the competency-centric model that trapped education programs into erroneously believing that these programs might develop enough people to have critical mass and change the organization. What we have seen over time, however, is that the competencies may stack up, but they do not add up.

Perhaps it is a misunderstanding of the purpose of a corporate university. There are many that do not meet the standards of a true corporate university yet call themselves by that name. Many are still operating like training departments and exist as a kind of covenant to the worker:

> When the concept of guaranteed employment died, we hardly even
> noted its passing. It was slowly and inexorably replaced by what we
> called the "New Social Contract" that went a bit like this: Employ-
> ees must bring value to the organization and they must determine
> what that value will be. In return, the organization would help
> ensure that that employee stayed, not employed, but employable.
> This means providing either the funding or the education or both
> to continuously rebuild and improve an employee's skills. We found
> that this was a good way to attract and retain workers in a tough
> labor market. It enhanced their morale and we believed that would
> improve productivity, etc. etc. [Kiely, 2002, p. 167].

Or it could be that we are so busy and the speed with which we need to upgrade skills is so fast-paced that we have gotten too caught up in the dance and have failed to go to the balcony. It is only from the balcony that we can see the patterns we are causing or the patterns we are missing:

In addition, the old calculation that, because of an ever-changing technology, an employee's skills would become obsolete every five years, has itself become obsolete: that number is down to every two to three years and counting. College degrees, including MBA's, now have a shelf life that is increasingly shorter. So we have seen our mission as keeping companies and employees current and productive by keeping them upgraded and updated on knowledge and information.

In a way, the increasing need for what we do has become part of the accountability problem; our attention has been focused on delivering goods that are changing daily to clients whose needs are shifting equally rapidly. So the service of education and development makes us significant partners in the enterprise. But delivering the goods is one thing, assessing the quality and usefulness of the deliverables is another, and if no one can tell whether the goods got delivered and whether they were effective, then the whole game is lost [Kiely, 2002, p. 167].

Whatever the cause, the problem is widespread and is so close to us we cannot see it. What really is our long-term goal? We are often so caught up in putting on training events and programs, finding the sexiest off-the-shelf stuff to give our folks so that they will rate the sessions highly, that we have lost sight of not only our greatest opportunity, but also our most certain purpose: to effect sustainable change in the DNA of the organization. Let me put it as directly as possible: if education does not focus on the organization's DNA, our programs will be at best a missed opportunity and at worst a disastrous waste of enormous amounts of money and time.

Describing the Elephant

Many people will argue that education always has an effect. The mind is not like a rubber band: once stretched, it cannot snap back to its original shape. Restated, when it comes to corporate education, there is no such thing as a neutral effect. The outcome will be either positive or negative. So if the rubber band theory is correct, when a person has been "educated," his or her mind has been stretched and expectations raised. But if this person is then ostracized or ignored when bringing these new attitudes and skills back to the workplace, the effect can actually be to drive people out of the organization, not bring them closer. Even in this simplest (and most typical) of examples, the theory of education as an employee retention strategy is flawed.

Consider these more-common-than-not scenarios:

• People leave a training session feeling enthusiastic due to a dynamic trainer or interesting content. The evaluation form has all smiley faces. And as the participants leave, they say, "This was a great session. Too bad I can't really use these tools back at work." The number one complaint among most participants in training and development programs is, "This is great, but I can't use it back at work."

A colleague of mine just brought to my attention the dilemma he faced with a very expensive training program he implemented in a large, international corporation. The program was to develop the director level of the corporation to be more aggressive, more empowered, and better leaders to move the company rapidly forward. After finishing twelve months of the program and developing two-thirds of the directors, the CEO and the vice presidents brought it to a grinding halt. Their reason: the directors were now too aggressive and had become uncontrollable. The company was not getting the intended result of the training: directors who would use the training to become better leaders to advance the company.

• The session was well received and people felt enthusiastic and rated the facilitator with all fives (five being best). As they leave, they say, "Have the vice presidents [or managers or supervisors] been through this class? My boss needs this more than I do!" This is the number two most common complaint.

• The sessions went extremely well, and the people learned most enthusiastically. When they left, they said, "Thank you. This is the best course I have ever had!" But when they went back to work, these costly sessions resulted in no observable differences.

Examples of massive cost and the minimal return are many and pathetic. Organizations pour massive amounts of money into developing their leadership, yet end up curious about why no behaviors are actually being changed.

Sometimes people further down in the organization don't change because they don't have to. One reason we have often heard is that the leadership and management turn over so frequently that the people actually doing the work believe that they can simply outlive the managers: "I don't have to change. My manager will turn over, and I will outlast him or her." This is a problem of the system itself that will continue to undermine any educational efforts.

• Different individuals go to different programs and return with a my-education-is-better-than-yours attitude. For years we have known that sending one person to a development program will often cause him or her to be ostracized. Try it: send someone to an executive program at one of the top academic universities costing eight thousand dollars and watch this person try to bring usable information back. His or her peers will simply roll their eyes and either think or even say out loud, "Oh, yeah, Jenny just went to Harvard" (accompanied by that certain face-and-hand nonverbal gesture). Years ago, a client decided that its leadership needed some modernizing. In a clever design, they sent some of their people to outside executive education programs and kept some at home to attend a customized development program run in-house. The end result was a clash over whose education was more relevant. After hundreds of thousands of dollars, the return on investment was zero or worse. It got so bad that people didn't want to bring up anything they had learned because it triggered competitiveness and undermined any shared learning.

• Training skills out of the context of the organization. I have seen several content-specific yet out-of-context programs that focused on skills but ignored causes of the problems addressed. For example, programs might offer training on conflict management because management sees too much disagreement or hostility in the workers. But without discovering the systemic issues inside the organization that cause most conflicts, the company is likely treating only symptoms. The result is that the cause remains in place, the symptoms pop up somewhere else, and nothing improves.

• People are in training and development programs too much of the time, actually lowering productivity significantly. A large company in a deregulating industry ran large and costly development programs that included nearly everyone in the organization, with the result that people were almost constantly in training. We noticed that the same faces kept showing up in the various programs, so much that we wondered when people had time for work. When we asked, we were told that this training was being used as a retention strategy. We had to point out that what this was really accomplishing was a bunch of highly skilled employees who were using this company to train them and then moving on to use the skills elsewhere.

Attempts to Ignore the Elephant

Too many organizations with corporate universities or training departments see a need for upgrading people's skills or to solve a problem in the organization, so they throw training at it like pasta thrown against the wall to see if it will stick. We are acting like training agencies whose job is to deliver a program and then go home with our consciences clear because we delivered it. But this is way wrong: the raison d'être of a corporate university ought to go much further:

> Corporate Universities have an even more vital mission—to ensure change and progress at the level of corporate culture. Today's business must go from being a mob of functioning individuals to a learning organization to a collective, "thinking" mind. This demands more than an expanded training and development model. It demands that Corporate Universities become a microcosm of the future organization itself. It means becoming "thinking" organizations that think globally, holistically, in nonlinear ways, and it means creating new ways of defining and measuring outcomes. It is time to recognize that Corporate Universities must be a different animal, whose purpose is to consistently, effectively, and efficiently enhance the culture of an entire organization. Training and development models tend to participate in the old, comfortable assumptions from academia that exclude wondering about whether we're necessary or expendable [Kiely, 2002, p. 166].

There are two sides to this coin: the first is the inadequacy of training and development to stick because the new skills are often countercultural, and the flip side is the missed opportunity to shape or fine-tune the organizational culture itself. And as the examples have shown, it's a case of asking the wrong question, solving the wrong problem, and treating symptoms rather than cause.

There is one other reason for the elephant remaining in the living room: we have been responding to what people have requested of us. There are three frequent reasons that educational programs are requested: to respond to a need, support a strategy for retention, or because we just think it is necessary and expected of the organization to give the people training programs.

Here is the real question: What behaviors, attitudes, and norms does an organization need to create and foster in order to best align to its strategy and goals; ensure the accomplishment of its strategy and goals; have and attract the most productive, effective, and efficient behavior; and ensure a place where people thrive and choose to stay? This requires learning that works, is sustainable, and makes a difference.

Giving the Elephant a Name

If any of the above scenarios set out above seems familiar, then we must be missing something in our educational model. Leah Houde, in "Aligning Education with Business Strategies" (2005), observes that "a sea change in thinking about corporate education is taking place—a shift in how we view it, as well as a shift in how we design and deliver education programs. Instead of regarding education dollars as a tiresome drain on profits—the first expense to be cut back in hard times—smart CEOs increasingly see education as a strategic asset, an asset that enhances the long-term value of the business."

Houde is making the argument that we need to align education efforts with business strategies. But even that noble effort will fall short if we do not focus our education efforts on the organization's culture. I have seen many organizations try desperately to align education and strategy, only to end up baffled about why their hard work failed to change anything. We have found that this failure is caused by failing to get at the culture—the DNA—of the organization, assessing it, understanding it, and changing it.

To put it plainly, the elephant in the living room, the obstruction that keeps educational programs from having the desired effect, is organizational culture. Organizational culture takes on a life of its own and is much more pervasive and powerful than the cumulative changes in individual competencies. We have to study this beast; we have to ask, "What is in the DNA of the organization that keeps people from adopting new behaviors and keeps them stuck in the old patterns?" For years, we have believed that the people themselves are resistant to change. In fact, it isn't the people. Rather, it is systemic: it is the culture that enshrines the old and resists the new.

Organizational cultures are persistent and stubborn and outlast everyone: the individuals in them, the managers and leaders who grapple with them, and the corporate universities that continue to throw simplistic and ineffective training at complex and culturally grounded problems. Entrenched elephants are not moved by something weak and peripheral going on somewhere over across the room. They yawn comfortably, they do not take notice, and it never occurs to them to move or change until someone comes with an approach that recognizes and adapts to and is powerful enough to move elephants.

Defining the Elephant

I am going to be a bit theoretical here to put the elephant in the right context. As you read these explanations, see if there is anything that sounds like your organization. Following this section, we'll apply this information directly to corporate universities. But to start, let's give organizational culture a definition.

Culture Defined

As a general definition, *culture* is clusters of patterns among groups of people—patterns of assumptions, beliefs, attitudes, behaviors, and ways of doing things. Organizational culture has to do with the hidden, underlying, systemic patterns in an organization. To some extent, an organization's culture can be created through the design of its structure, but it often comes about due to unintended consequences of the structure or perhaps lack of structure. Usually it's both ways: intentional and unintentional. Research shows that the synergy between people and structure makes culture much stronger than just the additive effect of these elements. It is nothing less than the "how stuff gets done" of organizations. To put it another way, "A culture is not simply a collection of human and physical resources but the pattern by which these are joined, balanced, and synthesized" (Hampden-Turner, 1990, pp. 12–13).

Social scientists and anthropologists have contributed several definitions. One of the most basic is, "By their very nature, cultural systems have taught people to think and behave differently from others; sometimes the differences produce behaviors that are polar opposites from one another. Because of the primitive, tribal need for belongingness and the intense desire to manage uncertainty, our cultural systems have also taught us to be suspicious of differences, to think ours is the superior culture" (Kiely, 2001, p. 193).

Out of the wilds and into the systemic, Hall in his seminal work wrote: "Anthropologists do agree . . . culture . . . is not innate, but learned; the various facets of culture are interrelated—you touch a culture in one place and everything else is affected; it is shared and in effect defines the boundaries of different groups" (1976, pp. 13–14).

Harris and Moran (1991) move from Hall's system emphasis to something more cosmological and developmental. A culture is "the way of living developed and transmitted by a group of human beings, consciously or unconsciously, to subsequent generations. More precisely, ideas, habits, attitudes, customs, and traditions become accepted and somewhat standardized in a particular group as an attempt to meet continuing needs" (p. 135).

Culture is learned, creates a sense of superiority and belonging, and is powerful and change resistant enough to be passed to succeeding generations. This set of themes is picked up in organizational studies as well. In my own research on international teams I found:

> Cultures evolve as a type of shared history because a group of people goes through a set of common experiences. Those similar experiences cause certain responses. The responses become a set of expected and shared behaviors. Those behaviors become unwritten rules, which become norms that are shared by all people who have that common history or are descendants of that original group.

By the time these commonalities become rules and norms, they have become pre-conscious, or even unconscious; they are a part of us. They become reality—truth, beauty, and justice, and we believe our norms to be the "right" ones and others to be weird, incomprehensible, rude or just wrong [Kiely, 2001, p. 194].

The false but pervasive perception from inside a culture is that its norms represent truth and objective reality. New organizations may not show much evidence of a definable culture, but when they are better established, "culture reflects assumptions about clients, employees, mission, products, activities, and assumptions that have worked well in the past and which get translated into norms of behavior, expectations about what is legitimate, desirable ways of thinking and acting. [These] are the locus of its capacity for evolution and change" (Hampden-Turner, 1990, pp. 12–13).

The anthropological view of international and ethnic cultures fits neatly like a template over the discussion of organizational culture, with the same characteristics and functions, the same problems, the same assets and opportunities. If we are to fulfill our mission, this is the level at which the corporate university must live.

Aspects of Culture

Three areas or characteristics or aspects of culture are especially relevant to the corporate university and educational interventions.

Myths or Beliefs. Similar to members of primitive tribal cultures, people come up with ways to explain themselves or things to believe about themselves. All cultures and subcultures develop their own stories over time consisting of narratives of their history, their values, their experiences, and their heroes and enemies. The power of the symbolic meaning of these stories for the culture is not to be taken lightly. These stories or perceptions are believed to be true and become the lens through which members of an organization view themselves. Because of this, mythos both helps and hinders the choices made within organizations. Discovering the myths in an organization may be more powerful than factual assessments or survey questionnaires. Myths tend to be self-fulfilling (creating a reality) and self-perpetuating as well. They might be specific subculture myths or large and amorphous myths. For example, complacency can be one of the most dangerous attributes. It can come about by benign neglect, or it could exist because of the organizational cultural mythos. The same is true of optimism or "we" cultures. Any myth taken too far can become a liability.

Rules and Norms. Norms are deeply held assumptions that turn into repetitive attitudes and behaviors. "Social scientist Susan Shimanoff observed that groups of people who share a culture or sub-culture seem to have sets of unwritten rules—rules that are so embedded in their culture they cannot even articulate them, let alone see them objectively" (Kiely, 2001, p. 194). The bottom line is that people in organizations watch how others survive and thrive and then emulate those same behaviors; over time these become norms. Norms may fall anywhere on the continuum between very productive and very dysfunctional or even dangerous. According to Schein (1992), norms might be observed behavioral regularities, group norms, espoused values, formal philosophies, rules of the game, aspects of climate, habits of behavior, and perhaps shared meanings and root metaphors, all powerful, all operating largely unexamined, and all capable of enhancing or seriously threatening the long-term viability of an organization.

Dimensions of Culture. As many as twenty of these aspects of culture have been studied over many decades (for a complete summary, see Hofstede, 1984, 1991; Harris and Moran, 1991; Hall, 1976). For our purposes, the following aspects of culture have the largest effect on the success or failure of educational interventions.

Tolerance for Ambiguity. For an organization to survive in the twenty-first century, its norms need to be flexible, resilient, and adaptable, especially in the face of rapid change. Culturally, however, these abilities (or lack of them) are deep-seated and cannot be changed just by willing them to be so; in organizations, tolerance for ambiguity appears all along the spectrum from low to high.

Tolerance for ambiguity "refers to the ability to react to new, different, and at times, unpredictable situations with little visible discomfort or irritation. Excessive discomfort often leads to frustration and hostility" (Harris and Moran, 1991, p. 104).

High tolerance for ambiguity might cause slippage, mistakes, or poor quality; low tolerance for ambiguity might cause a system to be so rigid it cannot adapt rapidly enough and cannot be innovative enough. The inability to see potential danger could occur in either case but for differing reasons, calling for differing solutions.

Power Distance. This dimension in an organization refers to perceived authority and how clearly the levels or hierarchy are delineated. For example, the perception of power is not only in the organizational chart design but also in the informal beliefs, norms, and myths. Cultures that revere their elders or prefer military-type command and control are called "high power differential." Cultures that believe all employees are created equal have strong norms regarding diversity and empower their workforce are considered low power differential. The power differential issue affects information flow as well as many other productivity issues, including risk aversion. High-power-distance cultures typically have top-down decision models. Low-power-distance cultures allow for more emergent processes and decisions.

Politeness Norm. This cultural dimension is one of the ways the high power differential plays itself out. It is a form of cultural etiquette or diplomacy closely related to the maintenance of face. Never underestimate the need of individuals to save face or to keep from losing face. Cultures that have a high power differential and a collectivist perspective have a strong politeness norm as well. An assessment of organizational politeness norms can be very revealing regarding vulnerability in the face of change. A strong politeness norm might be misinterpreted as respect for people or cultural sensitivity. Misunderstanding this concept can create a culture where people are unable to disagree. Over time this can be quite toxic in a culture. It isn't simply that people see problems or opportunities; it is that they aren't speaking up. It might be that the politeness norm is so strong that people have stopped looking altogether.

Context. The dimension of context refers to the need or lack of need for shared backgrounds and histories in order to create meaning. High-context cultures, which require fewer words and depend on the shared experience of members to generate meaning, are by nature more homogeneous and have more shared history. Low-context cultures tend to be more individualistic and heterogeneous, with multiple histories that were not shared. There is no pre-programmed memory of the system, so it takes more information to activate the system. The problem is that it increases the need for information handling, thereby increasing the mass and complexity of the system. The information must be explicit, verbalized, written down. Shared meaning and understanding take a lot longer and demand multiple explanations both verbally and in writing. These low-context cultures are more verbal and rely more on words and symbols to explain ideas and concepts. There is more likelihood of misunderstanding here; nonverbal behavior takes on less meaning or is misinterpreted. There is more documentation in these cultures, and the documents tend to be much longer.

As this relates to learning, the more we integrate heterogeneous cultures into teams of people who have to make collective decisions, the more low context we have to be. For example, as we implement a proposed paradigm shift, we must be low context at first. But eventually, to be maximally effective, we must consciously strive to become high context. This means sharing and discussing multiple similar experiences, sharing them in low-context verbal interactions, thus developing shared implicit codes and new myths. The more high context a team can become through initially low-context shared experiences, the more trust can develop and the more leaders will be able to foster growing collaboration, effective interaction, and having a different kind of dialogue. This is the best and most sustainable way to change the DNA in a system.

Collectivist Versus Individualist. This dimension refers to the general mentality of the people in an organization regarding the we-versus-me perspective. Many books are being written trying to help organizations get to the "we" perspective. To oversimplify, this means that when we make decisions, we make them with a focus on what's best for the group or organization rather than what's best for me and my career. Studies have shown that when the organization's mythos is that "we will be around forever," or, ironically, when there is more ambiguity and uncertainty in a system or less clarity of goal or purpose, people in all these situations will tend to make more self-serving choices. No amount of training, cajoling, therapeutic sessions, or rock climbing will change this to a sustainable collaborative culture.

Taming or Training the Elephant

Since the elephant is already in the house, we need an approach for using it to our advantage. The following steps can significantly strengthen the sustainability of educational interventions.

Step 1: Set the Organization's Strategy and Direction

First, you must determine the organization's strategy. Jay Galbraith's definition of *strategy* is "the company's formula for winning. The company's strategy specifies the goal and objectives to be achieved as well as the values and missions to be pursued; it sets out the basic direction of the company. The strategy specifically delineates the products or services to be provided, the markets to be served. And the value to be offered to the customer. It also specifies sources of competitive advantage and strives to provide superior value" (Galbraith, 2001, p. 10).

A warning here is that the old S.W.O.T. analysis model and asset-based strategy model are both too insular and internally focused. You must focus on the external opportunities and threats first. One of the dangers in using these models is that if you focus on what you have to offer first, you could be the best buggy-whip company in the world, but no one wants your product. The second reason is more insidious: you could get too caught up in your own corporate culture and beliefs, drinking too much of your own Kool-Aid. Remember that cultural beliefs are insidious. They tend to carry with them the nonobjective bias of superiority and optimism.

Also, forget the executive retreats that send a few executives off to write a mission statement and a value statement that will at best gather dust on the shelf or at worst become a joke inside the organization. (We have always thought that retreats are aptly named; we prefer to call what we do an "advance.") Getting buy-in from all stakeholders is a critical step, second only to determining the direction in the first place. You don't get buy-in by telling people; you get it by asking.

Step 2: Communicate the Strategy

Communicate the strategy clearly, concisely, and often. These sound bites must be stated the same way every time. Communication research has shown that just about the time you are tired of saying a particular message, people are just starting to hear you. Old research told us that people used to need to hear the same message three times before they let it sink in. We have learned that it is now up to five times. And if you change just one word of the message, you have changed the whole message. This is why educational programs need to use a common language among all sessions, courses, and facilitators.

If the strategy or direction changes, announce it as a change, and explain why. I am constantly amazed that so few people in an organization can articulate its strategy and direction.

Step 3: Position the Chief Learning Officer

The CLO or head of the corporate university must have a seat at the table and must be trained in how to listen for underlying problems and systemic issues. This also means that there must be an alignment between the corporate university and human resources. Note I said "alignment" between persons. There are many reasons that being both the HR person and the CLO could be a conflict of interests. There are an equal number of reasons that a lack of alignment between the two parties could paralyze the system.

Step 4: Assess the Current Culture

There are a few assessment instruments and tests available for culture assessment. Whichever one you choose, remember that what you are trying to find is the organization's mythos, its beliefs and values, its norms and rules. You are also looking to find out the complex answer to the simple question, "How does stuff get done here?" Anthropological assessment designs are best for this stage. Ask people to tell their stories about "how stuff gets done." Content analysis or narrative software can help you discover the patterns that exist under the surface of the obvious. We start to realize at this point that what we see at the surface does not get at the actual infrastructure of the organization's culture. That lies deeper, often at a level that is unarticulated. Several resources are available to help you at this point. I recommend no one single resource for all cases, but scanning the different models can help you determine which one will get at the real identity and the underpinnings of your organization. As a beginning, consider Cameron and Quinn's labor-intensive but excellent model appearing in *Diagnosing and Changing Organizational Culture: Based on the Competing Values Framework* (1999). You can also consult Kiely's *Creating an Intentional Culture* (2006).

For assessing how things really get done, you can discover and map sociograms of the actual paths of influence. The best resources for this are *The Social Life of Information* (2002), by John Seely Brown; *The Wisdom of Crowds* (2004), by James Surowiecki; and *The Hidden Power of Social Networks* (2004), by Robert Cross and Andrew Parker.

Step 5: Determine the Necessary DNA Changes

Get out of the dance and go to the balcony. Mine the appropriate data to find the patterns. After assessing the culture, determine which norms, values, beliefs, attitudes, and behaviors are going to enhance or obstruct the new learnings. Next, determine what systemic issues or structural design factors might be causing the behaviors we want to change or prohibiting those we want to introduce into the organization.

A classic example of this is one I ran into at a pharmaceutical company. The marketing vice president of the Americas called us in to help him strengthen his team of five to become the strategy team whose mission was to determine the direction that marketing should go in the future. He believed that he could no longer determine the trends without their input. Since they were the regional directors, they had the trending data and consumer information among them to make these collective and collaborative decisions. One look at the organization's structure told us it wasn't possible: these directors were all evaluated in competition with each other annually, very much by the theory of the zero-sum game. Every year the vice president measured the success of each region; only one region would be singled out to win the special prize, a trip to Whistler or Belize, but only one winner each year was selected.

When we told him there was no way we could turn these five into a collaborative team, he disagreed. They would be able to overcome the competitive nature of the reward model and collaborate when necessary, he insisted. But it was apparent to us that there was a system flaw built in that prevented their being able to collaborate with trust and good faith. When he still didn't see it, we conducted a 360-degree feedback instrument where the managers' superiors rated them, their subordinates rated them, and they rated each other. The superiors gave them a 4.5 on average out of a possible 5.0, demonstrating a great deal of faith in this group. Their subordinates gave them an average of 4.6, indicating very high trust. They rated each other at a 1.2! This is not an I'm-not-so-sure-about-you score. It is an out-and-out hostility score. A 1.2 means, "I don't trust you and I don't like you either." These scores were not earned because of the individuals themselves. They were caused by a system flaw that set up a lack of trust and a lack of collaboration.

It is important to remember that we get the behaviors we measure and reward, even when those rewards or reinforcements are subtle. Rensis Likert is reputed to have said that there is nothing good or bad about a group. A group can be a roadblock to progress, enforcing "group think" and conformity on its individual initiative. Under other conditions, a group can be a powerful synergism of talents, strengthening its members, speeding up the decision-making process, and enhancing individual and personal growth.

A serious word of warning, however: you can change the organization to be more efficient or productive and unintentionally destroy its heart. One way is by misunderstanding what is causing the problem. The politeness norm is a good example of a deceptive norm. It may look good on the surface, but it could have insidious undertones that cause dysfunctional behavior. One problem might be that the politeness is face-to-face only and people are behaving differently behind each other's backs. It could also be that the politeness and collaboration are sincere, but to a fault. We can be so much of a "we" culture that people are no longer able to disagree, causing a lack of innovation or risk taking. As a start, we like to use these three questions: What do we keep doing? What do we stop doing? and What do we change doing?

Step 6: Develop the Educational Programs

The curriculum or program design should have as its basic structure the changing or strengthening of the norms in the culture. To develop competencies without building the normative foundation is the tail wagging the dog. Again, the work you do will then stack up, but it will not add up. Even worse, no matter what you do, it will not be sustainable. This step has the following core substeps:

- Enlist a culture specialist to oversee the normative content of programs.

- Create a culture committee to oversee assessment and changes.

- Designate an integrator, and keep that person in place throughout. This can be the same person as the culture specialist.

This is another place where the corporate university model falls apart: too many program coordinators and no one person seeking to integrate and align all of the pieces. Nobody is looking at the whole picture. What usually happens here is that what was meant to be a culture-centric intervention becomes a catalogue of courses. Even if you are outsourcing all of the development and delivery of the programs, there should be one person who ensures integration of program content with the organization's strategy and direction; the new, emergent cultural norms; and the shared language among the various parts of the educational interventions. The integrator's role is also to create a new language; change the conversations inside the organization; and create new meaning, values, attitudes, and behaviors that adhere to the DNA of the culture rather than just in the intellectual databases of the participants.

Step 7: Vary the Methods of Delivery or Access to Learning

Learning is best accomplished by varying the methods by which to learn. Getting stuck on classroom delivery can undermine the sustainability of an educational intervention and seriously limit the ability to change the cultural norms. Thanks to a severely broken educational system, people are all too used to sitting, hearing, and forgetting. There are multiple methods that can be used, but two bear mentioning here as they relate to changing norms in a culture. First, it is best to build in real work experiences or applications that are accompanied by coaching and assessment. These experiences should be real and significant, not manufactured with an artificial purpose. Second, build ongoing learning communities or communities of practice with specific purposes and rules of engagement. The time spent in these communities needs to be focused on the application of the new learnings to real work situations. Having people just meet to discuss the abstract is a waste of time; moreover, the communities will break down, thus having a negative effect.

It is important to take people out of their comfort zone and their familiar context to learn new skills. The more you do this, the more the development is sustainable, and the more it changes the DNA of the organization. The best model for this type of educational intervention was designed by Duke Corporate Education (www.dukece.com).

Step 8: Build These Changes into All Educational Activities

Demand that each part of the program, whether experiential or classroom delivery, stay true to the common language and common cultural goals of the program. Get educators and consultants to communicate the strategy and work with each other and the culture committee to ensure alignment of content. Insist that educators and participants constantly connect the educational segments to the organization and ask what would need to change to be able to behave in this way. Hold the people involved accountable for staying aligned. This means a different type of evaluation from the typical smiley-face satisfaction survey done at the end of a "training" course.

Get regular feedback from the facilitators to see if there is anything going on that needs attention or should be rewarded.

Admittedly, this is time-consuming and complicated. But if you're going to spend the money and time, spending a little more time to coordinate effectively will ensure that you have accomplished something.

Step 9: Measure and Reward

Make the educational intervention become more sustainable by measuring, testing, and giving reinforcement along the way. For an excellent treatment on changing individual behaviors and ensuring sustainability, see Aubrey Daniels's *Bringing Out the Best in People* (1999).

In *The Corporate University Handbook* (2002), I proposed a new model for measuring the effectiveness and sustainability of educational interventions that goes beyond Kirkpatrick's well-known model of four levels to an eight-level model (for an indictment of typical measurement models and a proposed new model, see Kiely, 2002. Also see Chapter Seven, this volume):

Level 1: Participant satisfaction: Self-report measures of participant satisfaction

Level 2: Cognitive, acquired knowledge: Pencil-and-paper tests of multiple choice or essay to measure accumulated information

Level 3: Technical skill acquisition: Pre- and postmeasures and observations of specific, technical skill behaviors

Level 4: Attitude and perception change: Pre- and postnarrative design content analysis to demonstrate attitude and belief change

Level 5: Individual behavioral change: Pre- and postvideo or 360-degree evaluations (or both) using nonequivalent group design

Level 6: Individual behavioral change regarding application of new knowledge: Calculated return on investment on action learning projects to measure behavioral change and application of learning

Level 7: Critical mass change: Combining pre- and postdata within levels 1 through 6 to show cumulative and general results at each level

Level 8: Culture change: Triangulating measures of cognitive, attitudinal, and behavioral changes to cross-check reliability and validity of all three

Applying this model can provide a great deal of information about the usefulness of educational interventions.

Conclusion

Once again, we have met the enemy and it is us. We have been so caught up in our day-to-day work that we have failed to see the obvious: an elephant in the living room. It's big and it's pervasive. But if we acknowledge it, enlist it, and develop it, it will work in our favor. By designing and creating this intentional culture (Kiely, 2006), you can shift an organization in a matter of months rather than years with the least amount of disruption. Best of all, it will be sustainable, the organization will be nimble and successful, and people will thrive.

References

Brown, J. S. *The Social Life of Information.* Boston: Harvard Business School Publishing, 2002.

Cameron, K. S., and Quinn, R. E. *Diagnosing and Changing Organizational Culture.* Reading, Mass.: Addison-Wesley, 1999.

Cross, R. L., and Parker, A. *The Hidden Power of Social Networks.* Boston: Harvard Business School Publishing, 2004.

Daniels, A. C. *Bringing Out the Best in People* (2nd ed.). New York: McGraw-Hill, 1999.

Galbraith, J. R. *Designing Organizations* (2nd ed.). San Francisco: Jossey-Bass, 2001.

Hall, E. T. *Beyond Culture.* New York: Anchor Press/Doubleday, 1976.

Hampden-Turner, C. *Creating Corporate Culture.* Reading, Mass.: Addison-Wesley, 1990.

Harris, P. R., and Moran, R. T. *Managing Cultural Differences.* Houston: Gulf Publishing, 1991.

Hofstede, G. *Culture's Consequences: International Differences in Work-Related Values.* Thousand Oaks, Calif.: Sage, 1984.

Hofstede, G. *Cultures and Organizations: Software of the Mind.* New York: McGraw-Hill, 1991.

Houde, L. "Aligning Education with Business Strategies." *Chief Learning Officer Magazine,* Sept. 2005.

Kiely, L. S. "Overcoming Time and Distance: International Virtual Executive Teams." In W. H. Mobley and M. W. McCall (eds.), *Advances in Global Leadership.* Stamford, Conn.: JAI Press, 2001.

Kiely, L. "Measurement in Corporate University Learning Environments: Is It Gonna Show? Do We Wanna Know?" In M. Allen (ed.), *The Corporate University Handbook.* New York: AMACOM, 2002.

Kiely, L. *Creating the Intentional Culture.* Los Angeles: Libertas Press, 2006.

Schein, E. H. *Organizational Culture and Leadership* (2nd ed.). San Francisco: Jossey-Bass, 1992.

Surowiecki, J. *The Wisdom of Crowds.* New York: Doubleday, 2004.

Laree Kiely, Ph.D., CEO of the Kiely Group—Organizational Effectiveness Consultants—has over twenty-five years of experience consulting, researching, and teaching organizational behavior to businesses internationally.

She served as a faculty member of the Marshall School of Business at the University of Southern California for fifteen years, where she taught in the M.B.A. and executive education programs as well as served as director of the Center for Teaching Excellence. Prior to her appointment at USC, she directed technology services at First Interstate of California.

Kiely is the recipient of several teaching awards, including the Best Corporate Intervention award from the International Society for Performance Improvement; the USC Marshall School of Business Golden Apple Award for Teaching Excellence; and her course on "Negotiation: Plays, Ploys, and Pitfalls" was granted the Best Distance Learning Program for Corporate Development from IDLCON.

In addition to several papers and articles on business issues, Kiely is the author of "Measurement in Corporate University Learning Environments: Is It Gonna Show, Do We Wanna Know?" in *The Corporate University Hand-*

book; "Overcoming Time and Distance: International Virtual Executive Teams" in *Advances in Global Leadership, Volume 2;* and coauthor of *Taking Charge: A Guide to Personal Productivity* and *Everything's Negotiable.* Her award-winning program, *Managerial Communication: Tools for Leadership,* is aired regularly on PBS.

She received her B.A. and M.A. from the University of Colorado and her Ph.D. from the University of Southern California.

Mentoring is one of those functions that many companies are embracing. People who have had a mentor are grateful for the experience. Yet mentoring is often done on an informal basis, and its benefits are not maximized. I have heard Lynn Slavenski and her team at Equifax talk about how they have developed a mentoring process within their corporate university, and I knew that Lynn would be the best person to write this chapter and that Equifax would serve as the perfect case study. In this chapter, Lynn provides an in-depth discussion of mentorship and its benefits and describes the process she and her team implemented within Equifax University.

13

Mentoring Can Be Magic

Lynn Slavenski

ORGANIZATIONS TODAY ARE focused on growing the business. CEOs talk about it, books are written, and Wall Street demands it. Strategies are put in place in almost every company to achieve this goal, and talent is the key resource. Just as organizations want to grow, employees today also want to learn and grow and make a contribution. Management consultants at Boston-based consulting firm Bain & Co., have found that companies that nurtured their potential leaders averaged annual shareholder returns of more than 10 percent over a ten-year period. In contrast, the firms that in Bain's opinion placed little emphasis on cultivating leaders averaged returns of less than 1 percent a year. Mentoring is one of the most valuable and efficient strategies an organization has for developing its people.

The Corporate Leadership Council in 2001 did an extensive quantitative research project with over twenty companies on leadership and development strategies. Out of seventeen identified development strategies, mentoring was one of the top five, along with creating a development plan, interacting with peers, meeting with an executive coach, and the amount of decision-making authority. At Equifax we participated in the research study, and mentoring was found to be the third most important development tactic. Creating a leadership development plan was first, but this is also included in the mentoring program as an outcome. Table 13.1 shows the top ten tactics at Equifax.

Table 13.1. Importance Ranking of Development Tactics at Equifax

Specific Tactic	Type of strategy
1. Creating a leadership development plan	Feedback and relationship
2. Amount of decision-making authority	Experience
3. Mentoring	Feedback and relationship
4. Interacting with peers	Feedback and relationship
5. Meeting with a coach	Feedback and relationship
6. Feedback	Feedback and relationship
7. Working in new lines of business	Experience
8. Turning around a struggling business	Experience
9. People management skills courses	Education-based
10. Working in new functional areas	Experience

Note: The tactics are listed in order of appearance.

What Mentoring Is

A mentor is someone who will guide and coach. People can have many mentors during their career and even multiple mentors at one time. Mentoring relationships often grow naturally within and outside organizations. However, in a more formal, structured corporate mentoring program, mentors and protégés are matched, given specific roles, and usually a time limit for the official program is imposed.

Structured mentoring has these characteristics:

- Focuses on specific goals

- Has clearly articulated expectations for the mentor and the protégé

- Has planned activities to enable them to reflect and gain skills
- Includes evaluation

Structured mentoring is not:

- An opportunity for an experienced or higher-level person to tell his or her protégé what to do
- A one-way relationship that benefits only the protégé
- A perfect relationship without difficulty or challenge
- A relationship in which the experienced person always has the exact skill sets that the protégé needs
- A substitute for other types of learning such as e-learning, classroom, or personal networks

Mentors may be assigned to new employees to help guide them for a period of time. These mentors could be peers or others who provide the most basic information about the do's and don'ts not found in the official orientation or manual. Mentors assigned to new employees may also answer routine questions that save management time and make the employee feel more at ease in asking questions.

Mentoring may be used to grow high-potential talent within an organization, the topic of the balance of this chapter. In this case, a higher-level person is assigned to guide and develop the individual, usually over a specified period of time.

Potential Benefits of Mentoring

A key benefit is attracting key employees. Having a program in place sends a message that the organization cares about developing people, especially when these mentors are key officers in the organization. A mentoring program communicates a great deal about an organization's culture and the commitment of its officers to develop people. This also serves to attract people to the organization.

Besides attracting key employees, mentoring can help retain those with high potential. Assigning a mentor to a person is a signal that he or she is a key player. When people feel they are being invested in, they tend to stay. Even more specifically, protégés may share frustrations with their mentors that they don't tell their managers. Mentors can actually head off situations that could end up in the loss of a key person. Mentoring is also key in developing talent. Through a combination of feedback, exposure that they can give to the protégé, learnings that they share, and guidance that they give, mentors can help protégés to develop and move through the organization.

In addition to providing opportunities to acquire valuable skills and knowledge, mentoring involves the transfer of business-related social skills and political savvy within the work context. A mentor can help the protégé take calculated risks successfully to help this person grow and gain insight about his or her own behavior and its impact on others.

Mentors also gain. They often report that they learn more from their protégés than they think the protégés learn from them. Mentoring can provide insight for the mentor in diversity of thought across functional areas, generations, style, gender, and other topics. And since mentors are usually encouraged to teach through stories, institutional memory can be shared and passed on.

Thus, a good program can attract and retain high performers, improve job performance, reduce learning time, support knowledge sharing, and provide corporate socialization and networking. Mentoring helps the individual protégé, the mentor, and the organization.

Key Questions in Building a Mentoring Program

Each organization is different, but there are some key questions that always need to be asked when building a mentoring program is under consideration:

- Who needs to drive the program?

- What are the objectives of the program?

- Who is the target population of mentors and protégés? (This refers to the type and level of employees.)

- How will the protégés and mentors be selected?

- Should you use team mentoring? (In this, one mentor has more than one protégé, and they all meet together.)

- How many protégés will a mentor have at one time? (The number of protégés depends on the availability of mentors.)

- How long should the official mentoring period be?

- What will be the time commitment?

- What roles do you expect each person (protégés, mentors, managers of protégés, staff) to play?

- How structured do you want to make the process? For example, will they do a 360-degree feedback instrument or have a learning plan?

- How will you do the matching process? (How much and what kind of protégé input will there be, for example?)

- Do you want to use any computer-based systems for matching and tracking?

- How much distance mentoring should you do, and how should you manage it?

- What will be the plan if the pairs do not work or if the mentor leaves the company?

- How much instruction will you provide to mentors and protégés and in what form?

- How much tracking and follow-up will you do?

- How will you evaluate the program, and how often?

- What other opportunities will you offer the protégés, and for how long?

- What resources do you have to use for the following activities: selection of protégés and mentors, matching, materials development, or tracking and evaluation?

The Equifax Story

Equifax is a global information solutions provider with over $1.4 billion in revenues and 4,600 employees in thirteen countries. At Equifax, the CEO and chairman, Thomas Chapman, drove the mentoring program, which started in 1997. He deeply believed in coaching and mentoring key employees. He naturally coached his direct reports and often went down into the organization to coach others. He wanted to extend mentoring beyond himself to build a mentoring culture that would help develop and retain key talent, and he wanted it to be part of the "Equifax Way." In addition, he felt strongly that senior leaders needed to take responsibility to help develop talent for the corporation now and into the future. In fact, he expected all senior officers globally to be mentors.

Since he wanted the senior officers to drive the mentoring program, he asked them to kick it off in their areas. However, those of us in the corporate university who were administering the program learned quickly the second year that the kickoff needed to come from the CEO. Some areas did it well the first year, and some didn't. The program also did not have the cross-functional matches we needed to have.

Since the first year, Chapman has personally kicked off each program annually with a global conference call to all mentors, protégés, and their managers in the United States, Canada, Latin America, and the United Kingdom—about 150 people. The largest room at corporate headquarters is filled with people gathered around a huge table because Chapman wants to chat with them and feel close to them in the room and on the telephone. He talks about the importance of leadership and mentoring as a vehicle to develop leaders. Then past mentors talk about their personal experiences in mentoring. At the most recent session, someone asked how many officers had been protégés, and it was heartwarming to see how many hands were raised.

The Target Population

The target population is high-potential employees who are identified through the succession planning process. When we started the mentoring program, many protégés were vice presidents, but now the program reaches further down the organization, with protégés selected from the ranks of managers up to vice presidents.

Our mentors are at the very top of the organization: business leaders, staff heads, and their direct reports (senior vice presidents). The first year we had about a hundred people in the program: the officers wanted to get their key people in the program and they were also willing to mentor more than one person. We learned that this was a mistake: one protégé per mentor is plenty. This is especially true as a program continues over time. Now we limit it to fifty people globally. We have a potential pool of about sixty-five officers who could be mentors. Currently we have one mentor for one protégé and do not do team mentoring, where one mentor meets with a group of protégés.

One question I usually get asked is how we choose mentors or whether they volunteer. There is an expectation by the CEO that leaders need to be mentors, so we do not ask for volunteers to mentor. However, if we know someone cannot handle it in a year or can't do it this year, that is fine. We know that some officers are better mentors than others and have not asked all officers to be mentors, but we have asked most. At the beginning, when we had a lot of protégés, we needed almost all of the officers, and I learned that I don't always know who will be a good mentor. I thought the chief financial officer at that time would not be good in this role because he was not really a people person. In fact, he turned out to be great in this role. He took the program seriously and shared a wealth of information with his protégé. This experience helped me realize that a senior officer has something to offer, and if a more junior person has high potential, he or she should be helped to find this gift.

We outline these specific roles for protégés (the following excerpt is from Equifax's internal guidelines):

- *Take responsibility for meeting with your mentor at least 6 times during the program year and help them get to know you.* These meetings can be in person or by phone. The program also offers participants several activities that are designed to help you understand the areas where you need to grow. You are also expected to complete a short bio.

- *Learn about how others perceive you by taking an Equifax 360 Leadership survey and discussing the results with your mentor, manager, and employees.* The first activity/tool is the 360 Leadership Survey.

You will ask at least 5 direct reports or colleagues and your manager to complete the survey for you. You will also complete a survey on yourself. The report you will receive will let you know what areas of leadership you need to improve on.

- *Complete a learning plan and show some progress toward achieving it.* A critical part of the program is a learning plan. This process will help you start to plan out your career goals and how to achieve them. You can use the results from your 360 Leadership Feedback Report to help you create your plan.

- *Participate in offered learning activities*—any meetings or classes offered on-line or in person.

Another important person in this mentor–protégé relationship is the protégé's manager. The first time we had the CEO kickoff, we did not invite the protégés' managers. This was a mistake. These managers had sponsored the protégés, and therefore needed to be invited and informed as much as possible.

Mentor–Protégé Process

We give specific steps protégés can follow with their mentors at each meeting, and we give the mentor corresponding information. Nevertheless, these are just suggestions. We suggest a theme for each of the six meetings that they will have during the year (the following excerpt is from the company's internal guidelines):

1. Person

Meet with your mentor: Get acquainted and discuss "Who Am I?" Tell your mentor about your goals and expectations for the relationship. Discuss your background using your short bio. Talk about scheduling all the meetings for the year. *Get on your mentor's calendar!*

Use these discussion topics as a guide for the first meeting:

- The three most important strengths or skills you are currently using

- The most valuable parts of your education, background, or work experience

- The parts of your job that you most enjoy

- Your values and how they are reflected in your work

- Accomplishments you are most proud of

2. Perspective

At your second meeting with your mentor, use your 360 feedback report to discuss how others see you.

- Share:
  - How you think others within your organization see you.
  - Areas you feel are in need of improvement.
  - Ideas you have to enhance your reputation.
- Ask your mentor for suggestions for improvement.

3. Place

At your third meeting with your mentor, discuss the changes in the company and the world of work.

- Discussion topics:
  - Ask about the organization structure and trends.
  - Share where you think the most viable opportunities are for you.
  - Ask about the areas you think are growing.
  - Ask about the cultural dos and don'ts.
- Understand what information about the profession and industry you want to find out about.

4. Possibilities

In your fourth meeting, discuss what your options are. Review your possibilities:

- Consider a variety of options, including lateral and vertical moves.

- Share some of the options you are considering.

- Discuss obstacles and how to overcome them.

- Explain how you think you can enrich your current job—what you enjoy most and how you can increase what you enjoy.

5. Plan

At your fifth meeting with your mentor, you need to start designing a learning plan that will help you achieve your goals.

- Use your 360-degree feedback report and discuss the new competencies, skills, knowledge, or behaviors that you think you might need to achieve your goals.

- Discuss how you can get these skills and knowledge.

- Use ACE: assignments, coaching, education.

- Have your manager contribute to the discussion.

6. The Plan

By the time you have your sixth meeting with your mentor, you should have developed a learning plan to discuss and have presumably started on some activities.

- Go over the plan.

- Is it doable? Is it realistic?

Continuing the Journey

We remind participants that the learning from this process continues after the year is over. We tell them that their careers are just beginning and to take advantage of the contacts they have made, take action on their learning plans, and never stop learning and growing. They should schedule a few minutes every day to reflect on what has happened and plan for the future.

The mentoring period is set officially for one year. Many pairs have continued their relationship formally or informally past the year. However, mentors usually get a new protégé after a year, so the formal meetings diminish.

The requirement is to meet a minimum of six times, each for an hour. However, they usually meet from six to twelve times.

Protégés are expected to take responsibility to get on the calendar of the mentor. The first year, this was not clear. However, we also tell the mentors they need to be available. One clever protégé had a mentor who traveled a lot and was a business head starting a new business. He wanted to be a mentor, but they had difficulty establishing a time to meet. She volunteered to pick him up at the airport. She said it was wonderful. He was very prepared, and she had his undivided attention.

We at the corporate university provide some structure to the relationship, but in the end, each pair creates its own experience. Each protégé is asked to develop a career profile, do a 360-degree evaluation based on this, and have discussions with his or her mentor to put together a specific learning plan. The training also provides career development steps they can follow.

The Matching Process

There is a continuum of matching techniques in mentoring from self-matching (a mentor and protégé choose each other) to assigned matching. With self-matching, mentors and protégés may meet each other in a group setting and then propose matches. Programs are also available online where protégés select mentors who have entered their bios online; mentors can then accept or say they already have protégés.

At Equifax, we assign matches since this is part of a succession planning effort to build bench strength. We form a team of all the human resource consultants who meet with the manager of the protégé to discuss what the person needs to get out of the mentoring program—for example, exposure to another area, help with interpersonal skills, or understanding how to navigate the organization. The manager of the protégé can also propose a potential mentor. Then the team gets together and makes the matches. We consider the manager's thoughts but also determine what would help the overall business succession plan. We are very careful about matches with the most senior business leaders.

At first we did less cross-functional matching. Initially the senior leaders seemed to want to take care of their own. Now almost all the matches are cross-functional because the senior leaders recognize that this approach adds greater value to the organization.

Working cross-culturally is a challenge, but if the pairs want it to work, they will find a way. If they do not actually meet, we encourage them to make the relationship as personal as possible, for example, by sharing pictures of self and family. If they can meet at least once in person, the relationship works best. We do not fund this, but rather set up matches where we think this could happen naturally.

Not all matches work out, and sometimes the mentor leaves the company. Out of fifty matches a year, there have been about two or three each year that did not work out. In this situation, we usually match the person with someone else the following year.

Guidelines for Mentor, Protégé, and Manager

Doing a program globally and with high-level mentors has presented challenges. We do four things:

• *Guides.* We provide short guides for each person that define roles, actions, and timetables.

• *CEO kickoff.* The CEO kickoff, which lasts for about an hour and a half, sets the stage. The kickoff motivates, defines roles, provides the opportunity for officers who have mentored previously to share best practices (for example, by shadowing, introducing the protégé to other officers, inviting him or her to key meetings, reading key books together), and, most important, regains the commitment of the mentors.

• *Webinars and workshops.* We conduct a two-hour in-person workshop for those at corporate headquarters and a global interactive Webinar for remote participants. Mentors and protégés participate at the same time. In this workshop or Webinar, we explore the major steps of the career development process and the corresponding role of the mentor. Prior to the session, both take online tools that help them assess how well they perform in each of the career development areas shown in Table 13.2.

Table 13.2. Mentor Roles in the Career Development Process

Protégé's Career Development Area	Mentor's Role
Person: How am I?	Listen
Perspective: How do others see me?	Level
Place: What is changing in my world of work?	Look ahead
Possibilities: What are my options?	Leverage
Plan: How can I achieve my goals?	Link

Source: Adapted from The Career Power for Coaches Model from Career Systems International, A Beverley Kaye Company.

• *Newsletter.* A quarterly newsletter contains tips for participants' careers as well as where they should be in the mentoring process—for example, how many meetings they should have had and whether they have completed their 360-degree surveys.

The Twelve-Step Mentoring Process

The mentoring process looks like this:

1. Potential protégés are identified through our succession planning process.

2. A discussion is held with the person's leader or direct manager to reverify the program fit and determine what kind of mentor the person needs. Some managers may request a specific officer for their protégé. The local human resource consultant facilitates this process.

3. We conduct a matching meeting with all human resource consultants globally, the corporate university head, and the project person. At this meeting, we match mentors and protégés.

4. Mentors and protégés are informed of their match by e-mail and invited to the CEO kickoff. Managers and mentors receive notification before the protégés do.

5. Mentors and managers are asked to chat with each other about the objective of the match.

6. The CEO global kickoff is held about a month later.

7. A Webinar/workshop for mentors and protégés is held about two weeks after the kickoff.

8. After three months, the partners complete a short survey about where they are in the process.

9. Periodically the protégés get together to hear from key officers or discuss experiences.

10. We distribute a quarterly newsletter that contains reminders of where participants should be in the process, learning resources, tips, and other information.

11. We conduct evaluations midyear and at the end of the year through an online survey.

12. After the year is over, protégés continue to be invited to special events (for example, local presentations by key speakers).

Results

We measure success in three ways:

- Retention (through turnover)
- Growth (through promotion and movement rates)
- Satisfaction (through the midyear and final surveys)

Seventy-seven percent of the protégés have been promoted in a three-year period. Turnover has been 2 percent for people who have been through the program versus 10 percent for the organization as a whole. In addition, a high degree of satisfaction has been reported (Table 13.3).

Table 13.3. Protégé Satisfaction Survey Results

Satisfaction Measure	Percentage of Protégés Who Strongly Agree
Worthwhile program	94
Positive impact on career	72
Will definitely keep in contact	80
Rate experience from good to outstanding	90

Here are some sample comments from mentors:

"I took a very informal/semistructured approach to meetings. This (I believe) worked well!" (U.K. leader)

"Great program. My recommendation is that all protégés' names be tracked by HR to assure they will have the appropriate chance they deserve. I will continue supporting this program." (Latin America leader)

"I may have learned more than my protégé." (U.S. leader)

Protégés have offered these comments, among many others:

"I gained a relationship with a senior member of the Equifax leadership team, which provided me a safe environment to speak candidly and gain insight into the direction and behaviors of our leaders."

"I have gained greater insight and understanding of management at a senior leadership level. The program provided the opportunity to be privy to understanding the 'hows and whys' of some corporate decisions that are made. It also made me realize the importance of my role as a leader and the responsibility that comes along with it."

"The program is a great opportunity for an associate to gain insight from another level in their organization or even another area in our company. I think the exposure to the different areas and the world of the mentor is a tremendous learning tool. It is easy to think you know what roles people play in our organization until you have to actually see it for yourself."

At one time we tracked and monitored protégés' development plans. It became too time-consuming and ultimately the managers' responsibility. However, we are now considering some online products to help track development.

Lessons Learned

We have learned a great deal along the way. Among the lessons are the following:

- Too much structure (training, guidelines, paperwork) can suffocate all those involved. Too little structure can lead to less effective mentoring, poor communication, and protégés who put the responsibility on the mentor to make meetings happen or feel the program will solve all their career issues.

- Make sure you have true and visible commitment from the very top, especially if you want to use high-level executives as mentors.

- Put a clear limit on the number of matches you will make. This will make protégés feel special and also not let you overcommit yourself or the mentors.

- Monitor at the three-month mark to make sure there are no problems.

- Put time into the matching process but realize it will not be perfect. If protégés are high potentials, they will find a way to get exactly what they need.

- Finding out someone is not a high potential is important information.

- After the official program is over, continue to make protégés feel special. Give them the opportunity to attend special events (for example, local speakers). Even if they do not attend, they will know they are valued.

- Provide some opportunities during the year for protégés to get together with each other, at least in their locations. They like to meet and learn from one another.

- Not all protégés will put in the same effort, and that is okay. Organizations can give opportunities, but people need to take advantage of them.

- The managers are important.

- It will not be perfect.

Summary

If I had limited time and resources and could do only one development effort and if I had top-level support, I would do mentoring. Not only do the statistics say it works, but there are many side benefits:

- Mentoring tends to make the mentors better coaches to their own people and creates a culture of mentoring. It benefits the whole organization.

- It makes a huge statement to the entire organization about officer commitment to people and their development.

- Mentoring puts the responsibility for development in the hands of the protégé, where it should be. What they put into it, they will get out of it.

- Since the major cost is time, development continues even when hard economic times hit.

- The mentors will get as much out of this relationship as the protégés, and sometimes even more.

- This development takes place over time for the participant, but for the corporate university, most of the resource allocation is during the first two months. The process maximizes learning but minimizes corporate university resources.

When done properly, mentoring can be magic.

Lynn Slavenski, Ph.D., is senior vice president of global learning and organizational development and chief learning officer of Equifax University. She was formerly head of education and career development with Coca-Cola USA and head of training for Blue Cross/Blue Shield. She has experience in retail and government as well. She has done consulting for Bell South Enterprises, BellSouth Corp, the U.S. Department of Labor, Sanno Institute—Japan, Centers for Disease Control and Prevention, the American Red Cross, Prudential Bank, Georgia Tech, Fernbank Museum, Center for Puppetry Arts, and Campbell Soup. She was on the adjunct faculty of Mercer University in the business department.

Slavenski has published seventeen articles, including a chapter in AMACOM's *HR Yearbook*, and has given over forty presentations for professional organizations in the areas of assessment, performance reviews, career development, human resource planning, high-potential development and succession planning, culture change, mentoring, executive development, and corporate universities.

Slavenski has advanced degrees in career/organizational and human resource development and a doctorate in management. Equifax's training/education and culture change models have been benchmarked by HR Effectiveness, a leading national human resource database benchmarking organization, as well as many other companies.

She is a national board member of the Human Resource Planning Society (HRPS), former president of the HRPS Atlanta affiliate, former president of ASTD-Georgia, and former national head of career development for ASTD. She is on the board of Big Brothers/Big Sisters.

Merrill Anderson and I have crossed paths several times over the past ten years. When this book was in the planning stages, I came across an article that Merrill had written on the topic of executive coaching. This was an area that I knew next-generation corporate universities were getting involved in, and I was seeking a chapter and a case study on this topic. I subsequently discovered that Merrill had recently authored a book on the topic. When I contacted him, he readily agreed to contribute a chapter on executive coaching.

Fortuitously, he had recently completed a research study on coaching and had a great deal of current data. As a bonus, Merrill was also able to provide a case study of a company that had not only successfully integrated executive coaching into its corporate university but had also conducted a return-on-investment analysis of the coaching initiative that proved its value. In this chapter, he provides a discussion of executive coaching, the results of his research project, and a case study. He also shares strategies on how corporate universities can manage the executive coaching process.

14

The Strategic Contribution of Corporate Universities to Leadership Coaching

Merrill C. Anderson

LEADERSHIP COACHING HAS emerged as a powerful process to develop leaders in organizations. Coaching hit the corporate scene about fifteen years ago and has since expanded rapidly throughout the corporate world. Right Management Associates estimated the investment in coaching in the United States in 2004 was over $1 billion, with over 70 percent of Fortune 500 companies currently utilizing leadership coaching ("Corporations Using Coach Approach," 2005). Recent research conducted by MetrixGlobal and Linkage (2006) shows that this trend will continue or even accelerate.

MetrixGlobal/Linkage Coaching in Organizations Benchmark Study

The MetrixGlobal and Linkage Coaching in Organizations Benchmark study was designed to explore how leadership coaching is used and managed in organizations and to spot trends for the future. The survey was administered over the Internet in 2005 through invitations targeted to specific organization managers. The survey was completed by 216 people, two-thirds of them managers in learning, leadership development, coaching, human resources, or a line business function. The remaining respondents were individual contributors. Respondents were fairly evenly drawn from small (fewer than 1,000 people) to large (over 10,000 people) organizations. Some of the key findings include the following:

• Half of the survey respondents said that their organizations did more coaching in comparison to the previous year, while only 4 percent said that they did less. Looking ahead to the next year, three-quarters of the respondents said that their organizations would do more coaching, with a quarter of the respondents saying that this increase would be over 20 percent.

• Over 60 percent of the respondents said that it was extremely important that leaders become more effective coaches and that coaching becomes ingrained in the company culture. Accomplishing these objectives will be a long row to hoe. Less than 10 percent of the respondents rated their organizations as extremely effective in these two areas.

• In order for coaching to be successful and sustainable, it must be integrated with leadership selection and succession processes, according to over half of the respondents. Moreover, coaching outcomes must be linked to business outcomes, again according to over half of the respondents. And yet only 5 percent of the respondents rated their organizations as extremely effective in these two areas.

• Achieving strategic outcomes from leadership coaching in a sustainable way that delivers business value is the new agenda for internal learning and development functions. And yet currently, according to over one-third of the respondents, there is no centralized oversight or management of coaching. Only one-quarter of the organizations has a central group, such as human resources or a corporate university, managing leadership coaching. This is about to change. Over 40 percent of the respondents said that coaching will be more formally managed as a centralized initiative, while only 3 percent said that coaching will be less formally managed.

- The investment in building these centralized capabilities will be scrutinized, which opens up the topic of metrics. Only 15 percent of the respondents said that they currently evaluate the monetary benefits or return on investment (ROI) of coaching. However, 60 percent said that they expect to evaluate the ROI of coaching in the next two years.

Centralized learning and development functions, such as corporate universities, seem poised to play a pivotal and increasingly strategic role in managing leadership coaching initiatives. This will be a new journey for many organizations. It may be helpful to learn from one organization, a leading global professional services firm, how it embarked on this journey. Coaching began as a grassroots movement by several leaders. The corporate university of this firm channeled the enthusiasm and success of coaching into a major strategic initiative. Here is the story.

Transforming Coaching into a Strategic Initiative at Booz Allen Hamilton

Leadership coaching took root at this large, global consulting company in response to the development needs of individual leaders. Initially leaders who were interested in coaching contacted their corporate university or other sources to identify and engage a coach. At first, this approach seemed appropriate. However, as the number of coaching relationships grew and the firm's investment in coaching increased, questions began being asked about the business value of coaching. Most of the coaching relationships appeared to be successful. Several anecdotal stories floated through the organization about how leaders successfully applied what they learned from coaching to their work environment. There were also examples of where these relationships were not so successful. One of the challenges, of course, was how success was being defined. The personal success of the leaders being coached had to be balanced with the business success and the return the business was gaining from the investment in coaching.

It was clearly time for Booz Allen Hamilton's corporate university to step up and manage coaching as a business initiative. What was needed was solid information about how coaching was currently being done and the value it was adding to the business. Booz Allen Hamilton engaged MetrixGlobal, LLC to accomplish three activities:

1. Identify the current state of how coaching was being utilized in the company.

2. Learn directly from the senior leaders about their expectations for coaching.

3. Conduct an ROI study of coaching to demonstrate business value.

Identifying the Current State of Coaching

An e-mail survey was distributed to all leaders inquiring about their potential use of a leadership coach. The intention of this survey was to take a snapshot of how coaching was used in the firm. Also, by identifying the pool of leaders who were being (or had been) coached, the corporate university was in a stronger position to corral these coaching relationships into a strategic initiative.

The results of the survey revealed that leaders viewed coaching as a powerful developmental process. Coaching was rated as very effective by 86 percent of the survey respondents, and 95 percent would recommend it to a colleague. Over 80 percent of the respondents said that they significantly enhanced their leadership competencies through coaching. Although these results were promising, some leaders questioned the long-term impact and sustainability of coaching if it did not ultimately meet senior leader expectations.

Learning About Senior Leaders' Expectations for Coaching

Ten senior leaders in the firm were interviewed to gain their perspectives on and expectations for leadership coaching. These interviews were intended to provide the direction for the corporate university to manage coaching as a strategic initiative for the business. The better the coaching initiative met senior leader expectations, the greater the strategic value—and the perception of strategic value—that coaching would create. The senior leaders identified these top expectations from coaching:

- Increased productivity
- Retention of leadership talent
- Accelerating senior leader promotions
- Improved teamwork
- Increased quality of consulting services
- Increased diversity
- Increased team member satisfaction
- Increased client satisfaction

It was clear that sustaining coaching in the organization would require a demonstration that coaching was significantly meeting these expectations. Moreover, given the investment in coaching, it seemed important to show a return on this investment. A formal study of leadership coaching was planned and conducted. At the heart of this study was the set of eight expectations that senior leaders had for coaching. Each of these expectations would serve as a launching point to explore how leaders applied what they learned from coaching and the impact that these actions had in the organization.

Conducting an ROI Study on Coaching

Twenty-six of twenty-eight leaders in the target population were interviewed about their coaching experiences. These interviews honed in on how people applied their coaching to create value according to one or more of the eight value categories. When appropriate, this value was converted to monetary value, the effects of coaching to produce this value were isolated from other potential influencing factors, the total cost of coaching was tabulated, and the ROI calculated (Anderson, 2003). Specifically, respondents described specific actions that they took as a result of the coaching they had received. Then interviewers probed if and how these actions produced monetary benefits. If monetary benefits were produced, these were recorded for further analysis.

Respondents were asked to estimate, on a percentage basis, how much of the monetary benefit they would attribute to the coaching they received. This estimation isolates the effects of coaching to produce the benefit from other potential influencing factors. Next, they were asked how confident they were, on a percentage basis, in the isolation estimate that they made. This percentage value represents the error of the estimate. The lower, more conservative error value was used in the analysis.

Monetary benefits were discounted by the isolation and error percentages. For example, a benefit of ten thousand dollars with an isolation factor of 50 percent and an error of 80 percent would produce a benefit of four thousand dollars. The value of four thousand dollars is considered qualified after these discounts have been applied. Revenue increases were further discounted (by 35 percent) to factor out the cost required to produce the revenue. Therefore, only net revenue was considered in the pool of qualified benefits. Two extreme values (each totaling over a half-million dollars) were eliminated from the analysis (one from the team member satisfaction category and one from the quality of consulting category).

All monetary benefits were summarily reduced by an additional 50 percent to ensure a conservative set of monetary benefits. The intangible and monetary benefits were then probed according to the eight expectations of the senior leaders. Five of these expectations were realized by at least a third of the respondents:

• *Improved teamwork.* One leader, for example, cited improving teamwork as a key area of focus for the coaching, and she accepted her role in making this happen. Her coaching enabled her to be more aware of the impact she had on her team, and she was much more attuned to behaviors and reactions. As a result, she managed team meetings more effectively, and her team was able to accomplish more. She was also getting more buy-in on her ideas and proposals from peers and partners.

• *Team member satisfaction.* One leader said that he learned to consciously pay attention to individuals, to become a mentor, to make time for team members, and to accept that each person is different and there is no standard formula for working with others. As a result, he developed closer ties to people, especially with several high-potential and emerging leaders. Increased productivity and retention resulted from the higher team member satisfaction he helped to generate.

- *Increased retention.* One leader exclaimed that he didn't leave the firm because of his coaching experience. He was gratified that the firm was willing to invest in him. He described a situation whereby he had had "the rug pulled out from under me," but went on to say that the firm also provided him with a safety net: it was willing to pay for a coach. By working with his coach, he was better able to handle the twists and turns of his career. He credited coaching with keeping him in the firm.

- *Increased productivity.* One leader realized the impact that her poor communication skills had on her relationships with others: she was spending a lot of time rebuilding relationships. As a result of coaching, she became a much clearer communicator and better listener. These actions resulted in fewer mistakes and less rework by her team. She estimated that she personally gained at least two hours a week, and her team leaders gained at least four hours a week.

- *Increased quality of consulting.* One leader said that as a partial result of his coaching, he was able to open up a whole new venue of creating intellectual capital for the firm. His coaching enabled him to successfully interact with more senior-level clients. As a result, he positioned the firm for new areas of work and produced millions of dollars of increased revenue.

A total of $3.2 million in monetary benefits was identified by over 60 percent of the leaders. The total cost of the coaching was $414,000, producing an ROI for coaching of 689 percent. This ROI was impressive, but even more impressive was how it was delivered by realizing five of the eight expectations set forth by the senior leaders. Of course, this left three of the eight—accelerating senior leader promotions, increasing diversity, and increasing client satisfaction—as future opportunities.

Realizing these opportunities as well as continuing to drive business benefits from the other five sources of value required the corporate university to take a stronger hand in managing coaching as a strategic initiative. The corporate university was emboldened by these results to propose added investment for coaching. Recommendations were made to the senior leaders to support and enhance efforts to have the corporate university manage coaching as a centralized initiative. These recommendations included centralizing the management of the sourcing, qualification, matching, conducting, and evaluating of all coaching for the firm to achieve specific business objectives set by the firm's senior leaders. This coaching initiative was later recognized by an ASTD Excellence in Practice award.

Lessons to Draw from the Case Study

The case study shows how Booz Allen Hamilton blazed the trail that many other organizations are soon to follow. Four key lessons were illustrated about how to best leverage coaching as a strategic initiative for the business:

- Begin by understanding the current state of coaching in your organization.

- Capture the expectations of senior leaders for coaching.

- Demonstrate how coaching meets senior leader expectations and delivers a positive ROI to the business.

- Build capability and infrastructure to effectively manage coaching as a strategic initiative.

Understanding the Current State of Coaching

Coaching seems to spring up in many organizations as a grassroots movement. Leaders work with a coach, recommend coaching to other leaders in the organization, who then also engage coaches, and this cycle continues. At some point, the organization is sprinkled with many coaching relationships that represent a significant investment for the organization. Some centralized learning or leadership development functions may be tempted at this point to impose checkpoints or decision gates to approve all coaching engagements. However, gatekeepers control access; they do not create value.

The approach that the corporate university took in the case study example proved to be far more effective than gatekeeping. Their approach was to first understand how coaching was being used and the value that it was creating. What they learned was that coaching was more extensive than they imagined and there appeared to be a highly positive impact on developing leadership competencies. These findings begged the question about what value should be gained from coaching.

The corporate university was now in a stronger position to go to the senior leadership and, with a firm understanding of the current state of coaching, learn from the senior leaders in the organization about what they expected from coaching.

Capturing the Expectations of Senior Leaders for Coaching

Beauty is in the eye of the beholder, and in our case, the value of a coaching initiative is ultimately determined by how it is viewed by the senior leaders of the organization. A coaching initiative must not only deliver value; it must be seen as delivering value. Capturing senior leaders' expectations provides definition and clarity about how success for the coaching initiative will be defined. It provides a target for the corporate university to shoot for and suggests metrics that can be tracked.

In the case study example, the corporate university engaged a third-party evaluator to conduct conversations with each leader that were structured to gather quantitative as well as qualitative data. Rating scales enabled the expectation categories to be ranked according to perceived importance. Follow-up questions explored these expectations more deeply. When the results were fed back to the leaders, these conversations were used as additional opportunities to highlight common ground and create consensus about what can be expected from coaching. All leaders embraced the top eight (which were drawn from a much longer list) as their common expectations for coaching.

Demonstrating How Coaching Meets Expectations and Delivers a Positive ROI

As coaching has grown in popularity, the investment in it has increased accordingly. More and more, business leaders are asking about the return they are getting on their investment in coaching. Several ROI studies have shown that leadership coaching initiatives deliver 500 to 700 percent ROIs (Anderson and Anderson, 2005).

The ROI of the case study example was at the high end of this range. The monetary benefits were drawn from sources such as increased productivity and net sales, which have clear implications for the bottom line. As impressive as this high ROI may be, however, creating monetary benefits was not the reason that coaching relationships were initiated. The leaders being coached had their own reasons for engaging a coach, including building leadership competencies, improving the effectiveness of their teams, and collaborating better with their peers. Senior leaders do want to see that solid monetary benefits are being produced; however, they also want to see that these benefits are the outcomes of delivering the kind of value they expect.

In the case study example, the senior leader conversations revealed eight expectations that became the centerpiece of the evaluation. The ROI study served as the linchpin between the expectations and the value creation of coaching. The interviewing process enabled each respondent to explore and articulate his or her own story about coaching. Each coaching relationship was different, and each story of value creation was different. Collectively, these stories powerfully demonstrated how people applied what they gained from coaching to create value in their organizations. Categorizing these stories into the eight expectation categories demonstrated to the senior leaders how their expectations were being meet. These stories captured the hearts and not just the minds of the senior leaders. The $3.2 million in benefits and the 689 percent ROI were viewed as a credible and logical extension of the impact of coaching.

Managing Coaching as a Strategic Initiative

In the case study example, the monetary benefits and ROI clearly showed that coaching was delivering business value. The conversation quickly turned from leaders asking about the cost of coaching to inquiring about how best to invest in a more strategically positioned coaching initiative. This is the crux of the challenge: to make the transition from a collection of coaching relationships to a well-supported strategic initiative. Meeting this challenge does require investment to build the capability and infrastructure of the corporate university. Identifying potential coaches, qualifying coaches, identifying and selecting leaders to be coached, conducting sessions designed to facilitate the on-boarding process, monitoring progress of coaching, and a myriad of other activities all have to be supported.

The added strategic value of coaching more than compensates for the added investment in infrastructure. How valuable is increasing client satisfaction or increasing the diversity of leadership to better reflect the client base? These outcomes are valuable to the business. The real issue for corporate universities is not that they can create this kind of strategic value; it is that they don't make the case for the value they do create. In the case study example, the corporate university systematically built a powerful business case for increasing the investment in coaching. As a result, the senior leaders decided to increase the investment in coaching, and the corporate university was in a stronger position to maximize the strategic value from coaching.

How Are Corporate Universities Uniquely Positioned to Deliver Maximum Value from Coaching?

Given the trends revealed by the Coaching in Organizations Benchmark study, an important opportunity looms for corporate universities to manage the growth in coaching to accomplish strategic outcomes. These outcomes include ingraining coaching in leadership styles and company culture and embedding coaching in other people processes like succession planning. These outcomes have an impact on the entire business enterprise and are best addressed by a centralized function with a purview over the business enterprise.

Corporate universities and other centralized learning and development functions are well positioned to act on the four best practices identified in the prior section and deliver the strategic outcomes expected from coaching:

• *Corporate universities have strong relationships with the senior leaders.* Corporate universities are in the relationship business. While it may be tempting to think of them as primarily transactional in nature (delivering e-learning and student-days and processing a specified number of leaders through a program), it is the transformational capability that ultimately sustains a corporate university. Learning leaders must avoid the customer–supplier trap of meeting the stated requirements of the business leaders and elevate their contribution to meeting the underlying needs of the business. It is critically important for learning leaders to engage business leaders in conversations about root causes for business performance issues. Both leaders need to get below the symptoms to take meaningful actions that will improve performance. A learning leader who "just takes the order" for a learning program runs the risk of ill-serving the business leader and shortchanging the promise of a corporate university. A learning initiative may be effectively delivered; however, if the initiative does not improve performance, it will not be successful no matter how flawless the execution.

Over time, the relationship between learning leaders and business leaders deepens and grows. Learning leaders learn more about the business, and business leaders learn more about learning. Together both come to understand the contribution that learning makes to close part of the performance gap. In the case study example, the senior leaders and learning leaders clarified expectations for what coaching would contribute to the business. Eight specific areas were identified. The evaluation of coaching revealed that many, but not all, of these areas were addressed. Subsequent conversations between business and learning leaders focused on how to increase the strategic impact of coaching. Their relationship continued to deepen as they worked together to achieve shared business goals.

• *Corporate universities can integrate coaching into other leadership development initiatives and the overall leadership supply process.* The Coaching in Organizations Benchmark study revealed that while over half of the respondents felt that it was extremely important to integrate coaching with other people processes, only 5 percent of the respondents reported that they were extremely effective in doing so. There is a gap here, and it is a gap that corporate universities can bridge for organizations. Coaching can be integrated with the corporate university's other leadership development initiatives. For example, a leadership team development initiative can also include individual coaching with each of the leaders. This would enable leaders to better prepare to understand the team dynamics, anticipate potential issues, and more effectively contribute to the team process.

Coaching can also contribute to other people processes. For example, as part of the succession process, leaders can be selected for coaching to accelerate their readiness for promotion or added responsibilities. Leadership selection can be done in such a way to advance aspirations for a more diverse leadership team. Newly promoted or hired leaders can receive coaching to increase their near-term success in their new positions. All of these contributions are made possible by virtue of a centralized function that can more successfully integrate people processes.

• *Corporate universities have the infrastructure in place to manage the administration of a coaching initiative.* Corporate universities typically have in place the management and administrative infrastructure required to design, develop, and deliver a wide variety of learning initiatives. For example, intranet Web sites communicate new learning programs, learning project managers are in place to execute these programs, and processes are in place for vendor management and accounting program deployment. It is relatively straightforward then to use or adapt this infrastructure for a leadership coaching initiative. Web sites can be used to educate leaders about coaching and its potential, project management processes can be applied to the coaching initiative, and accounting and charge-back systems can be readily used.

• *Corporate universities can evaluate the impact and ROI of coaching.* Sustaining a corporate university requires articulating the business value that this centralized function delivers. Cost savings are important but generally not sufficient to make a sustained business case for a corporate university. Value delivered by the corporate university over and above the value that would be delivered by autonomous business units must be demonstrated. This takes us into the realm of ROI. Monetary benefits and intangible benefits are like two sides of a coin. It is important to tell both sides in the value story for business leaders. Intangible benefits, while perhaps more important than the monetary benefits, may alone not be enough to build a business case for coaching.

In the case study example, the corporate university presented a powerful business case for coaching by demonstrating the monetary benefits as well as the intangible benefits. The ROI of nearly 700 percent clearly delivered the message that coaching had bottom-line value. The senior leaders understood this message and viewed coaching as an investment in the business rather than a cost to be minimized. They quickly focused on how best to leverage coaching as a strategic asset and, working with the learning leaders, decided to make several investments in the coaching initiative.

The Coaching in Organizations Benchmark study suggests that leadership coaching will grow in organizations and gain greater traction. Coaching will be integrated with leadership styles and ingrained in the culture of the organization. Corporate universities and other centralized learning functions can play a pivotal role in making these strategic outcomes a reality. Indeed, corporate universities may be best positioned to achieve these outcomes. The success and sustainability of coaching in organizations may depend on how well corporate universities plan, manage, and administer coaching initiatives.

References

Anderson, D. L., and Anderson, M. C. *Coaching That Counts.* Boston: Elsevier Butterworth-Heinneman, 2005.

Anderson, M. C. *Bottom-Line Organization Development.* Boston: Elsevier Butterworth-Heinneman, 2003.

"Corporations Using Coach Approach." *Dallas Morning News,* Aug. 17, 2005.

MetrixGlobal & Linkage. *Coaching in Organizations Benchmark Study.* 2006. merrill@metrixglobal.net.

Merrill C. Anderson, Ph.D., is a business consulting executive, author, and educator with twenty years of experience improving the performance of people and organizations. He is the chief executive officer of MetrixGlobal LLC, a professional services firm that partners with business leaders to maximize the value of people and change initiatives. He has over eighty professional publications and speeches to his credit, including his latest books, *Coaching That Counts* and *Bottom-Line Organization Development.* Anderson was recognized as the 2003 ASTD ROI Practitioner of the Year, and his work with clients has been recognized as best practice by numerous professional industry groups. He may be reached at merrill@metrixglobal.net.

Jack Gregg is thoughtful as both a practitioner and a scholar in the area of corporate education. He has worked in the field from both the provider side (at universities) and the corporate side, most recently as the founding dean at Northrop Grumman's SPACE University.

Many organizations have developed career path models, usually within the context of the human resource function. In this chapter, Jack discusses how career path management is best done when coupled with curricular design, which makes a good case for career path management to be part of the corporate university's activities. Jack describes the plan that he and his organization developed for integrating career path management within their corporate university.

15

Career Path Management

USING STRATEGIC CURRICULA TO DEVELOP PEOPLE AND BUILD COMPETITIVE ORGANIZATION CAPABILITIES

Jack Gregg

THERE IS A COMMON THREAD in the major themes now emerging for the next generation of corporate universities: forward focus and learning accountability. How does the new corporate university add value to the firm beyond the simple metrics of attendance, percentages of courses completed, or cost efficiencies of class production? The focus has shifted away from the simplistic "how much and how many" to "who needs to be developed, and why is it important to the firm?" This change is not evidence of corporate altruism; it is pragmatic learning in its most essential form. Implicit in this new perspective is the shift from learner-driven to organization-driven learning process. This is not a subtle shift.

The old models of learning assume active ownership by the learner, an assumption steadily being driven out of the corporate university model. If Peter Senge's promise (1990) of the benefits of a learning organization is to be fulfilled, so goes the assumed logic, then the organization must take control. When it comes time to have that chat with your boss about next year's development plan, it is less about what you want to be when you grow up than what the company is willing (or unwilling) to do to remake you within the confines of the company's inventory of critical skills.

In many firms, it used to be generally accepted that the manager was ill prepared to advise his or her employees on professional development. To be fair, most managers have not been trained how to be organizational academic advisers. Their sophistication is not much better than the average high school career counselor ("I see you've taken four years of woodshop, wrestling, and water polo. Have you thought about a career as a graphic artist?"). But with the new shift to learning by design, these skills will soon change ("I see you have a rap sheet as long as my arm for stealing hubcaps and petty larceny. Have you thought about a career in local city politics?").

More to the point, the new manager will advise the employee based on a set of clear information about corporate strategic needs (critical skills) and measurable employee performance standards (capabilities). The comparison of organizational critical skills and an employee's capabilities yields an inventory of development options. But this gap analysis produces a potential list of learning experiences only for the employee. What of the needs of the company?

A career path approach takes the advising process one step further. More than just finding the learning gaps and scheduling available classes, this methodology begins by determining the skills and behaviors a typical employee needs in order to excel at a current position (remediation) or advance on a career path to a new position (growth and advancement). This curriculum may consist of a variety of learning activities that may include standard courses, university-based degrees or certificates, stretch assignments, and job rotation. Table 15.1 provides some examples of learning experiences other than classes that have proven to be successful in developing managerial competencies.

The shift in new process methodology is from fixing employee skill deficits to enhancing current strengths that align with a specific career development plan. Moreover, this plan is a standard approach for all similar employees. For example, a beginning carpenter who wanted to become a master carpenter would follow the same development steps to advance along a career path as every other carpenter. This is not a customized approach. At

---

Table 15.1. Learning Experiences That Drive Career Growth

Unfamiliar or new responsibilities
Proving yourself under pressure
Developing something new in the organization
Fixing inherited problems
Downsizing decisions
Dealing with problem employees
Delivering under pressure
Managing a complex organization
Role overload
Managing external pressures
Having to influence without authority
Adverse business conditions
Lacking senior management support
Lacking support from peers and others
Dealing with a difficult or incompetent boss

Source: Adapted from McCauley, Ruderman, Ohlott, and Morrow (1994).

the end of the day, some would become master carpenters, and others would not. But if the curriculum for the common career development path was rigorous and valid, those who would become master carpenters would be well qualified to do the job.

Linking Career Paths and Curricula

Career path management is a standardized approach to professional development driven by the strategic needs of the organization rather than the individual goals of the employee. Career paths are common curricula designed by the firm to define the scope and metrics of organizational learning for specific career goals. If you follow career path A, you will be qualified to become a project manager; if you follow career path B, you will fulfill the basic requirements for leadership; and path C might lead you to become a master carpenter. And because the career path curricula are defined, funded, and measured by the organization, they reflect both the long-term and annual needs of the company. If the long-range strategic plan calls for entering a new business in commercial finance, then career path F will support the organization's need to educate people to fill this capability gap. If the annual goal is to switch from manual slide rules to newfangled calculators, then this critical skill becomes part of the short-term annual plan and is integrated into the career paths that include this skill in the curricula.

An organization may define different types of career paths depending on the degree of complexity it wishes to impose on the development of its employees. Table 15.2 provides an example of several general career path categories. A firm may wish to subdivide these categories further into specific career paths to suit tactical needs.

Table 15.2. An Example of Career Path Categories

	Path	Description	Comments
1	S-path	Silo	Stays within his or her core process area
2	L-path	Leadership	Those with high potential or others in preparation for leadership role
3	X-path	Crossover	Supports moving from one silo to another
4	U-path	Update	Keeps current with job, certifications, etc.
5	A-path	Assimilation	New employee orientation
6	R-path	Rotation	Job rotation support
7	Z-path	Nonspecific	Designed with specific short-term objectives

Linking Career Paths and Employee Desires

One way to create a draft set of training paths is to listen to employees through a simple survey. Table 15.3 shows how employee desires can be mapped to existing career paths.

Table 15.3. Linking Career Paths to Employee Desires

What Employees Say They Want at Work	*Suggested Career Path to Help Them Get There*
Advancement	L-path
Skills proficiency	S-path, U-path
New challenge at work	X-path
Explore new options	R-path

From the perspective of the company, there are the benefits of focused funding around strategic critical skill development (for example, no more M.B.A.s for cafeteria workers who really want to be something else). From the employee perspective, there are limits to learning. The ambitious cafeteria worker who aspires to greater things must now fund his M.B.A. on his own.

In a large, complex organization where everyone is assigned to a career path, the benefits must be balanced with the risks. For a mature firm in a stable business sector (for example, transportation, city government, manufacturing, retail), the notion of a clearly definable career path is a clear way to add value to new or potential employees who are looking to establish a career through educational opportunities. Such organizations often operate in an environment of collective bargaining and can leverage career path learning with union contracts as a way to benefit worker job value beyond the standard suite of salary and benefits.

For a firm that operates in an environment of continuous change and innovation (such as high tech, entertainment, engineering, and advertising), the critical skill sets of an employee may change rapidly over time. This means an employee who starts out on a career path may find that his or her curriculum requirements have changed because the career goal has changed due to customer demands, market competition, technology, or economic shifts. For example, the introduction of power tools would alter the content of a curriculum for a master carpenter just as the introduction of desktop spreadsheet software has altered the career requirements of a certified public accountant or an accounts payable clerk.

Traditional university curricula have dealt with the unpredictability of change in content by building electives into the mix. These elective courses act as variables in the equation and allow for course corrections along the career path. The corporate learning environment has more flexibility and can simply redefine a career path at any time. The consequences of this are less than at a university, where a course catalogue acts as a contract with the student. The company has only the obligation to publicize the change and recast the career path curriculum around the new operating goals.

Implicit is the notion of a long-term commitment to employee development. Once a structure of career paths is in place that defines the organizational advancement options for everyone, there is an implied agreement that if an employee embarks on a career path, he or she will be able to claim rudimentary competency for a new position. This is not to say there are any guarantees—such decisions are always left to managers to determine—but the company is now on the hook for supporting the career paths it wishes to strategically promote within the organization. This is a considerable financial and political commitment.

This commitment comes in the form of a recurring learning budget to support courses, learning and development for organizational staff, and the career path process itself. A mistake would be to assume that once a structure is designed, developed, and implemented, there is little left to do. Support of the career path approach bears organizational costs that add to the corporate university's operating overhead. Even if supported by a comprehensive learning management system, these costs appear as ongoing development charges to refine, redesign, and measure outcomes on an aggregated curricula level in addition to the singular course level.

It is this additional financial burden that may inhibit a fully comprehensive career path model. Instead, a targeted approach of specific curricula for specific key job categories may be used to phase in the career path process. In this way, short-term pilot outcomes and administrative costs may be measured against expectations.

Research on Career Path Models

Surprisingly, there is little formal research specifically applied to the topic of developing a career path model in complex organizations. A literature review of this topic reveals only the most cursory information about the nature of career path development. Less attention is devoted to the actual methodology.

Some earlier work on organizational effectiveness suggests that development of adult learners is best supported by a two-pronged approach that involves both the employee and the organization (Bass, 1990). Gaertner (1988) suggested that a career should conform to and align with an organization's strategic focus. Furthermore, there is evidence that career growth is augmented by the employee's license to move relatively rapidly and regularly within the organization. This freedom of mobility and development is often a precursor to a position of leadership (Veiga, 1981).

Van Erde and Thierry (1996) revisited Victor Vroom's early work (1964) on developing an expectancy theory model and concluded that motivation for organizational success is dependent on a combination of three factors: (1) the worth or value the individual places on the expected outcome (valence) of the learning experience, (2) the employee's assessment of the likelihood that the energy invested in the learning activity will lead to the expected deliverable (instrumentality), and (3) an employee's measure of his or ability to perform to expected levels of success in the task (expectancy) once the learning activity is complete. As applied to career path management (CPM), this model defines a learner's self-efficacy or the confidence he or she may have to complete a given career curriculum (Stajkovic and Luthans, 1998).

Similarly, goal theory holds that specific (learning) goals will lead to higher levels of workplace performance than generalized goals. This suggests that the more explicit the nature of the curriculum developed in the CPM is, the more likely it is that the outcomes will have real impact on the organization and the successful career growth of the individual learner (Locke and Latham, 1990). Even more significant is the research about the degree of difficulty of curricular goals. Donovan and Radosevich (1998) concluded that the greater the learning activity stretch is, the greater the learning is. In short, they found that "performance generally improves in direct proportion to [learning] goal difficulty" (p. 309). This no-pain-no-gain approach goes directly to the heart of the critical importance of infusing rigor in corporate curriculum development. This is especially true in the case of leadership development.

What follows in this chapter is a result of conversations with other practitioners and members of the consulting community who toil in this field. There is, of course, a great deal of additional research on the components of this discussion, such as curriculum development, assessment, the employee review process, and the role of the organization as an instrument of strategic learning. It is not the purpose of this chapter to recapitulate this reference list but rather to validate and define the need for more formal career path research as a next step in the evolution of this discipline.

Getting CPM Under Way: The Assessment Process

The CPM starts with a series of needs assessments: (1) the initial career survey assessment for the firm that defines the scope of career paths to be developed and supported, (2) the long-range strategic assessment of critical skills needed to compete in the future marketplace, (3) the annual tactical competency assessment that defines the firm's ability to deliver products and services to customers today, and (4) an employee performance assessment that provides data about workforce ability. Workforce ability can be defined at the unitary (individual) level, the department or center level, the division level, and, finally, aggregated across the firm.

It is important to keep this multiple perspective in mind in the initial stages of design because at some point, it may be important to consider developing one division differently from another, or one department within a division differently from another within the same division, or even developing individuals differently within a specific department. Furthermore, from a companywide perspective, knowing the full breadth of workforce capabilities may provide additional insight into the firm's ability to enter new markets, the need for specific recruitment tactics, and even the degree of redundant skills or out-of-date skills that have an impact on overall workforce cost inefficiencies. (Although these data could well be used as a basis for building a layoff list, this is not the intent of a career path assessment process.)

Initial Career Survey

The assessment process can be thought of as a series of concentric circles (see Figure 15.1). The outer circle is a contextual assessment that should be done early on to clearly define the setting or environment of the other assessments; this is the organization's long-term strategic drivers. This high-level exercise should not be concerned with the actual curricular content of the career path. This initial phase is less about the actual content in the learning plan than about defining the learning outcomes (in terms of career objectives) that the learning process will support. As we move toward the center of the circle, we factor in short-term objectives and finally individual competencies and gaps. Figure 15.1 illustrates this taxonomy.

Figure 15.1. A Taxonomy of Learning Objectives

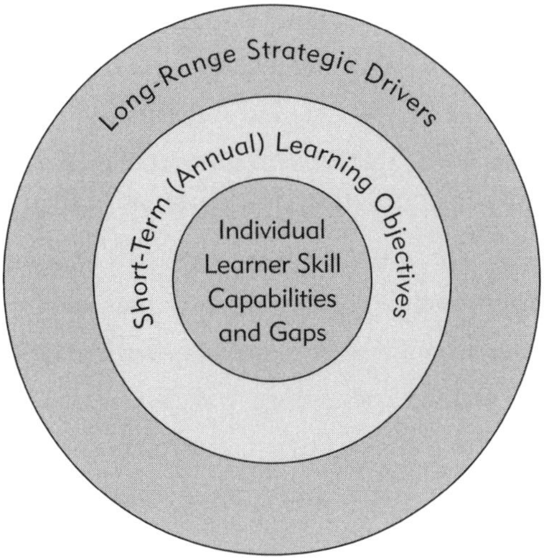

For example, a professional services consulting firm may start by cataloguing an array of career goals for employees. In this case, these career paths may include a wide range of positions, from full partner to technical support, with a variety of specialties and intermediate steps defined. To become a partner in the firm, there may be several positions (mailroom clerk, associate consultant, senior consultant, and so on) that an employee has to master first, each one representing a career path. The goal of this initial organizational assessment is to catalogue an inventory of possible career paths and decide which of these paths are to be supported by a curriculum. In the example, the decision to support a career path for a senior consultant may be easy, but the decision to support a career path for a full partner—or a mailroom clerk—may not fit with the financial goals or the political ethos of the organization.

Strategic and Tactical Assessments

After the initial career path inventory is established, it is time for operational assessments. These are in the form of the strategic assessment and the tactical assessment. The strategic assessment may be driven by a document such as the organization's long-range strategic plan. This document outlines the future state of the business and is valuable for the career path exercise because the future capabilities needed to run the business may not be in place today. Typically a company's long-range strategic plan may not provide an easy-to-find list of skills, but it will set out a general road map to defining these skills. If the nature of the skills needed to compete in future markets cannot be clearly defined, it will be difficult to teach to these skills. Thus, as the career path is outlined and defined, there will be some elements that can be provided with internal resources, some that will be better provided by external providers, and other elements that may be harder to define or provide at all.

The tactical assessment is easier in scope but still time-consuming. The result of this exercise is to gather a comprehensive picture of the critical skills needed to run the business today. This assessment may be executed as a demand survey for current courses offered. If the current inventory of courses is limited, then the needs assessment will have to be designed from the bottom up with attention to identifying what is necessary to train or replace the current workforce.

Employee Competency Assessment

The last assessment is of the employees themselves. By this time, a solid grasp of both long-range and short-range learning requirements will have been defined, and this list may be used as the benchmark by which employees can assess their competencies. This can be a simple self-assessment where the employee rates himself or herself on a Likert scale ("expert," "very competent," "competent," "need competency training"). Given the shortcomings of self-rater data, it may be advisable for the employee's skills to be rated by his or her direct supervisor. Figure 15.2 shows the relationship of the assessments with each other and how gaps emerge from the survey findings. It points to how the interrelationships among long-range critical capabilities, short-term skill needs, and employee/learner capabilities help to define the learning gaps.

Figure 15.2. Identifying Learning Gaps

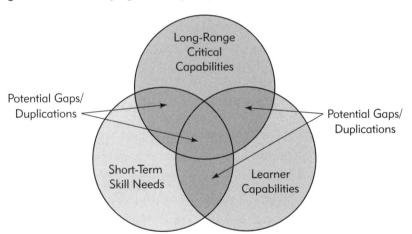

A Pilot Program

The assessment process can be quite daunting the first time. Since it is important that assessment take place annually, the costs associated with the process should be built into the annual corporate university budget. It is advisable that the initial round of assessments be done on a very manageable (small) scale. It is far more manageable to identify only one or two career paths that seem likely to have some impact on the firm. This review may be against the initial career path inventory assessment for the firm. Then, with these career paths in mind, assess the long-range strategic plan and the annual operating plan for future and current skills needed to support these plans. Next, create a straw-man or draft curriculum based on findings from the two needs assessments. Finally, select a target segment of the workforce that is likely to follow the chosen pilot career paths and assess their skills against those identified in the draft curriculum.

It may be worthwhile to speak directly to the role of mandatory training and required certifications in this process. Many organizations devote a significant percentage of their annual training budget to mandatory training and certifications, including environmental health and safety training. This will take place with or without the CPM. As a result, the career path should be designed and developed separately from mandatory training interventions. This segregation of learning content will also keep associated costs separated so that the true financial accounting of the career path can be tracked and analyzed with minimal influence by other training initiatives.

How CPM Benefits the Organization

At this point, it might be worthwhile to ask why an organization would want to go through this meaty process. Even more important, why would a corporate university take on the management of a comprehensive career path model for the firm? Just because someone identifies a potential learning activity doesn't mean that it necessarily fits with the purpose or direction of the corporate university. There are lots of learning activities that take place without the help of the corporate university. For example, does the corporate university support all assimilation for new employees? Maybe. Is the corporate university responsible for leadership development? Yes. Does the prep cook in the company cafeteria take a class through the corporate university if she wants to become the head chef? No. These issues are a matter of scope. Each company may approach the scope of the learning and development function differently, but the unifying theme of what makes a corporate university differ from a simple training department is how development is valued within the firm. The more that learning and development is considered central to the core mission of the firm, the more likely it is that the franchise of the corporate university will be strategic.

Organization development refers to enabling the growth of the enterprise. This differs in perspective from individual development in the way the value of learning is expressed. Individual development puts the employee first; organization development advocates for the firm. It is a matter of priority and expected return on the learning investment made to make the organization more competitive and viable to shareholders.

Organizations develop in different ways for different reasons. Among those reasons are regulatory compliance (mandatory training such as environmental health and safety certification), changing economic landscape, employee recruitment and retention drivers, and new business initiatives. These are all good reasons to support organizational learning with an organized learning and development (L&D) operation and a corporate university. But none of these reasons is altruistic. None presumes that the development of the individual comes first.

What seems clear now, as corporate learning finds its place more securely entrenched in commercial organizations, is an emerging view of the internal L&D organization as a partner. This partnership identifies local internal customers within the organization and then develops and provides accessible learning to that internal customer base. This often occurs as knowledge management, succession planning, new employee assimilation, organizational change process, leadership development, career path management, employee professional development, and university relations. The corporate university may play an active role in some or all of these activities as the facilitating arm of the L&D strategy, or it may exist in parallel to these other activities. Either way, the modern L&D view is one of multiple constituents centered on development: organization development, individual development, or both. Career path development is an example of an initiative that develops the individual and the organization together.

Beyond the internal partnerships that exist between the corporate university and the internal customer base, there are other external relationships that the corporate university often brokers: partnerships with local universities and colleges and vendor relationships with content providers and with contract labor who may assist with course development, instruction, or special projects.

More Than Just Course Work and Traditional Classes

In building robust and rigorous curricula for strategic career paths, several forms of learning interventions can be used to populate the model in addition to the more conventional instructor-led training courses traditionally offered at most firms. E-learning courses, either developed internally or provided as part of a vendor contract with a provider, can also be mapped to the critical capabilities identified for the career path curriculum.

Beyond courses, either instructor-led training or e-learning, there are stretch assignments, special projects, conferences, job rotation tracks, and even on-the-job-training that can, and should, populate the curriculum map.

A Note on Team Development and CPM

This discussion has centered on the process of developing the individual in an organization. The CPM process may also be applied to group or team development, an approach that may be especially effective when a special project team is created to solve a technical problem, launch a new product, or enter a new market. This is a specialized application of CPM and involves a customized developmental curriculum. The primary focus of this chapter is CPM as applied to individuals, not groups or teams, within an organization.

A Case Study at Northrop Grumman

This case describes a process to create a plan in order to implement a CPM model in a complex organization using a multiphase approach. The case outlines the key design decisions in the process. Some elements of the plan have been edited and modified in order to focus on the key learning opportunities. This case is intended to represent a work in process to avoid any disclosure of or reference to proprietary information about the organization.

The narrow focus of the case around building a working plan is a way of demonstrating and validating the time-phase (gradual step-by-step) implementation approach. While it is tempting to overengineer the career path model, it may be best to isolate one or two discrete career path curricula for the sake of working through elements of definition, design, implementation, user acceptance, and assessment metrics. Once the pilot career paths are launched, there will be enough institutional learning in place for the career path team to intelligently chart the next phases of the implementation rollout.

The Organization

Northrop Grumman Space Technology (NGST) is a sector of Northrop Grumman Corporation, a Fortune 50 international engineering-driven technology firm of approximately 130,000 employees worldwide. Its primary business areas are satellites and other leading-edge defense-related technical and scientific applications.

The commercial scientific and engineering environment is highly competitive for top talent, and firms like Northrop Grumman Corporation and its NGST sector are in a constant talent war for practitioner scientists and specialist engineers who can bring highly prized talents to their workforce portfolio. The combined pressures of pending baby boomer retirements, increased international competition for engineers with up-to-date technical skills, and the much publicized acknowledgment that engineering schools are incapable of supplying the huge demand for these specialists has elevated the topic of talent acquisition and employee retention to the top of the list for many presidents and CEOs of technology and engineering organizations. In addition to these industrywide issues, NGST learned from employee polls that it was losing employees who were dissatisfied with the lack of clarity provided by NGST about how success was defined and what future career prospects existed.

NGST's workforce consists of approximately ten thousand highly educated individuals, including nearly five hundred Ph.D.s and several thousand specialists with master's degrees. This division was acquired by Northrop Grumman Corporation within the past five years, and enterprisewide corporate learning policies were not fully established. One of the new directives of the corporate office was to slow the high turnover rate of highly specialized technical talent who were often wooed and poached by direct competitors in the sector's market space.

Background

Recruitment and retention of employees wasn't the only reason the project received a green light from senior management. NGST had long held sway as the place to go when nearly impossible high-tech solutions needed to be created and turned into practical applications. Before acquisition by Northrop Grumman Corporation, the legacy company managed this well, but after acquisition, the business model shifted from one of a supplier to that of a business integrator. Now NGST was expected to work with suppliers, customers, and strategic partners as the prime contractor. The name given to this new business mind-set was "Major Prime." Other competitors had already moved in this direction, and NGST needed to make the shift to a Major Prime culture in order to keep up and compete in the new market arena. The lack of clearly defined career paths put talent in dead-end stovepipes that inhibited senior management's ability to leverage talent across the sector.

Furthermore, NGST was experiencing the same problems as many other knowledge-worker-dominated organizations. Most companies in a broad variety of economic business arenas struggle with such questions as how noncore specialists feel valued and achieve successful career growth so that they want to stay and contribute their talents to the organization.

In law firms, it is the attorneys who become partners, not the administrative staff. Likewise, in large professional services firms, it is the consultant, not the technical support person, who has the fast track to senior partnership. In the health care industry, the advent of managed health care created a dual track to senior leadership where both physicians and those with an M.B.A. might obtain the corner office—still with a preference for the physician executive. In higher education, leadership at all levels requires time spent in the classroom and the doctorate. It is rare to find a university president who has advanced from a purely administrative career.

Aspiring managers and leaders in specialist-centric organizations such as these want to know if they should invest time pursuing a career with a firm that is not likely to promote them to their full professional aspirations. Ambitious high-potential employees no longer settle for vague promises that "cream will rise to the top." They want to know if there is a defined career path that will get them where they want to go.

NGST was no different. As a technology and engineering firm, the business was traditionally led by engineers, who moved up the ranks into administrative and leadership roles. Engineers were like the lawyers, doctors, and deans, as in the examples above, who had a clearly assumed line of sight to the top of the organization chart in other arenas. But what of the others at NGST who were not engineers? Were they out of the running? Where were their career paths? And if there were no clearly defined career paths to the top, then why should the best and the brightest stick around?

Choosing an Approach

At NGST there were several options in considering a course of action to create a career path model. The first option was to create a comprehensive map of career path curricula and turn the key to start the new process activities all at once. The second option was to choose a few strategic career paths and implement them as a pilot program. The third was a hybrid of the first two options: a time-phased rollout of career paths where a universal map would be created and then a selected set of career paths would be engineered and implemented over the course of the rollout. The third option was chosen so that there would be some sense of continuity and commitment for the project over time in terms of funding, staffing, technology, support, and other resources.

At the time of the initiation of this project, there were some significant resource limitations placed on the project. At NGST it was assumed that in order to adequately track and manage participants on multiple career paths, a robust technological infrastructure would be required. For firms with a learning management system, this capability would be present and adaptable as part of the support element of the project. Unfortunately, this was not the case at NGST at the beginning of the project. This shortcoming was one of the primary resource constraints on the forward momentum of the project. Further risks identified as potential inhibitors to success included unclear notions of benefits by senior leadership in the core internal customer areas, an overburdened CPM project staff, and loosely defined benchmarking that caused some concern about the full skill set needed to accomplish the project.

Nevertheless, human resource (HR) leadership had the foresight to see how creating an executable CPM system would create clarity of expectations around the fundamental relationship between the individual employee and the organization in the long term.

Defining a Process

NGST is a process-driven organization and a dedicated subscriber to Six Sigma methods. This means that it is imperative to the operational success of NGST that clear processes be in place so that everyone, from internal suppliers and stakeholders to internal and external customers, knows how the process works and who is responsible for making it work. A person who is responsible for the care and feeding of a process is called a process owner. Process owners reside at all levels in the organization (not just managers are process owners), and the greater the clarity of the process, the less opportunity for extra cost of execution or for unanticipated or immeasurable outcomes. Thus, at the beginning of the CPM project, it was generally recognized that the process to define and manage career paths was at least as important as the actual career paths that may be developed.

The plan was to begin with a series of assessments that would collect data in three dimensions necessary to build the model: an assessment of critical skills needed to prepare the workforce for future initiatives (strategic assessment), an assessment of capabilities needed to accomplish current commitments (tactical assessment), and an assessment of employees' mastery of these skills (competency assessment). A comparison of these assessments would yield a gap analysis that would result in a road map for development activities.

A key mapping element of the Six Sigma methodology is simplistically characterized by the SIPOC model: supplier, input, process, output, customer (both customer and supplier may be internal to the firm). In essence, this model says that if you know what your customer needs and the capabilities of your suppliers, then you can define and map the inputs and outputs to the process. At the core are the actual process steps. What makes this model significant is that it creates a standard approach to process definition and straightforward metrics for success, and it acknowledges that the process resides in a greater environmental context that integrates with other processes (other SIPOCs). For the CPM process, the customers were defined as shown in Figure 15.3.

Figure 15.3. SIPOC Model

Suppliers	Inputs	Process	Outputs	Customers
Senior management	Long-term goals		Long-term capabilities	Senior management
Division management	Annual goals		Yearly training needs	Division management
Business management	Financial constraints		Financial accountability	Business management
Department management	Learning gaps identified		Skill gaps closed	Department management
Employee	Development needs		Development fulfilled	Employee

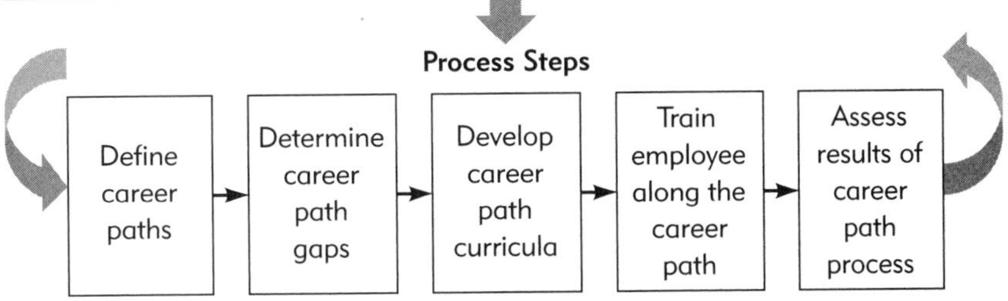

Process Steps

Define career paths → Determine career path gaps → Develop career path curricula → Train employee along the career path → Assess results of career path process

As Figure 15.3 shows, often the same stakeholders are both suppliers to and customers of the process, as is the case here. Employees and managers supply inputs to the process and are also often the customers of the process outputs. Inputs are the needs of the organization and the individual. Outputs are changed behavior as a result of learning or other developmental activities. The process is essentially a gap analysis driving curriculum development activities.

After the SIPOC is defined and the needs assessment data are reviewed, several pilot career path curricula models are selected that best suit the stated long-term career development goals of NGST (recall Table 15.2). From the plan, it was determined that the S-path (the silo path that promotes a career path within an employee's given area) and the X-path (the crossover path that allows for growth outside of an employee's area) would be developed first. These were chosen to test the efficacy of the process.

Mapping Capabilities to Content

The next step is to create a capabilities inventory for the career path template selected as the basis of the pilot. The purpose of clearly defining a capabilities inventory for each career path is to create a robust view of the skills needed to function in the organizational role. NGST's plan was to begin the curriculum development process with a clear vision of what the curriculum would support: the potential new role of the employee after he or she completed the career path.

The pilot career path is the S-path, or silo path. Specifically, it was a career path for career growth within the HR enabling function: the HR manager career path. The career path is defined by the role that represents the outcome of the CPM process. In this case, the question asked was, What capabilities are needed to qualify someone to be an HR manager?

At this point it should be noted that not all capabilities are substantiated by typical educational interventions. Mainstream education theory supports the notion that learning can have an impact on behavior change. In other words, if an identified skill or desired capability is a recognized behavior, then someone can be taught how to modify (improve or learn) that behavior. There are some career path capabilities that may be initially identified that will end up outside the ken of an executable curriculum. For example, capabilities that are more accurately defined as talents, attitudes, values, intuitive process, and so on are generally not trainable. If these are identified as part of an inventory of potential capabilities, then they may be best omitted from a structured career path curriculum. Table 15.4 lists the typical capabilities needed to fulfill the role of an HR manager at an average U.S. firm.

Table 15.4. Capabilities for a Human Resources Manager Matched to Curricular Elements

Role Learning Objective	Curriculum Activity Element
Able to execute annual employee review process	1. In-house course ABC 2. Conference BCD 3. E-learning element CDE
Able to interpret the political realities of the department to mitigate conflict	1. Capability is a value: not supported by a curriculum element
Completion of undergraduate degree	1. Undergraduate degree
Able to work well with user community as internal consultant	1. Stretch assignment with another sector 2. In-house course DEF
Able to create and manage department budgeting process	1. In-house course EFG 2. Rotation assignment FGH 3. Special project team assignment

Degree of Specificity: Generalist Versus Specialist Approach

In Table 15.4, a straightforward approach is used to represent the capabilities that support the NGST HR manager role. This simple model adopts a generalist perspective of the role. However, another approach exists that demands a greater degree of specificity about the role function. The degree of specificity about the career path curriculum can easily create an overengineered model that may be too tightly coupled with limited curricula, to the point that employees and managers have little flexibility when executing career path development. Figure 15.4 shows an outline of the degree of inherent complexity when more levels of specificity are burdened on the CPM model.

Figure 15.4. Mapping Curricula to Specific Roles Within the HR Function

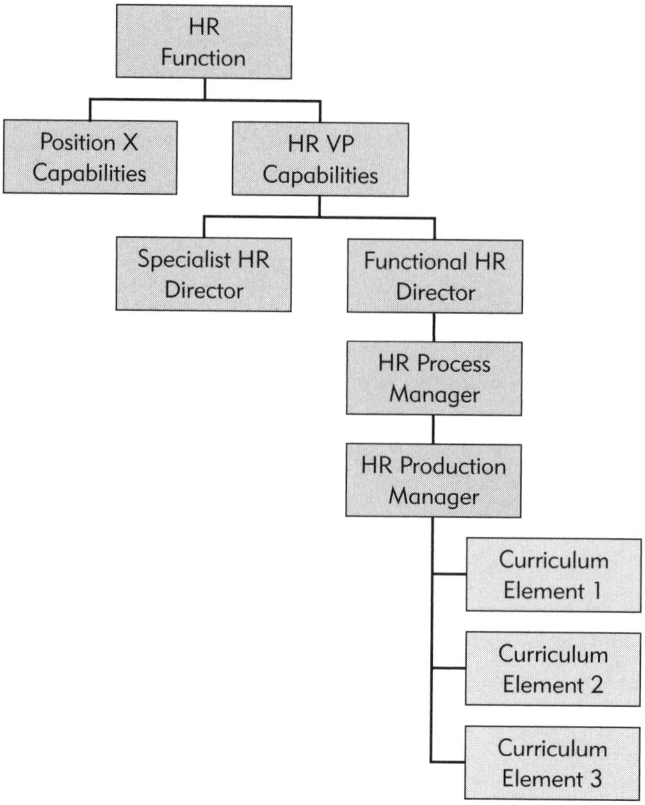

As can be seen in Figure 15.4, the more specific the role is, the more specific the curriculum. There may be isolated cases when this makes sense, but if one of the deliverables of a robust CPM model is adequate talent pool leading to fluid succession capabilities, then the extra effort spent in building a highly specialized workforce will thwart this effort. As such, NGST decided not to overly specify the capabilities needed for the pilot CPM program.

Preplanning Foundational Considerations

When building a career path curriculum based on role capabilities, it is important to define the learning metrics as early as possible. For example, if the required capability is an undergraduate degree, a simple check box will suffice. More often, though, the measure will demand a greater degree of assessment, as in the case of managing the budgeting process or acting in a consultant capacity as shown in Table 15.4.

Metrics are meant to measure the successful change or acquisition of new functional skills. Often training managers track attendance, cost per training hour, or yield efficiencies per course offering. But it was agreed that none of these measures would have a real impact on organization development in executing a new CPM. Metrics and accountability are owned by the CPM process owner. If CPM resides within the corporate university, then the university owns the process. But the expectations of the internal customer units will drive the level of reporting and accountability.

NGST selected a time-phased implementation approach. This meant that the implementation team would use the initial career path as a pilot to test its methodology, collect usable measurable data about the viability of the career path approach, begin the process of (pre)selling the concept to line department managers and employees, and develop a useful set of communication and training tools to facilitate the steps of the process.

Change Management: Setting Expectations for User Acceptance

The final phase of the pilot is to introduce the new career path model to users in the NGST community. The primary customers were department managers as well as employees, so a comprehensive communications plan was planned to describe the nature and purpose of the project, announce the project critical dates, and provide Web access for users to learn more about upcoming developments as they occurred.

The pilot also planned for a user training plan, designed to create, deliver, and explain the functionality of the new process; identify critical stakeholders; and present a time line for implementation. Because the pilot targets a specific segment of the NGST population, the training curriculum must be customized to address specific voice-of-the-customer concerns about how work processes will change as a result of the new CPM initiative. Part of the pilot design is to collect feedback at the end of the new user training and again three months after implementation in order to gauge how the new process is being accepted and identify unanticipated problems in design, communication, and user acceptance.

Case Coda: Issues of Conformity

It is anticipated that as a result of the pilot implementation, the Space Technology Sector will receive some visibility by other NGC business sectors as an early adopter of CPM methodology. This recognition within the greater organization may initiate an enterprisewide community of practice that may serve to set common standards and practices around process, governance, assessment, and shared learning.

Given the nature of one of the primary drivers for initiating a CPM methodology—the need to compete for top talent in a competitive workforce marketplace—a substantive policy issue may evolve: conformity.

Conformity is a natural outgrowth of any mature business model where leading players tend to influence the organizational activities, structures, and policies of others who function in the same market space. For example, all U.S. physicians conform to common professional training, ethics, and measures. Even competing railroad companies conform to the same track gauge. In the case of CPM, the question may well be defined as whether our version of career paths conforms to other career paths in other similar companies in our market space.

This question addresses the Major Prime perspective of defining common standards for an entire value chain of strategic players rather than investing in the development of a unique (read: proprietary) and unscalable infrastructure. In short, the question becomes, Should we enter into a substantive ongoing dialogue with customers, suppliers, strategic partners, and competitors to create conforming standards within the industry, or should we choose to abstain and live apart from supporting such an open system? The risk of abstention is that others will carry on the conversation without you and end up creating operating standards for you without your input no matter how excellent your process or elegant your design. Sony learned the hard lesson of taking the nonconformist path with BetaMax.

Summing Up the CPM Modeling Process

Career path management is a framework of professional development that clearly defines the right learning for the right person in the right amount at the right costs and at the right time. The architectural structure of this framework is a series of interconnected mini-curricula that provide both the learner and the organization with a clear understanding of the steps and resources needed to advance from one role to another. This structured approach is a major shift in the direction of organization development. Instead of allowing professional growth to be a learner-driven process, with the implicit high costs of development and delivery that a demand-driven model presents, this process is driven by the firm. The result of this supply-side approach is that costs and capability development are transformed to controllable variables and are articulated to building future capabilities to meet the long-term strategic goals of the organization.

The career path model process starts with a series of assessments that lead to an understanding of organizational learning gaps. Curricula for each career path are defined by the role to be developed. The degree of specificity about career path curricula is recommended to be more general than specific in the development phase to allow for flexibility and growth of the model. Conformity of career path models emerges as a critical concern for the firm, with the caveat that the consequences of nonconformity may inhibit future talent acquisition and employee retention success.

The Northrop Grumman Space Technology case showcases a time-phased pilot approach with the assumption that a successful pilot is scalable to the greater organization. Although the case outlined high-level activities in a large firm, the career path model process is easily implemented at organizations of any size. The greater the complexity of the implementation plan is, the greater a case may be made for robust (and expensive) technology support in the form of a learning management system or similar tracking software.

What's Next for CPM

Currently CPM curricula are designed and developed as customized efforts within individual firms. As CPM process benefits become more generally accepted, it is expected that there will be increased standardization from commercial vendors and others who wish to serve this emerging market. This will facilitate the transferability of employee skills through standardized company learning transcripts and greater opportunities for valuing employees' past learning achievements beyond their current employer.

References

Bass, B. M. *Bass and Stogdill's Handbook of Leadership: Theory, Research, and Managerial Applications.* (3rd ed.) New York: Free Press, 1990.

Donovan, J. J., and Radosevich, D. "The Moderating Role of Goal Commitment on the Goal Difficulty-Performance Relationship: A Meta-Analytic Review and Critical Reanalysis." *Journal of Applied Psychology,* Apr. 1998, pp. 308–315.

Gaertner, K. N. "Managers' Careers and Organizational Change." *Academy of Management Executive,* 1988, *2,* 311–318.

Locke, E. A., and Latham, G. P. *A Theory of Goal Setting and Task Performance.* Upper Saddle River, N.J.: Prentice Hall, 1990.

McCauley, C., Ruderman, P., Ohlott, P., and Morrow, J. "Assessing the Development Components of Managerial Jobs." *Journal of Applied Psychology,* 1994, *79*(4), 544–560.

Senge, P. *The Fifth Discipline.* New York: Doubleday, 1990.

Stajkovic, A. D., and Luthans, F. "Social Cognitive Theory and Self-Efficacy: Going Beyond Traditional Motivational and Behavioral Approaches." *Organizational Dynamics,* Spring 1998, p. 66.

Van Erde, W., and Thierry, H. "Vroom's Expectancy Models and Work-Related Criteria: A Meta-Analysis." *Journal of Applied Psychology,* Oct. 1996, pp. 548–556.

Veiga, J. F. "Plateaued Versus Nonplateaued Managers: Career Patterns, Attitudes, and Path Potential." *Academy of Management Journal,* 1981, *24,* 566–578.

Vroom, V. *Work and Motivation.* Hoboken, N.J.: Wiley, 1964.

Jack Gregg, Ed.D., is the dean of SPACE University, the corporate university for the Northrop Grumman Space Technology sector. Prior to this position, he spent over fifteen years in higher education administration, where he held the position of assistant dean of continuing education, directed M.B.A. programs at two major universities, and started numerous self-support programs, including the Office of Executive Education. Gregg is an adjunct professor, a published writer, a consultant, and an often-requested speaker. His primary areas of research are leadership, the use of influence in organizations, and the strategic use of organizational learning.

Succession planning is one of those topics I always thought was a no-brainer: have a plan in case there is a vacancy in a key position. It always amazes me when I hear about an organization that finds itself with a sudden opening and no plan in place to deal with it. Some companies do have succession plans, but only for a small handful of senior-level jobs, and not for every mission-critical position in the organization. And even organizations that are serious about succession planning usually have it as a function separate from the corporate university. This has always baffled me, as picking a likely successor is only the first step in succession planning; providing development for selected individuals to get them ready for the next position is just as important, and that always seemed to me to be a corporate university function.

It has been gratifying to see increasing numbers of corporate universities involved in the succession process. When I heard Lynn Schmidt tell the story of how she and her team did succession at Nextel, I thought it would be a good story for this book. She impressed me when she described it as succession management instead of succession planning. The idea that a corporate university would manage a process makes a lot more sense than merely having a plan. In this chapter, Lynn explores the concept of succession management and tells the story of its implementation at Nextel.

16

Succession Management in Corporate Universities

Lynn Schmidt

WHAT DOES AN ORGANIZATION need to do to ensure that it can remain competitive in a highly competitive environment? The answer is to implement a succession management process. An effectively designed and implemented succession management process can ensure leadership continuity, minimize retirement or other turnover disruptions, and retain key talent. Leadership continuity within an organization is essential for success. Leadership continuity is the result of identifying and developing high-potential leaders who are ready to implement the vision, mission, and strategy of the organization. These leaders need to be able to move into mission-critical positions as openings become available. Having those critical positions vacant for a significant amount of time leads to lost productivity and lost revenue, and that can be the downfall of an organization.

The aging of the baby boomer population is causing many organizations to experience a gap in leadership talent as boomers start to retire. Leadership talent is becoming a desired asset for organizations to acquire from outside (as opposed to developing internally). Leaders who have a successful track record can easily move from job to job and from company to company. This acquisition of leadership talent from the outside is often an indicator of high turnover in the leadership ranks. A succession management process can be an important vehicle that enables an organization to retain key talent. Succession management is no longer merely something nice to have; in today's environment, it has become a business imperative that enables an organization to remain competitive.

A succession management process focuses on identifying and developing internal talent to fill mission-critical positions. It requires creating a talent pool of high-potential candidates who have not only been selected, but are also being developed to move into positions with expanded responsibilities. Succession management is larger in scope than succession planning; it includes both the identification and development of high-potential candidates. In contrast, a succession planning process is defined here as a process that is focused on identifying successors for specific positions. Succession planning, often referred to as replacement planning, identifies but does not develop high-potential candidates or successors. Leaving out the development process creates a significant gap. The development process is what ensures that the leaders will be ready for the next job move within the organization. Identification without development is like a hot fudge sundae without the ice cream: a critical component for success is missing.

There are many factors to consider and questions to be answered when designing and implementing an effective succession management process. The process needs to be tailored to meet the needs of the organization. The General Electric succession management process is considered the grandfather of today's succession management processes, but that doesn't mean that every organization can implement the General Electric process without modifications. Time, money, and support all play a role in designing the best process for an organization.

These questions should be considered when designing and implementing an effective succession management process:

- How do you get started?
- Who owns the succession management process?
- Who manages the succession management process?
- Should you implement succession planning or succession management?
- How do you identify high-potential candidates?
- What are talent review meetings?
- What do you tell the high-potential candidates?
- How do you develop high-potential candidates?
- Do you buy or build a database?
- What measures can you use to determine success?

The following case study discusses how succession management was designed and implemented under a corporate university umbrella in Nextel Communications, a Fortune 500 company. The case study provides examples of how the ten questions listed above were addressed and the lessons learned.

Succession Management at Nextel Communications

In early 2002, the decision was made to centralize all training and development at Nextel Communications and create Nextel University. At that time, Nextel, a provider of an array of digital wireless communications services, generated revenues of approximately $6 billion and employed around seventeen thousand employees. Training and development were provided to employees within a decentralized training structure. Functional training groups resided autonomously in the field and provided primarily management, technical, customer service, and sales training. The reason for the centralization of training was to realize economies of scale, reduce duplication of effort, and gain consistency in training content and delivery.

Nextel University, once implemented, was managed by a vice president of learning and development who reported directly to the senior vice president of human resources. The university consisted of several functional institutes that managed the previously decentralized functional training responsibilities. Instructional design and training administration were also centralized within the university structure.

Coinciding with the creation of Nextel University was the decision to implement a succession process at Nextel. In the past, the company had been primarily focused on employee and management development. There was no process in place to identify or develop high-potential leaders or to determine the successors for mission-critical positions. Many in the organization believed that a succession process would create leadership continuity and help to retain key talent. In order to address these needs, the Leadership Institute was created within Nextel University. The Leadership Institute was responsible for succession management including both the identification and development of leadership talent. A director was selected to lead the Leadership Institute and to design and implement the succession management process.

Leadership Institute

The Leadership Institute was formed in August 2002 in order to identify and accelerate the development of the organization's future leaders. The objectives of the institute were to continuously improve leadership talent, create succession depth, reduce retention risk, and enhance the diversity of the leadership team. Within the Leadership Institute were three functional areas of responsibility. The first area was the succession planning process, which identified high-potential leaders and handled the administrative aspects of the process. The second area of responsibility was the development of leaders—the other half of succession management. This included the development of all directors and above in the organization, as well as accelerated development for selected high-potential employees. The third area of responsibility was a diversity initiative. This included establishing a diversity council, determining diversity metrics, and creating a mentoring program.

Since the Leadership Institute was a start-up, organization staff needed to be hired to support the purpose and objectives of the institute. Based on the three functional areas of responsibility, the director of the Leadership Institute hired three direct reports. One managed the succession planning process, another the leadership development process, and the third the diversity initiative. Although each had distinct responsibilities, there was overlap among the roles as they all contributed to the success of the overarching succession management process. This required the Leadership Institute team to work closely together. One of the first steps taken by the Leadership Institute was to name the succession management process at Nextel. It was called the Leadership Development Program (LDP). The goal for the program was to eventually cascade down to include senior managers. Figure 16.1 shows the Leadership Institute's responsibilities under the university umbrella.

Figure 16.1. Nextel University and the Leadership Institute

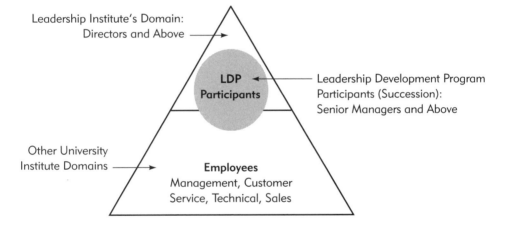

It was determined that Nextel would first implement the LDP for the top two tiers of executives at the company: the chief executive officer, the chief operations officer, and their direct reports. These were the top seventeen positions in the company. The process for these mission-critical positions would include replacement planning (naming specific successors for those positions), along with accelerated development plans for the successors. During the process of creating and implementing the LDP, the ten critical questions set out earlier in this chapter needed to be answered.

How Do You Get Started?

The way to get started is to learn as much as you can about the succession management process in a short amount of time. What is most important is that what is learned about the process is customized for your organization. There are a variety of ways to learn more about succession management. Some of the best ways to get started are using research to learn about best practices, reading books, and benchmarking with others. Many organizations, including the Corporate Leadership Council and Cutting Edge Information, have conducted research studies on succession management and have reports providing the findings of these studies that can be purchased. Another way to learn about best practices is to read scholarly and practitioner journal articles on the topic.

There are also many books that address succession management. A few that may be helpful are *Effective Succession Planning: Ensuring Leadership Continuity and Building Talent from Within* (2001), by William J. Rothwell; *Grow Your Own Leaders* (2002), by William C. Byham, Audrey B. Smith, and Matthew Paese; *The Leadership Pipeline: How to Build the Leadership Powered Company* (2001), by Ram Charan, Stephen Drotter, and James Noel; *The Extraordinary Leader: Turning Good Managers into Great Leaders* (2002), by John H. Zenger and Joseph Folkman; and *High Flyers: Developing the Next Generation of Leaders* (1998), by Morgan W. McCall Jr.

Last but certainly not least, one of the best ways to get started on creating and implementing a succession management process is to benchmark with your peers in similar businesses. You can learn from them how they customized their succession management processes and what works best in your industry. There are many excellent succession management processes; what is important is that the process is customized to work in your organization so that it will be successful.

Who Owns the Succession Management Process?

There may be a number of owners of the succession management process. Those individuals and their roles need to be determined early on. At Nextel the key stakeholders in the process were the CEO, the chief operations officer, and the senior vice president of human resources. Without the support of these three individuals, the process would not have been a success. Top-down support is a requirement of a successful succession management process; it needs to start at the top and work its way down into the organization. Those top-tier positions are critical to the organization. In addition, the LDP participant, the direct manager of the LDP participant, and the human resource department, along with the Leadership Institute, were owners and had roles in the process.

The Leadership Institute, in partnership with human resources, had the responsibility to support the managers and the LDP participants throughout the process. This included providing support for:

- Candidate selection
- Communication
- 360-degree assessment
- Individual development planning
- Development efforts
- Tracking progress against goals

The direct manager of the LDP participant was another owner of the process and had the following responsibilities:

- Ensuring fair and accurate assessment on leadership potential
- Congratulating and announcing the selection to the LDP participant
- Setting expectations on development outcomes, time, and resource commitments
- Supporting the LDP participant throughout the process

The LDP participant was also an owner of the process and was responsible for these roles:

- Making the decision to participate in the program
- Actively taking advantage of the individualized development support provided
- Achieving expected development outcomes

Who Manages the Succession Management Process?

The management of a succession process can reside in a variety of places within an organization but is often found within the HR function. Often the identification process and the development process reside within different HR functions and are managed by different people. In this case, the Leadership Institute was created specifically to manage both the identification and development processes. This was a distinct advantage as the two responsibilities are strongly linked and need to work closely together. Because this was a start-up function, the Leadership Institute had the responsibility to create, implement, and maintain the succession process. The following is not an inclusive list, but it does identify the most critical items that were included in the Leadership Institute's succession management responsibilities:

- Leadership competency modeling
- Identification and selection process
- Database administration
- Coordinating and facilitating talent review meetings
- Communication vehicles for the LDP
- 360-degree assessment
- Individual development planning
- Mentoring
- Coaching
- Lateral, rotational, and enrichment assignments
- Leadership training and education
- Program evaluation and return on investment

Should You Implement Succession Planning or Succession Management?

Succession planning is comparable to replacement planning and involves only the identification of successors. Succession management is focused on identifying and developing successors as well as a talent pool. This talent pool consists of high-potential leaders who aren't necessarily targeted for a specific job but would be able, depending on the additional development they receive, to move into several different jobs within the organization.

Many organizations decide to implement succession planning only. The problem with that choice is while the successors have been identified, most aren't ready to move to the next higher-level job. Because development is not a focus in succession planning, the leaders are identified but not developed with an accelerated focus. When the higher-level position becomes available, those designated successors are often not ready to make the move.

At Nextel, the decision was made to implement a succession management process that included replacement planning for the top seventeen positions in the organization as they were considered critical. The potential successors for those jobs would be both identified and developed. That is where the succession process started at Nextel. The next step was to identify and develop a talent pool of leaders. The Leadership Development Program was created to identify and develop the successors and the high-potential leaders who would be in the talent pool. Figure 16.2 shows the components of the succession management process developed by the Leadership Institute.

Figure 16.2. Nextel's Succession Management Process

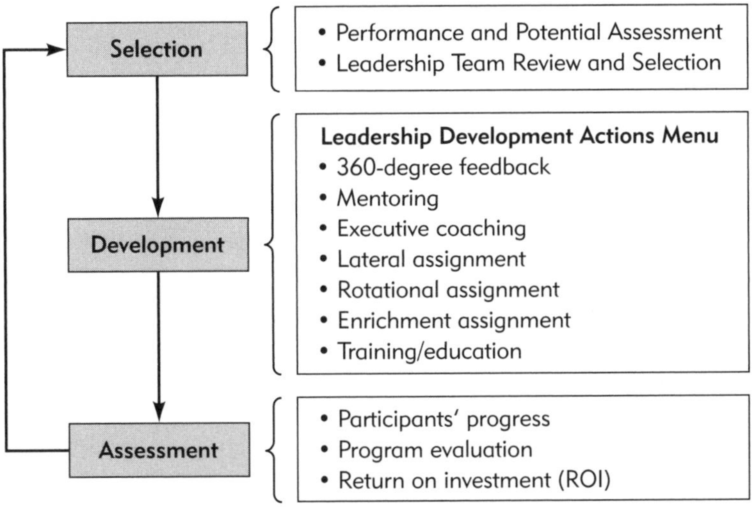

How Do You Identify High-Potential Candidates?

There are often a variety of criteria that are collected and reviewed when determining who the high-potential candidates are within the succession management process. The criteria can be broken into two categories: criteria based on past and current performance and criteria based on future leadership potential. This is an important distinction, as leaders may excel in their current jobs but lack the potential to move into higher-level positions. Not all high-performance professionals demonstrate high leadership potential. It is important to consider both types of criteria when determining the potential of a leader. The Leadership Institute created an assessment process with two components that addressed past and current performance, as well as future potential: the most recent performance review rating, including a rating on the leadership competencies and a rating on the performance objectives, and leadership potential ranking.

The most recent performance review rating contained two components. The first was the rating on the leadership competencies: how the job got done. The leadership competency model was created by the Leadership Institute in partnership with the senior executives at Nextel. It was a competency model customized to meet the needs of the organization. It contained competencies that focused on what was needed to do the job today and also competencies that had a focus on what it would take to move the company forward into the future. The leadership competencies were included in the performance review and evaluated at the same time as the performance objectives. These same leadership competencies were also evaluated as a part of the 360-degree feedback process that all LDP participants took part in. These competencies were identified:

- Shaping strategy
- Driving execution
- Financial acumen
- Industry knowledge
- Seasoned judgment
- Drive for stakeholder success

- Fostering open dialogue
- Entrepreneurial risk taking
- Cross-functional capability
- Inspiring trust
- Empowering others
- Attracting and developing talent
- Career and self-direction
- Building organizational relationships

The second component of the performance review rating was the rating on the performance objectives: what was accomplished as it related to the business objectives of the organization. The overall performance review rating showed the leader's current ability to do the job, including both how the job got done and what was accomplished. The overall performance review rating provided the assessment criteria based on past and current performance. Only leaders who received the top performance review ratings made it to the next step and were evaluated on their leadership potential.

In order to have assessment criteria based on future leadership potential, the Leadership Institute, in partnership with Nextel's senior executives, determined the five criteria to use to assess leadership potential:

- Demonstrated ability to learn quickly and apply learning to the job in ways that add value
- Demonstrated self-awareness of his or her own strengths and weaknesses and actively seeking feedback to make meaningful changes in his or her own behavior
- Demonstrated ability to build and lead a diverse team with complementary strengths that excels under all conditions
- Demonstrated ability to influence and collaborate with other functions to accomplish goals that impact areas beyond his or her function
- Demonstrated drive and desire to achieve, excel, and advance in the company

The overall assessment process used to select the high-potential leaders included the most recent performance review rating and the leadership potential ranking. Once both pieces of information were collected for all employees, the employees were then force-ranked by their current manager. Leaders with the highest performance review rating and the strongest leadership potential ranking were considered high-potential leaders and rose to the top during the forced ranking. Then a percentage of these high-potential leaders were put on the list to become part of the talent pool and participate in the Leadership Development Program. The next step was to hold a talent review meeting to determine the candidates to be in the talent pool.

What Are Talent Review Meetings?

Talent review meetings are a critical component of the succession management process. These meetings, often referred to as calibration discussions, are held to review, discuss, and approve the selected high-potential candidates. The purpose is to ensure a consistent selection process and include a variety of perspectives concerning each candidate. All managers who have put candidates forward as high-potential leaders should attend the talent review meeting. The meetings should be held as often as the selection process takes place. In some organizations, the selection process takes place only once a year. In others, it takes place two or three times a year.

The first phase of the succession management process at Nextel involved replacement planning for the top seventeen positions in the company: the CEO, the COO, and their direct reports. Based on this structure, the Leadership Institute held two separate talent review meetings. The first involved the CEO and his direct reports and the second the COO and his direct reports. Each of these talent review meetings was approximately three hours in length and followed this agenda:

1. Introduction

    - Purpose, goals, and success measures
    - The role of the senior leaders
    - Leadership development strategy overview

2. Candidate overview and actions discussion

- Functional goals and challenges

- Candidate strengths, development needs, and development suggestions

- Discussion to finalize candidates

3. Discuss next steps

The Leadership Institute staff worked closely with each executive who would be attending the talent review meeting to ensure that the executives understood the purpose of the meeting and that the candidate data were complete and in a consistent presentation format.

Once this first phase of the succession management process was complete, the Leadership Institute began working on the second phase of the process: each functional executive and his or her direct reports assessed and selected candidates. Each of these functional teams became the participants in the talent review meeting for their function. The talent review meetings were held twice a year: once in the first quarter and again in the third quarter.

What Do You Tell the High-Potential Candidates?

To tell or not to tell the selected high-potential candidates is an important question that must be addressed as part of the succession management process. There are pros and cons to either decision. The decision to tell is often more applicable to an organization with an open environment, where all types of information are shared openly within the organization and there are no secrets. The upside of telling is that it may increase the retention of candidates. The downside is that it may cause dissatisfaction among noncandidates. The decision not to tell is applicable to a more closed environment within an organization. The problem is that typically nothing can be kept a secret within an organization. The upside of not telling is that no expectations have been set for the candidates. The downside of not telling is that there will be minimal, if any, impact on the retention of the key talent. Not telling also makes development planning more difficult.

Nextel made the decision to tell, with caveats. All of the selected and approved candidates became participants in the Leadership Development Program managed by the Leadership Institute, and the candidates were informed by their managers that they had been selected to participate in this program. The decision was made to not use the terms *high-potential* or *successor,* and it was made clear to each selected candidate that participating in the Leadership Development Program was no guarantee of advancement or compensation changes. Continuous participation in the program was not guaranteed either, as participation status and selection were reviewed and updated twice a year to reflect dynamic business and individual development needs. In addition, all employees at the company had the opportunity to create individual development plans, which ensured a more inclusive development process. The Leadership Institute staff prepared a frequently asked questions document for managers so that they would be able to address employee concerns about not being selected to participate in the LDP. It was considered important to do everything possible to ensure that the succession management process was legally defensible and not discriminatory. The decision to tell with caveats allowed Nextel to maximize the associated benefits of the process and minimize the potential downsides.

How Do You Develop High-Potential Candidates?

The development plan for high-potential candidates needs to be focused, customized to the individual, and accelerated to ensure that the candidates are ready for the next position when it becomes available. The Leadership Institute staff believed that leaders are most effectively developed through on-the-job experiences. In addition, it is important to include mentoring or coaching as appropriate. And based on the individual development plan, it may be necessary to include some education or training, or both. The candidates selected to participate in the Leadership Development Program first completed a profile form that provided previous job information and desired career goals. Then they participated in a 360-degree feedback process and used those data to complete their development plans. Figure 16.3 shows the initial development process for the selected candidates.

Figure 16.3. Leadership Development Program Process

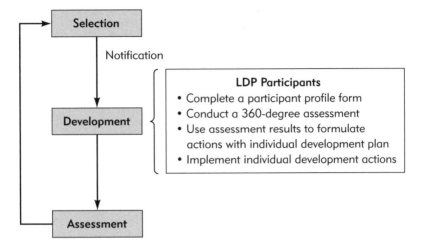

Once the LDP participant completed the 360-degree feedback process, a variety of development options were made available through the Leadership Institute based on the customized individual development plan. Those development options included lateral assignments, rotational assignments, enrichment assignments, mentoring, executive coaching, and training/education. The 360-degree feedback process was to be revisited by each participant ten months after the first assessment to see what changes had taken place. Each participant's progress was monitored by both the participant's manager and the Leadership Institute staff.

Do You Buy or Build a Database?

When creating and implementing a succession management process, it is important to give thought to how the data will be managed. As the program grows, so will the amount of data to be tracked. Decisions need to be made about buying or building a database to manage the data. Both alternatives have pros and cons. Buying a database can save time and you will often get more features. But buying can be more expensive, require customization, and have less flexibility. Building a database takes more time and often has fewer features. But building a database is less expensive and allows for customization and flexibility.

The Leadership Institute explored the option to buy a database and reviewed a variety of software packages. The Leadership Institute staff made the decision to initially track the data using an Excel spreadsheet. This would allow the staff to determine what data needed to be tracked before making an investment to buy or to build. Often a start-up program will experience a variety of changes while it is in the pilot phase and it is best not to make a significant investment until you know what data need to be included in the database.

What Measures Can You Use to Determine Success?

As with any other program, it is important to determine how the success of the succession management process will be measured. There are tangible measures such as retention, advancement, and performance. There are also intangible measures such as satisfaction measures. By determining what will be measured, success can be ensured and continuous improvements can be made to the process. It is important to tailor the measures to meet the needs of your succession management process.

The Leadership Institute staff selected several measures to monitor:

- Internal promotion rate of candidates
- Retention of candidates
- Diversity of candidates
- Satisfaction levels of candidates, their managers, and executives
- Executive recruiting expenditures
- Time to fill positions
- Completion of development plans and development actions
- Perceived return on investment or impact on the bottom line

How to measure the perceived return on investment of a leadership development initiative can be difficult. A recommended resource is *The Leadership Scorecard* (2004), by Jack J. Phillips and Lynn Schmidt.

Lessons Learned

Leadership Institute staff learned several lessons as they created and implemented the succession management process at Nextel:

- Make sure the process you implement fits your organization's culture. Research, read, and benchmark; then customize the process.

- Create a process focused on development. Replacement planning is not enough. The selected candidates will need focused, customized, and accelerated development in order to be ready for the next position.

- Involve and educate the executive team. Ensure that they are active participants throughout the process.

- Ensure the process is legally defensible. Review your customized succession management process with the legal team.

- Create your database, at least an interim one, prior to implementation.

- Be flexible and allow for continuous improvements.

During the pilot phase, the process will need to change as you implement your own lessons learned.

Conclusion

Succession management is an important process to implement in an organization. It can help an organization remain competitive by creating leadership continuity, minimizing turnover disruptions, and retaining key leadership talent. It is critical to implement not only succession planning, but a full succession management process that includes identification as well as development. The development for the selected high-potential candidates needs to be focused, customized, and accelerated. There are many questions that need to be addressed when a succession management process is being designed and implemented. The answers will help to customize the process for the organization.

A succession management process can be effectively managed under a corporate university umbrella. It can be useful to have both identification and development managed by the same organization as the two components need to work closely together. But regardless of who owns the management of the process, all of the stakeholders must understand their roles. Their full participation is needed for the succession management process to be successful. Measures need to be included in the process so that success can be tracked and communicated. If all of the critical factors are in place, an organization will have a succession management process that will provide the benefits needed to keep the organization competitive.

References

Byham, W. C., Smith, A. B., and Paese, M. *Grow Your Own Leaders.* Upper Saddle River, N.J.: Prentice Hall, 2002.

Charan, R., Drotter, S., and Noel, J. *The Leadership Pipeline: How to Build the Leadership Powered Company.* San Francisco: Jossey-Bass, 2001.

McCall, M. W., Jr. *High Flyers: Developing the Next Generation of Leaders.* Boston: Harvard Business School Publishing, 1998.

Phillips, J. J., and Schmidt, L. *The Leadership Scorecard.* Burlington, Mass.: Elsevier Butterworth-Heinemann, 2004.

Rothwell, W. J. *Effective Succession Planning: Ensuring Leadership Continuity and Building Talent from Within.* New York: AMACOM, 2001.

Zenger, J. H., and Folkman, J. *The Extraordinary Leader: Turning Good Managers into Great Leaders.* New York: McGraw-Hill, 2002.

Lynn Schmidt has twenty-one years of experience as a learning and organization development professional within Fortune 500 corporations. She is currently first vice president for executive development and leadership at Countrywide Financial. In that role, she has responsibility for executive-level development initiatives including education, 360-degree feedback, and coaching. She is the former vice president of learning and development for

Charter Communications. In that role she had responsibility for all learning and development functions at Charter, including organization development, management, leadership, human resources, sales, technical, customer service, and curriculum design and development. In her previous position, as director of Nextel Communications' Leadership Institute, she had responsibility for succession management, identification and development of high-potential candidates, diversity and mentoring programs, and executive development. Schmidt has previously had responsibility for performance consulting, management and employee training curricula, new employee orientation, distance learning, instructional systems design, competency modeling, and employee satisfaction surveys.

In addition, Schmidt has extensive experience in the field of measurement and evaluation. She is certified in ROI evaluation and served as chairperson of the ASTD ROI Network Advisory Committee in 2003 and 2004. In 2002 she received the Jack and Patti Phillips ROI Practitioner of the Year Award. She authored a case study for the ASTD *In Action* casebook *Measuring Learning and Performance*, on evaluating soft-skills training. She has conducted several ROI/impact studies on programs such as change management, time management, performance management, and diversity awareness. She is an editor and contributor of the 2003 ASTD *In Action* casebook *Implementing Training Scorecards* and is coauthor of *The Leadership Scorecard*.

Schmidt has presented at numerous national and international conferences on topics such as leadership development, succession management, creating the corporate university, training scorecards, and measurement and evaluation. She has taught both needs assessment and measurement and evaluation at Georgetown University. She has a B.S. in business administration and M.B.A. and M.A. degrees in human and organization systems, and she is pursuing a Ph.D. in human and organization development. She can be contacted at lynn.schmidt@comcast.net.

Although a relatively small number of people work in the world of corporate universities, one of the curiosities is that two of us are named Mark Allen. Mark W. Allen is the chief consultant and strategist of Corporate University Xchange (he is referred to in this book as Mark W. Allen since, well, W is his middle initial and I don't have one). Someone once accused me of creating him as a fictional alter ego, but I can assure you that given that my name is Mark Allen, if I were to create a pseudonym for myself, I could come up with something more creative than Mark W. Allen.

Mark has worked with countless corporate universities during his many years in this business and has agreed to share his expertise in this book.

Some organizations view knowledge management as another failed flavor of the month type of fad, while others see it as an organizational savior capable of realizing hundreds of millions of dollars in cost savings. Many of the failures are a result of viewing knowledge management as a technology issue instead of a people issue.

Among the key issues in knowledge management are the acquisition of knowledge (also known as learning) and the sharing of knowledge. Therefore, it is clearly a people issue. As such, it certainly can be argued that corporate universities should be involved in knowledge management. In this chapter, Mark describes how corporate universities can oversee the knowledge management process. He uses several corporate universities as illustrations of how to successfully implement knowledge-sharing communities.

17

The Role of Corporate Universities in Knowledge Management and Knowledge-Sharing Communities

Mark W. Allen

THIS CHAPTER DISCUSSES knowledge management and knowledge-sharing communities, their role within corporate universities, and the requirements for their success. Examples are drawn from Caterpillar University, the Great Harvest Bread Company, and other exemplary learning organizations.

The Business Case for Knowledge-Sharing Communities

Caterpillar University's communities of practice—the Caterpillar Knowledge Network—delivered over $14 million worth of value to community members in 2005 on a budget of $500,000 and with a staff of three, supporting over four thousand communities of practice across its value chain. Caterpillar's

Thanks to Reed Stuedemann and Dave Vance of Caterpillar University for sharing what they have learned.

Knowledge Network is one of the most valued and successful components of its award-winning corporate university.

Knowledge-sharing communities form around narrowly defined business activities: bolt fastening, drive shaft maintenance, or knowledge network community management, for example. Members pose questions on topics important to their business: "We are having a problem with drive shaft life. Does anybody else have this problem?" Answer: "We used to have the same problem until we changed the type of grease. Try using . . ." Discussion threads like these generate an average of six hundred dollars in value per discussion for each employee who poses a question and an average of twenty-five hundred dollars when value chain partners become involved. (Note that the $14 million calculation is actually conservative since solutions benefit more than just the initial person who posed the question. For example, extending drive shaft life benefits everyone in the drive shaft community, not just the initial questioner.) Since its inception in 1999 and its integration into Caterpillar University two years later, Caterpillar University's Knowledge Network has become an integral and important part of how the company operates. Even the CEO is an active participant.

Everyone in the organization benefits when knowledge circulates. And people value what they learn from others in the network. How often have we heard people say that what they liked most about a particular training program was "the opportunity to network with other participants"?

The business case for including knowledge management as a component of an organization's overall learning strategy is clear. With a clear strategy and effective practices to support knowledge sharing, performance continues to improve. The challenge is for the organization to support knowledge sharing in a way that works. To avoid sidetracks, it is helpful to look at how other corporate universities have addressed this opportunity and examine what has worked and what has not.

Role of the Corporate University

An important reason for the success of Caterpillar's Knowledge Network is Caterpillar University. The knowledge network operates within the context of a world-class corporate university that includes the following components:

- A highly engaged governing board

- A chief learning officer with an in-depth understanding of the business

- An excellent strategic planning process that ensures alignment of learning investments with needs that are enterprisewide, business unit specific, regional, and individual

- Effective leadership for all major learning program and service areas, including the Caterpillar Knowledge Network

- An annual Business of Learning Plan, a strategic learning plan that focuses learning and development initiatives on key business priorities

- Strong internal and external alliances

- Effective brand development, marketing, and communication

- A strong benchmarking capability for evolving organizational performance

- Importantly, a comprehensive and practical approach to measurement; senior executives at Caterpillar understand the return on investment for Caterpillar University and the Caterpillar Knowledge Network

The Caterpillar Knowledge Network has been successful in part because of this supportive framework. Knowledge management initiatives that operate outside such a context tend to fall short on alignment to business initiatives, lack an effective approach to measurement, don't always operate with a clear strategy, focus more on the technology or taxonomies than on connecting people, fail to gain traction, and consequently fall short of expectations. All of these reasons explain why many knowledge management initiatives have failed.

Knowledge-Sharing Strategy

Caterpillar University's strategy is simple: focus on connecting people, not on content. Some organizations focus on building content libraries with mixed results: a few staff use them, and others don't. In contrast, Caterpillar University provides communities with the tools for developing their own resource libraries as they see fit, minimizing overhead while ensuring that documents are relevant, useful, and up-to-date. It reflects a view that knowledge-sharing communities ought to be self-originating, self-managing, and self-sustaining and that community members ought to have the right to vote with their feet.

This philosophy toward knowledge sharing elevates the importance of knowledge-sharing roles and usability: two additional areas of focus for Caterpillar University.

Knowledge-Sharing Roles

The important roles within Caterpillar's Knowledge Network are as follows:

• *Knowledge-sharing manager:* Manage the knowledge-sharing network. This is a full-time position, supported by a staff of two.

• *Community managers:* Identify experts, review and approve formal knowledge entries and keep them up-to-date, oversee community discussions, and serve as role models for community members. These are volunteer positions—one per community. People like to help each other solve problems. Experienced staff enjoy sharing what they have learned, that is, giving back. When community members are appreciated and recognized for the contributions they make, they actively share knowledge. When an environment of trust is established, they do not hesitate to ask for advice from other members of the community. Generosity, appreciation, and trust keep knowledge circulating. An important role of any community manager is to help establish an environment that supports this kind of open exchange and inquiry. Knowledge sharing breaks down in environments where members are afraid to ask questions that they view as "stupid" and hesitate to offer suggestions that might appear inadequate.

• *Community delegates:* Assist managers and take over community management responsibilities when managers are absent.

• *Experts:* Possess a high degree of skill, knowledge, and experience relevant to the needs of their community. They share their expertise with other community members and author and assist in reviewing knowledge entries. These are volunteers identified by the community manager. A community can have multiple experts, and experts can serve in more than one community.

Usability

To realize its vision, Caterpillar University had to provide knowledge-sharing capabilities that were as easy to use as e-mail. They discovered early on that the biggest barrier to participation was users' fear of appearing to be stupid because of the technology. They worked closely with the National Center for Super Computing to overcome this challenge and regularly refine the platform to improve its usability. The design is heavily driven by customer preferences. Ongoing usability engineering has contributed significantly to success. A new user can create a community in three to four minutes. Today the Caterpillar Knowledge Network supports 41,000 members and over 190,000 memberships across the value chain. More than half of the company participates in one or more knowledge-sharing communities.

Security

Caterpillar University's knowledge network is very open, with access offered across its value chain. The more open the borders are, the more important the security is. Each community has a security profile that safeguards access to discussions and knowledge entries. Access is controlled through a security identification.

Disaster Recovery: Knowledge-Sharing Communities in Action

Do communities of practice have a role in helping to respond more rapidly and effectively to earthquakes, tidal waves, hurricanes, epidemics, and other natural disasters?

On July 13, 2004, Parsons Manufacturing, one of Caterpillar's important suppliers, was hit by a tornado that leveled its business. Although none of the 180 employees working at the Parsons facility when the tornado hit were hurt, the business itself and its buildings were devastated.

Parsons specializes in making small batches of complex metal parts for a host of Caterpillar products. It had been supplying 6,936 different part numbers for 220 Caterpillar products. At the time the business was leveled,

Parsons had 7,000 purchase orders to fulfill for supplying Caterpillar's assembly lines in fourteen Caterpillar facilities. The threat to Caterpillar production was significant.

Caterpillar quickly assembled a cross-functional team to help Parsons restore operations. The team formed a community of practice and used the knowledge network to facilitate communication, collaboration, and coordination of recovery efforts across Caterpillar departments, geographies, and facilities. They used the knowledge network to identify experts across the company to assist in each aspect of the recovery. Altogether, seventeen Caterpillar departments were involved in supporting Parsons.

Through the knowledge network, all recovery processes were rapidly developed and staffed, alternative sources were identified for 50 percent of part numbers within two weeks, within ninety days Parsons had the roof back on, and ninety days later it was fully operational. A consulting company that supported the project said it was the most rapid disaster recovery their company had experienced. The speed, efficiency, and effectiveness of the response testify to the strength of knowledge-sharing communities in action.

Diversity, Knowledge Sharing, and Natural Selection

The Great Harvest Bread Company is a franchise of several hundred retail stores that bake and sell bread made from milled-in-the-shop Montana wheat. Great Harvest gives its store owners the freedom to do whatever makes sense within their stores. Then, through their learning community, owners discover, explore, and replicate what works best. By supporting diversity and knowledge sharing, Great Harvest has created a true learning organization.

It is helpful to understand how Great Harvest uses performance measurement data to support continuous improvement through its learning community. Every store owner has the opportunity to join the Numbers Club, to share in-depth store performance data with all other store owners in the club. Owners open their books and share best practices and lessons learned. The company uses these data to identify the top performers in each area. By benchmarking themselves against other members, owners quickly discover opportunities for improvement. They also discover which stores are most successful in each area and why. Members are encouraged to visit and study the practices of top performers. The company also facilitates franchise owner discussions and knowledge sharing through its Breadboard site, posts case studies, and more. Through store visits and online discussions, members quickly learn how to replicate the successes of the highest-performing stores.

Experimentation at the local level supports continuous innovation for the company as a whole. By identifying those stores with the highest levels of performance and supporting knowledge sharing across the company, good ideas continue to spread.

Professional Service Firms

Professional service firms are in the knowledge-sharing business. The knowledge of their staff is their product. As such, they have developed some of the most advanced knowledge bases for sharing knowledge among professionals who work on similar customer engagements. Some firms employ hundreds of staff in this area. In contrast, most corporate universities need simple, low-maintenance methods for supporting knowledge-sharing communities. But there are still lessons to be learned from the practices that professional service firms have developed. For example, one professional service firm ensures that knowledge sharing becomes an integral part of how each associate works by using knowledge-sharing tools in all corporate university programs. Another forms course participants into an ongoing community of practice to support action learning assignments. Some mandate community participation and schedule formal community meetings. Professional service firms with highly developed knowledge management capabilities include Capgemini, Ernst & Young, Deloitte, Accenture, and IBM. These same firms also have established highly effective corporate universities because of the importance of human capital to their businesses.

In a similar way, Corporate University Xchange has developed its Collaboratory, a knowledge base for learning executives. The Collaboratory includes case studies, design tools, research reports, methodologies, and best practices and lessons developed from years of corporate university research. Community members access the following knowledge categories:

- Corporate university design
- Governance and alignment
- Strategic planning
- Partner and vendor management (including corporate-college partnerships)
- Funding
- Leadership development
- Learning technology
- Globalization
- Measurement
- Marketing, brand development, and change management

Community members discuss common needs and share practices, lessons learned, tools, content, and more with other members in the network.

Preserving Baby Boomer Expertise

Baby boomers are starting to retire and take their expertise with them. That's a big threat for organizations like Caterpillar, where the average employee age is forty-seven. It was, in fact, one of the drivers for developing the Knowledge Network. Effective knowledge management is an important component of the solution for addressing this looming challenge.

The pending retirement of baby boomers is a significant issue for U.S. government agencies. Large numbers of senior executives have left the U.S. federal government, taking with them difficult-to-replace knowledge and skills. Many more will qualify to retire over the next few years, including half the senior executive service, who serve in key positions below top presidential appointees.

Knowledge-sharing networks help to address this challenge by connecting people across generations and geographies, facilitating rapid access to senior expertise, accelerating the speed of knowledge transfer from one generation to the next, providing effective channels for supporting that transfer, and providing the means for expertise to be recorded and preserved. It is not a complete solution, but it is an important component for many organizations that must solve this problem. The problem is not unique to North America. Manufacturing companies, governments, and many other organizations around the world will be hit hard without an effective approach to knowledge management. (For additional information on solutions for addressing this challenge, see Allen, 2002.) The corporate university has an important role to play in addressing this challenge.

Benjamin Franklin's Junto

Knowledge-sharing communities are not a new phenomenon. Benjamin Franklin formed one in 1777 in Philadelphia. He called it the Junto, using the Latin word for meeting. It included a dozen local businesspeople who gathered every Friday night to explore questions Franklin would pose on a range of topics designed to further "mutual improvement and knowledge." Part of what they sought to learn was why some local businesses flourished while others failed, but their focus was much broader than business improvement. In his autobiography, Franklin (1962) described the Junto as follows:

> I should have mentioned before, that, in the autumn of the preceding year [1727], I had formed most of my ingenious acquaintance into a club of mutual improvement, which we called the JUNTO; we met on Friday evenings. The rules that I drew up required that every member, in his turn, should produce one or more queries on any point of Morals, Politics, or Natural Philosophy [physics], to be discuss'd by the company; and once in three months produce and read an essay of his own writing, on any subject he pleased. Our debates were to be under the direction of a president, and to be conducted in the sincere

spirit of inquiry after truth, without fondness for dispute or desire of victory; and to prevent warmth, all expressions of positive opinions, or direct contradiction, were after some time made contraband, and prohibited under small pecuniary penalties.

The Junto was highly effective in developing practical solutions to social challenges. Its members developed the first public lending library in the United States, the first volunteer fire department, the first hospital, and a learning academy that became the University of Pennsylvania, and their businesses flourished. A key reason for their success was the leadership that Franklin provided and the guidelines he established early on—important for today's community managers.

Evolutionary Stages of Knowledge-Sharing Networks

It may be helpful to think of organizational support for knowledge sharing as evolving along a continuum (the evolutionary stages described here are not linear):

- Knowledge sharing is driven by individual initiative. Individuals seek out what they need with limited organizational support.

- Regional networking and regional knowledge sharing occur in some parts of the organization, with very little sharing across organizational boundaries, even at the executive level.

- Support for in-person networking opportunities exists for executives and others.

- Knowledge repositories are organized by the sales organization or information technology, with no coordination across disciplines.

- Sales staff can query other sales staff for support on sales opportunities.

- Knowledge management is formalized by the organization and staffed as part of the overall corporate university strategy.

- The organization develops a formal knowledge management strategy that supports knowledge-sharing communities.

- Guidelines and infrastructure for formal communities are established.

- Subject matter experts are identified within many business areas.

- Procedures are implemented to capture and record subject matter expertise.

- Knowledge taxonomy and knowledge repositories are managed and maintained.

- An infrastructure is developed to support self-creating and self-managing communities.

- Value chain partners are engaged.

- Knowledge sharing is managed successfully across the organization, delivering increasing value to the organization, its partners, and those it serves.

- Knowledge sharing has become an integral part of how people work together to solve problems and improve performance.

Where does your organization fall along this continuum?

Organizational Origins and Development

In many organizations, the knowledge management system originates outside the corporate university and sometimes predates the development of the corporate university, as was the case at Caterpillar. Over time, the knowledge management organization evolves to take on many of the components of a corporate university, including an advisory board, alignment processes, and performance metrics. As knowledge management develops, the overlaps between knowledge management and the corporate university become increasingly obvious, and the two organizations merge, with knowledge management becoming an important component of the corporate university. Both organizations gain strength from such a merger, and the whole company benefits. This was the case at Caterpillar, Milliken, and other organizations that have developed highly successful knowledge management solutions.

Best Practices

Following is a summary of best practices to consider:

- Keep the scope of each community narrow, and clearly state its purpose.

- Organize communities around key business activities or goals.

- Start by focusing on a handful of areas that are a priority for your organization.

- Require that each community appoint a community manager with a clearly defined role.

- Elect community managers with the leadership skills needed to support open inquiry and exchange.

- Acknowledge and reward knowledge sharing.

- Establish an infrastructure and guidelines that enable community self-management.

- Identify experts in each area, and provide quick and easy access to them.

- Provide members with intuitive tools for posing questions to the group and searching the knowledge base.

- Engage members by posing questions related to current challenges and organizational goals.

- Implement after-action reviews to learn as much as possible from failures and successes. Institutionalize this as part of community activity.

- Provide a simple means for experts to record their knowledge.

- Leverage your organization's diversity as an asset.

- Encourage regional diversity and innovation, and replicate the most successful practices that evolve.

- Develop performance measures that community members can use to benchmark their performance, and identify top-performing members from whom others can learn.

- Establish performance measures for business activities, publish a list of the top ten groups, and offer groups the opportunity to benchmark themselves against the top ten.

- Establish knowledge sharing as a core competency for all staff. Build it into competency models.

- Tell the story. Measure the impact of communities, and publish the results.

- Establish role models.

- Provide an easy means for groups to develop case studies and agree on best practices.

- Keep in mind that what constitutes best practice changes as conditions evolve. Establish a shelf life for knowledge, and assign community managers, experts, or other knowledge owners responsibility for refreshing or deleting outdated practices. Unlearning is as important as learning.

- Benchmark other corporate universities to learn from their successes and failures.

- Establish and publish a mission for knowledge sharing.

- Reward senior executives who encourage knowledge sharing. Publicize their participation in communities.

- Don't fall into the technology trap. Keep the focus on connecting people, not the technology. Technology is only an enabler. Technology-focused solutions fizzle.

Low-Hanging Fruit: Quick Access to Internal Experts

One of the simplest knowledge management tools to implement, and one of the most useful, is a searchable directory of experts listing each person's e-mail address and areas of expertise. Microsoft has developed a useful internal solution (Expert Finder), which gives staff an easy way to locate and e-mail internal subject matter experts.

There are many different methods for sharing knowledge. The following lists illustrate some common knowledge-sharing channels:

Important Knowledge-Sharing Channels

- Community discussions
- E-mail
- In-person meetings, including dedicated knowledge-sharing sessions
- Virtual meetings
- Mentoring sessions

Methods for Identifying and Retaining Knowledge

- Member queries and discussion threads
- Expert interviews
- After-action review meetings
- Online surveys
- Member research
- Knowledge base searches

Common Knowledge Base Items

- Case studies
- Procedures
- Tools and templates
- White papers
- Links
- Lists of communities, experts, and members

Outline for Capturing Best Practices

1. State the problem.

2. Describe limitations inherent in previous approaches to the problem.

3. Explain what the problem was costing the organization, partners, or clients. Include financial measures or other measures particularly relevant to your organization.

4. Describe what you did differently, providing as much detail as possible.

5. Tell what worked and why.

6. Tell what didn't work and why, so that others can avoid the same sidetracks.

7. Describe the benefits achieved using as much concrete data as possible. Link those benefits back to the measures discussed in step 3.

Critical Success Factors for Launching Knowledge Sharing

- Focus on business priorities.
- Start simply.
- State the mission.
- Articulate the strategy.
- Set clear expectations.
- Gain executive support.
- Magnetize participation.
- Measure performance.

Sample Mission Statements

"To improve individual and organizational performance by enabling rapid access to essential knowledge and expertise."

"To facilitate on-demand access to internal know-how and collaborative problem solving wherever and whenever it is needed."

Definitions

Community of practice: A group of people with a common interest who improve organizational performance by learning from each other's know-how and experience.

Knowledge base: An online repository of expert practices and lessons learned, often including case studies, tools, templates, procedures, lists of experts, samples, white papers, reference materials, and useful Web links.

Knowledge-sharing network: An organizationwide network of knowledge-sharing relationships that accelerate performance improvement by supporting rapid discovery and on-demand access to new knowledge whenever and wherever it is needed.

Summary

People naturally enjoy solving problems together and sharing what they have learned. The drive to help each other is innate. The most successful knowledge-sharing managers tap into this. Instead of creating communities, they create environments in which communities can develop on their own accord to address common challenges across the organization. They establish roles and guidelines for maintaining successful communication, and then get out of the way. By keeping the focus on connecting people, not on technology, they have created networks that deliver significant value for their organizations and customers.

References

Allen, M. "Responding to the US Federal Government's Human Capital Management Issues." *Corporate Universities International,* 2002, *8*(6).

Franklin, B. *The Autobiography of Benjamin Franklin.* New York: Touchstone, 1962.

Mark W. Allen is a senior adviser to chief learning officers on all aspects of learning and development strategy, organization, and operations. He was president and CEO of Corporate University Xchange from 2001 to 2004 and currently serves as the company's chief consultant and strategist. His areas of focus include corporate university design, development, and management; corporate learning transformation; leadership institute development; corporate–college partnership development; learning organizations; and knowledge management. He has delivered corporate university consulting engagements for a wide range of clients, including Caterpillar, the Centers for Disease Control and Prevention, Defense Acquisition University, General Motors, IBM, and many others.

18

Wisdom Management

THE MISSING LINK BETWEEN LEARNING AND PERFORMANCE

Mark Allen

WE HAVE BEEN TALKING for many years about how important it is to have continuous learning in the workplace. Then came the notion that our workforces were composed of knowledge workers. More recently, we have been focusing on managing the knowledge in our organization and sharing it (see Mark W. Allen's thoughts on this in Chapter Seventeen). So why is it that if we have such a focus on learning and knowledge, we are still not always seeing the productivity gains that are supposed to accompany all of these advances in learning and knowledge? In Chapter Seven, Jack and Patti Phillips tell us that 60 to 90 percent of all job-related skills and knowledge acquired in a program are not being implemented on the job. So why is it that the world of workplace learning has a flurry of activity but a shortage of meaningful results? The reason is a failure to employ what I call *wisdom management*.

We've all seen it happen. We offer a course that is well designed and delivered expertly. The feedback we get was that everyone liked it and found the content interesting. Yet everyone went back to work Monday morning and didn't do anything differently. We get caught up in the immediate demands of the job and don't change our behaviors. I think we've all taken a course that we found to be interesting and full of good stuff, but we never implemented any of it in the workplace. Many of us have not only taken that course, but designed it or maybe even taught it.

The disconnect is between getting the material into our heads and applying it and using it in the workplace. As challenging as training is, it is a whole lot easier to help someone learn something than it is to get him or her to use it.

What Is Wisdom Management?

Buckman Laboratories does a world-class job in knowledge management, and it is one of the leading benchmark companies in this area. The CEO, Bob Buckman, says that the knowledge continuum looks like what is shown in Figure 18.1. He defines wisdom as "the creative use of knowledge" (Harvard Business School Publishing, 1999). I believe the third arrow in Figure 18.1 is where we have the disconnect between our learning efforts and the desired results. The missing link is between our ability to give people the knowledge and skills they need and our ability to get them to use it in ways that benefit the organization.

Figure 18.1. Knowledge Continuum

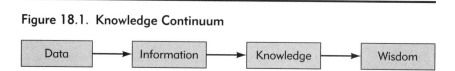

This book is devoted to telling stories about how corporate universities have managed processes to deliver improved results. Mentoring is not a new idea, but in Chapter Thirteen, Lynn Slavenski writes about how her corporate university manages the mentoring process so that Equifax can get full value from its investment. Similarly, many companies have some form of executive coaching, but in Chapter Fourteen, Merrill Anderson tells us how a corporate university can manage the process to ensure results. The importance of knowledge in the workplace is not a recent idea, but only in the past ten years have organizations embraced the concept of knowledge management, which is predicated on managing how organizational knowledge is acquired, stored, and, most important, shared.

What we have not done is managed the process of how knowledge is used. That is where wisdom management comes in. I define it as follows: *wisdom management is a planned and systematic process by which an organization manages how its employees use and apply their knowledge and skills in ways that benefit the organization.*

In Chapter One, I defined a corporate university as being responsible for "conducting activities that cultivate individual and organizational learning, knowledge, and wisdom." While most corporate universities can honestly say that they focus on learning and knowledge, how many actually work on cultivating wisdom? I do not usually see a lot of hands go up when I ask this question of corporate university professionals.

Not surprisingly given the nature of this book, I am advocating that the corporate university be the locus for wisdom management within an organization. It is no longer enough for us to give people knowledge and skills; we need to make sure that they are being used.

Linking Program Design and Measurement of Results

The importance of using newly acquired knowledge is certainly not a new one. Donald Kirkpatrick hit on this over fifty years ago when he created his four levels of evaluation. Kirkpatrick said that workplace training can be evaluated at four levels: reaction (how people feel about the course), learning (whether they actually learn something), behavior change (whether they do anything differently on the job after taking the course), and results (whether the organization sees improved results due to the training). The Kirkpatrick model for evaluation is still in use, virtually unchanged, more than a half-century after its birth. Why? Because Kirkpatrick got it right.

It was not enough to just ensure that learning took place. Learning without behavior change doesn't affect performance. In short, we wanted people to do things differently. But even behavior change alone is not sufficient: those changes could produce positive results, negative results, or no change whatsoever in results. Remember that training is predicated on a desire to improve performance. Therefore, to truly know whether training has been beneficial, we need to measure if performance (individual or organizational) has improved.

The true genius of Kirkpatrick's model is not just that it's the gold standard for evaluation; it is also a lodestone for training design. If we know a training program is going to be evaluated at level 4 (that is, we are going to measure whether it has generated improved results), then we are more likely to design the training in a way that should get us the results we want. By building in the evaluation at the start, we help to ensure meeting our goals in the design and delivery phases. Thus, evaluation is not something done after the fact; it is built in up front.

So how do we ensure that we can get measurable results? First, we need to clearly and specifically define what success would be. We need to articulate precisely what the results we want are before we begin to design the training. Once defined, we can then focus on achieving those results. And creating a program that delivers the learning that people need to achieve the goals is not sufficient; we need to build in a mechanism that ensures that the learning is operationalized into behaviors.

Linking Learning and Action

Once again, there have been programs through the years that have not only attempted but succeeded in ensuring transfer of knowledge and skills to the workplace. Since 2002, Pepperdine University has delivered a nine-month certificate program to Boeing on leading change. The major assignment that participants work on is a job-related change project. Rather than read case studies of other companies, each student crafts a custom change project that is a real-world work issue. Throughout the nine months, students work on this change project on the job concurrent with the course. At the end of the course, they report on their successes and failures in implementing their change project. This project was a big reason that this program was so appealing to Boeing. In addition to getting twenty employees better equipped to lead change, it also gets twenty real-world change projects completed during the nine months by employees under the mentorship of Pepperdine's faculty.

Approaches to learning that attempt to link course work to real-world job issues are not new. The field of action learning is predicated on this concept. What is new in wisdom management is the idea that all development efforts should be linked directly to real-world application and that this process should be managed centrally by the corporate university.

Applications Gone Awry

Before I give an example of a company that is doing this and doing it well, let me provide two examples that illustrate both how critical it is and how it can go awry.

Several years ago, I designed a two-week executive program for a company that sent a group of nineteen vice presidents to Pepperdine University from all over the United States and Canada. The program was designed to meet the organization's goals, the vice presidents were enthusiastic participants, and the faculty delivered the program with aplomb. At the end of the two weeks, the company's CEO, who had flown in to see the participants present their end-of-course projects, told me that the money he spent on this course was the best investment he ever made.

To someone who designs executive education programs, this was the holy grail of all compliments. Not only was a CEO giving high praise, but he was using the right language: he didn't talk about the expense; he referred to it as an investment. We're always trying to get executives to refer to workplace learning as an investment, not an expense, and this CEO was saying that it was the best investment he ever made.

Here's the punch line to the story: the company received virtually no value from its investment in this seemingly successful program. In a bit of poor timing, an announcement that the company was being acquired by a competitor was made the week following the program. The new owners, rather than trying to capitalize on the investment that the previous regime had made in this group of vice presidents, viewed them as redundant or replaceable. Within a year after the completion of the program, twelve of the nineteen were no longer with the company. Within five years, only two vice presidents remained.

While it might seem like a waste of money to invest in a two-week program for executives who are leaving the company, it's much worse than that. The diaspora of vice presidents did not lead them into other industries: the executives all went to work for competitors, so this company ended up investing heavily to provide knowledge and skills for a cadre of executives for its competitors.

Acquisitions and layoffs are not the only culprits when it comes to not realizing full value (or any value) from investments in education. Sometimes inattention is culpable, as the following example illustrates. There's a company that spends heavily on tuition reimbursement for its employees to earn degrees at the associate, bachelor, master, or even doctoral level (and I used the word *spends* instead of *invests* intentionally), but its inattention to putting the skills of its graduates to use has resulted in this investment looking more like a mere cost. There is one positive organizational benefit: the tuition policy certainly drives retention. The high retention rate of employees in this company debunks the myth that companies are losing money when they pay for tuition and the employees flee to other organizations. In truth, employers who don't educate suffer from turnover, while those who do educate have a high retention rate. Remember the winning answer if anyone ever asks you the ill-conceived question: "What if I train them and then they leave?" The appropriate answer is, "You're asking the wrong question. A better question is, 'What if I don't train them and they stay?'"

While the employees at this company certainly love the tuition benefit, there is one complaint that has been a constant refrain. When employees complete their newly minted degrees, they are not treated any differently from those who have not been to school. There is no preference shown in promotion, there is no career path planning (as described in Chapter Fifteen), and there is no plan to use the employees' new knowledge and skills to benefit the organization. After a while, the employees, frustrated by the lack of promotion accompanying their new degrees, change their complaint. Ultimately the frustration comes out as, "I don't even care about promotions. I want some new responsibilities and a chance to use my new skills."

Here we have a case of a company spending tens of millions of dollars on tuition annually while having an educated workforce that is begging to put its skills to use, but the company has not yet figured out a way to match company needs and employee skills in a way that capitalizes on the considerable expenditures the company is making without a strategic intent behind it.

All of this leads us to a company that has a plan for getting it right. Enclos Corp., profiled in Chapter Nine, has developed a plan to put the notion of wisdom management to use.

Wisdom Management at Enclos Corp.

Enclos is the first company to embrace wisdom management, and it has not only formalized a system for operationalizing it, it even uses the term *wisdom management.* Enclos is a specialty contractor that works on high-end construction projects and is dependent on having people with the right skills and experience to manage these projects.

When they heard about wisdom management, the people at Enclos University were quick to adopt the concept because there was a clear need for it. As the company grows, it has more of a need for senior project managers—people who can manage a construction contract of $25 million or more. In the past, it has taken Enclos ten to fifteen years to develop a senior project manager who is ready to take on projects of that size. Given the company's ambitious growth goals, a decade or more to develop people into the senior project manager role was no longer a luxury it could afford.

The first breakthrough for Enclos was when its leaders realized that if the company was to grow, they needed to change the mind-set from a focus on building buildings to a focus on building a company. The real epiphany came when they realized the only way to do that was to shift the focus to building people. That was when Enclos decided to create and invest in Enclos University. The corporate university is a core part of the company's growth strategy and has been successfully implemented and integrated into the company, despite the company's relatively small size (roughly 450 employees).

Historically, new employees began on smaller projects and worked their way up to larger ones, first reporting to other project managers and then managing small projects on their own. Under this process, it took ten to fifteen years before a person was deemed ready to take on a senior project manager role. Before Enclos University was created in 2004, managers were responsible for developing employees. There was always a tension between the desire to give people the various experiences they needed to develop versus the immediate needs to complete construction projects. At the forefront of the minds of project managers was the need to complete the projects successfully, on time, and profitably, not to develop employees.

This is where a desire to implement wisdom management came in. With Enclos University in place as an accepted part of the company, there came a realization that Enclos could not develop people with training, classes, and e-learning alone. Although training was important, according to Lee Steffens, the director of Enclos University, "Managers were hung up on that one aspect and were neglecting other developmental experiences." As we all know, there is no substitute for experience, but rather than waiting around for a decade and a half for someone eventually to acquire the requisite experience, Enclos University mapped out what the necessary experiences are. It certainly helped that Steffens was a former senior project manager himself.

The first step was to look at the career path. Typically a new employee would enter as a project coordinator. The next steps up the ladder were assistant project manager, project manager, and finally senior project manager. It was taking a minimum of four years to progress from newly hired project coordinator to project manager. So the first question Enclos asked itself was, How can we accelerate to progress to project manager so that the process takes less than four years?

In order to do that, Enclos had to determine what the necessary steps were along the way (and it was certainly not putting in time until the four-year anniversary was celebrated). Enclos mapped out the six necessary steps in the development of project managers:

1. Hands-on field experience

2. Experience in a fabrication plant

3. Work on an engineering team

4. Work in the sales and estimating functions

5. Management experience

6. Manage a mock-up job as if they were the project manager in charge

Once the necessary steps were mapped out, Enclos realized that someone could acquire the necessary experience in two to two and a half years instead of the four or more that had been the case. Thus, the wisdom management plan was to ensure that people acquired the necessary experience and did so in a timely manner.

While it was Enclos University that created the plan and the process, the responsibility for execution lies with the supervisors and managers. The key to making a plan like this succeed is to hold the managers accountable for developing their people. Managers typically will not focus on developing people as a core part of their job unless they are held accountable. At Enclos, managers were historically held accountable for completing projects on time, on budget, and with high quality. In order for the wisdom management plan of accelerating development to work, Enclos cannot solely rely on its university to develop its people.

Now the organization and the project managers need to delicately balance the desire to have the best person working on a job versus the desire to develop that person. Some of Enclos's projects last as long as two and a half years. In the past, an assistant project manager would get to know the job intimately and would stay on a project for its entire duration. While this person would be the best choice to help manage the project, the two and a half years in one place would not help his or her development. Naturally, a senior project manager with a need to complete a major job on time and within budget does not like to have his or her best person rotated out of the job, so Enclos University is very involved with the personnel planning for each job.

The director of Enclos University is in contact with supervisors at least once every two weeks to make sure developmental goals (not construction goals) are being met. In the initial stages of wisdom management, Enclos University feels it needs to manage the process meticulously. The new wrinkle to the organization is that now managers are held accountable for people development as well as putting up buildings. Steffens, the Enclos University director, notes that it is a "huge culture change for us."

The next step in an employee's development at Enclos is to progress from project manager (project managers oversee jobs in the range of $8 million or serve as the number two person on $25 million jobs) to senior project manager (who can run a $25 million job). This had been taking six or more years (after the minimum of four years to get to project manager). So the whole process was taking anywhere from a minimum of ten to as many as fifteen years. The first step will be to reduce the time to project manager from four years down to two or two and a half years. Enclos is in the midst of doing that right now. The next step will be to repeat the mapping and rotation process for project managers to get the developmental time to senior project manager down from the minimum of six years that it is currently taking. The goal of the wisdom management project at Enclos is to reduce the time it takes to develop a senior project manager from ten to fifteen years down to no more than eight.

If Enclos can succeed, there are tremendous business advantages. Although the development process requires a great deal of attention, it will be much more efficient to focus that attention for eight years rather than spread it out over fifteen. More important, Enclos has ambitious growth goals, but it can bid on only jobs it has the capacity to complete and deliver with quality. By developing more project managers in a shorter period of time, Enclos is building its capacity to generate revenue.

The key to the initial success of wisdom management at Enclos is the complete support of the company's executives. The executive team has fully supported Enclos University since its inception and has thoroughly embraced wisdom management. The president trumpets this process when he speaks to employees, and the vice presidents have given it their full support.

The other key is having the corporate university as the integrator of all developmental processes. Rather than the university being responsible for training and the managers being responsible for development (as is the case in many organizations), Enclos, although small, has entrusted all of its development efforts in Enclos University. Thus, the university has on its to-do list training, e-learning, research and development, knowledge management, and wisdom management. By having a single entity, Enclos University, responsible for all of these functions, the company sees greater efficiencies in its investment in people; more important, there is also greater effectiveness in its development efforts by not having these functions scattered throughout the company.

It's too early in the process for Enclos and Enclos University to declare victory, but they are certainly well on their way.

Core Principles of Wisdom Management

For years we have excoriated companies for not investing in the development of their people. By not investing, these companies were not developing their organizational capacity or the capabilities of their employees.

In time, we came to realize there was something worse than this. It was that companies were investing/spending/wasting money on people development but seeing no return. While the company that was doing nothing got nothing, at least it wasn't wasting money. Companies that were doing it poorly were also getting little or no return, but they were also wasting money and lots of time (people hate sitting in training classes that have no value, and employees have traditionally failed to complete valueless e-learning programs).

Wisdom management refers to processes designed to ensure a return on the investment in developing people. It can take any number of forms, from the career path management being used at Enclos to action learning to any number of techniques designed to ensure that classroom learning is translated to behavior change in the workplace, which is translated to value to the organization.

The exact form that wisdom management will take in any organization depends on a number of factors, but here is a list of the steps needed to ensure a successful wisdom management application:

1. *Figure out exactly what the developmental needs are of your organization and its people.* Too often I see organizations use a shotgun approach to training and development. They throw a bunch of stuff out there and hope that something sticks. I am frequently asked if I can evaluate a training or development

program (if the question comes after the program has been delivered, but the organization is just now asking the question, it's usually a lot harder to evaluate and a lot less likely to be successful). The correct answer usually is, "It depends." It depends on their answer to the question, "What were you trying to achieve with this program?" I am amazed at how often people struggle to answer this question. If you don't know what you were trying to do, I can't tell you if you succeeded. Sometimes when I ask a corporate university director why the organization established a corporate university, I get an answer like, "To develop a world-class workforce." (This, I suppose, distinguishes it from those companies that desire to have a mediocre workforce or an adequate one.) I can't measure "world-class workforce." Sometimes the people involved really haven't thought it through and don't really know what the phrase means. Other times, after some prodding, they can articulate what they mean. In order for the phrase to have some meaning, they need to define *world-class workforce.* They need to explain the difference between what they have now and what they envision as a world-class workforce. They need to describe what it would look like if they had it. If they can answer these questions, it can be measured.

Of course, the key isn't just being able to measure what you're striving for; it's being able to define it. If you can clearly articulate what it is that you are trying to accomplish, you have a chance of succeeding. If you can't define it, you can't achieve it.

2. *Once you have figured out the needs, determine the best means of giving people the required knowledge, skills, and experience.* People used to think of corporate universities as a catalogue of classes. As we now know, there are numerous methods for developing people beyond classroom training (see the list presented in Chapter One, as well as the concepts presented throughout this book). Select from the long menu of choices (in many cases, the best solution will be a combination), and try to execute as well as possible.

3. *Ensure a method of translating the development intervention into behaviors that have an impact on performance.* Whether you have chosen classroom training, e-learning, coaching, mentoring, job rotation, or puppet shows as your means of development, good execution means there is some means of translating that developmental activity into behaviors that matter.

For example, the confidential nature of most executive coaching relationships means the company doesn't always know what's going on between the coach and the executive. They don't really have to know what is being discussed, but they need to know what the results are. Why was that person given a coach in the first place? Was there a specific performance area that needed improvement? An executive coach should not be a perq; it should have a solid developmental goal behind it. If you can define the goal, then maybe you determine that an executive coach is the best way to achieve the developmental goal. However, it is not enough to merely make this determination and then hire a coach. Both the coach and the executive should know what the desired outcomes are of the coaching intervention. This way, they can work toward meeting the goals. But remember that the goals need to be clearly articulated; "become a better communicator" is a difficult target to hit because it is ill defined. So before embarking on the intervention, make sure everyone is clear about what is expected of them in terms of observable behaviors and, more important, specific results.

Although this may seem as if I am advocating a detailed measurement system, the goal is not evaluation but implementation. By specifying the desired outcomes, you are more likely to achieve them. The goal is not, "Spend three months working with a coach" or "Take an executive development class for the next two weeks." The goal is, "Reduce the number of employee grievances against you to zero" or "Learn to create a marketing plan that complements the company's strategy." Clearly stated goals with measurable outcomes will get the results you want.

The key is to always ask the question, "What do I need to do to ensure this developmental activity delivers the behaviors I want to see and the results we need to see?" If you impose on yourself the discipline to keep asking this question, you will find yourself focusing more on delivering the behaviors and results and less on the activity itself. Remember that the key is not designing a great-looking curriculum and getting a terrific instructor; it's getting results.

If you develop this discipline and change the focus to these sorts of questions, you will shift the mind-set to one of wisdom management, and you will more consistently achieve the results you strive for.

Reference

Harvard Business School Publishing. *Buckman Laboratories* (video 800–502). Boston: Harvard Business School Publishing, 1999.

Mark Allen, Ph.D., is an educator, consultant, author, and speaker. He is the editor of and a contributor to *The Corporate University Handbook* (2002) and the author of numerous articles on the topic of corporate universities. An internationally recognized authority, he is a popular speaker and has published and presented research on corporate universities and nontraditional higher education throughout the world. Other research interests include the assessment of training and development programs and the evaluation of teaching and learning in postsecondary and adult education. He serves as a consultant to both new and mature corporate universities.

Allen is a participating faculty member in Organization Theory and Management at Pepperdine University's Graziadio School of Business and Management, where he also served for ten years as director of executive education. An award-winning teacher, he also teaches at Pepperdine's Graduate School of Education and Psychology.

Previously he was program director in executive education at the University of Southern California's Marshall School of Business, where he developed a variety of highly successful executive education programs. He has also held managerial positions at several organizations.

Among the organizations he has worked with are 3M, Boeing, Caesars World, the Los Angeles Police Department, Verizon, Southern California Edison, Farmers Insurance, Enclos Corp., Infonet, Safeguard, Samsung, Hughes, Kaiser Permanente, and the government of Taiwan.

Allen has a B.A. in psychology from Columbia University, an M.B.A. from Pepperdine University, and a Ph.D. in education from the University of Southern California. He can be reached at mark.allen@pepperdine.edu.

INDEX

Pfeiffer Publications Guide

This guide is designed to familiarize you with the various types of Pfeiffer publications. The formats section describes the various types of products that we publish; the methodologies section describes the many different ways that content might be provided within a product. We also provide a list of the topic areas in which we publish.

FORMATS

In addition to its extensive book-publishing program, Pfeiffer offers content in an array of formats, from fieldbooks for the practitioner to complete, ready-to-use training packages that support group learning.

FIELDBOOK Designed to provide information and guidance to practitioners in the midst of action. Most fieldbooks are companions to another, sometimes earlier, work, from which its ideas are derived; the fieldbook makes practical what was theoretical in the original text. Fieldbooks can certainly be read from cover to cover. More likely, though, you'll find yourself bouncing around following a particular theme, or dipping in as the mood, and the situation, dictate.

HANDBOOK A contributed volume of work on a single topic, comprising an eclectic mix of ideas, case studies, and best practices sourced by practitioners and experts in the field.

An editor or team of editors usually is appointed to seek out contributors and to evaluate content for relevance to the topic. Think of a handbook not as a ready-to-eat meal, but as a cookbook of ingredients that enables you to create the most fitting experience for the occasion.

RESOURCE Materials designed to support group learning. They come in many forms: a complete, ready-to-use exercise (such as a game); a comprehensive resource on one topic (such as conflict management) containing a variety of methods and approaches; or a collection of like-minded activities (such as icebreakers) on multiple subjects and situations.

TRAINING PACKAGE An entire, ready-to-use learning program that focuses on a particular topic or skill. All packages comprise a guide for the facilitator/trainer and a workbook for the participants. Some packages are supported with additional media—such as video—or learning aids, instruments, or other devices to help participants understand concepts or practice and develop skills.

- *Facilitator/trainer's guide* Contains an introduction to the program, advice on how to organize and facilitate the learning event, and step-by-step instructor notes. The guide also contains copies of presentation materials—handouts, presentations, and overhead designs, for example—used in the program.

- *Participant's workbook* Contains exercises and reading materials that support the learning goal and serves as a valuable reference and support guide for participants in the weeks and months that follow the learning event. Typically, each participant will require his or her own workbook.

ELECTRONIC CD-ROMs and Web-based products transform static Pfeiffer content into dynamic, interactive experiences. Designed to take advantage of the searchability, automation, and ease-of-use that technology provides, our e-products bring convenience and immediate accessibility to your workspace.

METHODOLOGIES

CASE STUDY A presentation, in narrative form, of an actual event that has occurred inside an organization. Case studies are not prescriptive, nor are they used to prove a point; they are designed to develop critical analysis and decision-making skills. A case study has a specific time frame, specifies a sequence of events, is narrative in structure, and contains a plot structure— an issue (what should be/have been done?). Use case studies when the goal is to enable participants to apply previously learned theories to the circumstances in the case, decide what is pertinent, identify the real issues, decide what should have been done, and develop a plan of action.

ENERGIZER A short activity that develops readiness for the next session or learning event. Energizers are most commonly used after a break or lunch to stimulate or refocus the group. Many involve some form of physical activity, so they are a useful way to counter post-lunch lethargy. Other uses include transitioning from one topic to another, where "mental" distancing is important.

EXPERIENTIAL LEARNING ACTIVITY (ELA) A facilitator-led intervention that moves participants through the learning cycle from experience to application (also known as a Structured Experience). ELAs are carefully thought-out designs in which there is a definite learning purpose and intended outcome. Each step—everything that participants do during the activity— facilitates the accomplishment of the stated goal. Each ELA includes complete instructions for facilitating the intervention and a clear statement of goals, suggested group size and timing, materials required, an explanation of the process, and, where appropriate, possible variations to the activity. (For more detail on Experiential Learning Activities, see the Introduction to the *Reference Guide to Handbooks and Annuals*, 1999 edition, Pfeiffer, San Francisco.)

GAME A group activity that has the purpose of fostering team spirit and togetherness in addition to the achievement of a pre-stated goal. Usually contrived—undertaking a desert expedition, for example—this type of learning method offers an engaging means for participants to demonstrate and practice business and interpersonal skills. Games are effective for team building and personal development mainly because the goal is subordinate to the process—the means through which participants reach decisions, collaborate, communicate, and generate trust and understanding. Games often engage teams in "friendly" competition.

ICEBREAKER A (usually) short activity designed to help participants overcome initial anxiety in a training session and/or to acquaint the participants with one another. An icebreaker can be a fun activity or can be tied to specific topics or training goals. While a useful tool in itself, the icebreaker comes into its own in situations where tension or resistance exists within a group.

INSTRUMENT A device used to assess, appraise, evaluate, describe, classify, and summarize various aspects of human behavior. The term used to describe an instrument depends primarily on its format and purpose. These terms include survey, questionnaire, inventory, diagnostic, survey, and poll. Some uses of instruments include providing instrumental feedback to group members, studying here-and-now processes or functioning within a group, manipulating group composition, and evaluating outcomes of training and other interventions.

Instruments are popular in the training and HR field because, in general, more growth can occur if an individual is provided with a method for focusing specifically on his or her own behavior. Instruments also are used to obtain information that will serve as a basis for change and to assist in workforce planning efforts.

Paper-and-pencil tests still dominate the instrument landscape with a typical package comprising a facilitator's guide, which offers advice on administering the instrument and interpreting the collected data, and an initial set of instruments. Additional instruments are available separately. Pfeiffer, though, is investing heavily in e-instruments. Electronic instrumentation provides effortless distribution and, for larger groups particularly, offers advantages over paper-and-pencil tests in the time it takes to analyze data and provide feedback.

LECTURETTE A short talk that provides an explanation of a principle, model, or process that is pertinent to the participants' current learning needs. A lecturette is intended to establish a common language bond between the trainer and the participants by providing a mutual frame of reference. Use a lecturette as an introduction to a group activity or event, as an interjection during an event, or as a handout.

MODEL A graphic depiction of a system or process and the relationship among its elements. Models provide a frame of reference and something more tangible, and more easily remembered, than a verbal explanation. They also give participants something to "go on," enabling them to track their own progress as they experience the dynamics, processes, and relationships being depicted in the model.

ROLE PLAY A technique in which people assume a role in a situation/scenario: a customer service rep in an angry-customer exchange, for example. The way in which the role is approached is then discussed and feedback is offered. The role play is often repeated using a different approach and/or incorporating changes made based on feedback received. In other words, role playing is a spontaneous interaction involving realistic behavior under artificial (and safe) conditions.

SIMULATION A methodology for understanding the interrelationships among components of a system or process. Simulations differ from games in that they test or use a model that depicts or mirrors some aspect of reality in form, if not necessarily in content. Learning occurs by studying the effects of change on one or more factors of the model. Simulations are commonly used to test hypotheses about what happens in a system—often referred to as "what if?" analysis—or to examine best-case/worst-case scenarios.

THEORY A presentation of an idea from a conjectural perspective. Theories are useful because they encourage us to examine behavior and phenomena through a different lens.

TOPICS

The twin goals of providing effective and practical solutions for workforce training and organization development and meeting the educational needs of training and human resource professionals shape Pfeiffer's publishing program. Core topics include the following:

Leadership & Management

Communication & Presentation

Coaching & Mentoring

Training & Development

e-Learning

Teams & Collaboration

OD & Strategic Planning

Human Resources

Consulting

What will you find on pfeiffer.com?

• The best in workplace performance solutions for training and HR professionals

• Downloadable training tools, exercises, and content

• Web-exclusive offers

• Training tips, articles, and news

• Seamless online ordering

• Author guidelines, information on becoming a Pfeiffer Affiliate, and much more

Discover more at www.pfeiffer.com